HIGH PLAINS
YESTERDAYS

FROM XIT DAYS THROUGH DROUTH AND DEPRESSION

John C. Dawson, Sr.

EAKIN PRESS ✦ Fort Worth, Texas
www.EakinPress.com

Heritage Edition

Copyright © 1985
By John C. Dawson Sr.
By Eakin Press
An Imprint of Wild Horse Media Group
P.O. Box 331779
Fort Worth, Texas 76163
1-888-982-8270
www.EakinPress.com
ALL RIGHTS RESERVED
1 2 3 4 5 6 7 8 9
ISBN-10: 1-57168-406-9
ISBN-13: 978-1-57168-406-6

All royalties to be earned from sale of this book have been donated by the author in equal shares to Dalhart's XIT Museum Trust Fund and Dalhart's Memorial Park Cemetery Perpetual Care Fund.

ALL RIGHTS RESERVED. No part of this book may be reproduced in any form without written permission from the publisher, except for brief passages included in a review appearing in a newspaper or magazine.

*For the memory of
my mother and
my father.*

*And all along we have kept a
kind of hold on the human
side of life . . .*

> — Letter to John C. Dawson
> From his mother,
> Willie Catherine,
> December 5, 1929

Contents

Part One: THE FIRST GENERATION SETTLERS
Introduction to Part One ... 2
Beale Queen and Childhood Memories ... 7
Dalhart in 1909 ... 15
The Rita Blanca and Lessons in History and Nature ... 21
Val Powell's Blacksmith Shop and Joe Langhorne's Barbershop ... 31
Legendary Eugene Logan ... 37
Andy James and The James Brothers Ranch — Part One ... 43
Andy James and The James Brothers Ranch — Part Two ... 50
Symbols of Change and I. J. Gushwa ... 57
Dalhart Life and Lore and Shorty No Legs ... 65
Pioneer Doctor: G. W. Dawson ... 72
Pioneer Doctor's Wife: Willie Catherine ... 88
The Errant Jackass and How to Raise Tumbleweeds ... 103
My Friend: Al Dalton and Bill Bennett: Gentleman ... 112
Dalhart's Angel of Mercy: Mrs. E. R. Stewart ... 118
Dalhart's Golden Cycle and W. H. Lathem ... 124
Jim Webb's Head — Or A Stranger's Mysterious Death ... 134
Number 126 and Prohibition's Children ... 139
The Prairie Fires and Bertie Whaley Cecil ... 148
The "Worst" Blizzards and Sam Wohlford ... 152
The Skunk in the Opera House and Return of a Native ... 163

Part Two: SURVIVORS OF THE DUST BOWL
Introduction to Part Two ... 178
The Black Dusters ... 180
Homesteaders' Struggles: C. C. Lucas Family ... 191
John McCarty, Albert Law, and the Weather Reports ... 215
A Long Dead Outlaw Brings a Sense of Relief
   from Drouth and Depression ... 228
Digging Out ... 237
Index ... 267

Illustrations

Part One: THE FIRST GENERATION SETTLERS

Map
U.S.G.S. Map: The High Plains	xiv

Paintings
Pristine Channing	13
Robust and Rowdy Dalhart	14

Drawings
The Commercial Hotel, 1903	58
The Trans-Canadian Sanitarium, 1912	78

Photographs
Author, John C. Dawson, 1985	x
Author, Dalhart, 1910	20
The Felton Opera House, 1908	59
The De Soto Hotel, 1910	61
Old Family Picture, Father	73
The "Last Man Out" Card	87
Old Family Picture, Mother	89
Willie Catherine Dawson, circa World War I	101
The Old Home Place in Dalhart	98

Part Two: SURVIVORS OF THE DUST BOWL

Painting
After the Storm	176

Photographs
April 14, 1935, Dust Storm, Colorado	188
April 14, 1935, Dust Storm, Colorado	189
The Granddaddy Black Duster	190
Abandoned Farm of the 1930s, Cimarron County, Oklahoma	207
Abandoned Farm of the 1930s, Coldwater Area	208
Abandoned Farm of the 1930s, Baca County, Colorado	209
A Normal High Plains Sandstorm	210
Deserted Homestead of the 1930s, Dallam County	211
Drifting Soil in Hartley County, Texas, Farmyard	212
A Field Blown Out Ten Feet Deep	213
The Barbed Wire Crows' Nests	214
Albert Law, of *The Dalhart Texan*	216

Foreword

By Jenkin Lloyd Jones

[Editor and Publisher of *The Tulsa Tribune*, Tulsa, Oklahoma; writer of widely circulated syndicated weekly column; author of *The Changing World.*]

On a gray November morning some years ago I stopped at a little crossroads cafe somewhere west of Amarillo for a cup of coffee. A tall, grizzled ranchman ambled in, waved a general greeting, and settled on a stool.

Someone called out, "Bill, you still feudin' with old man Throckmorten?"

"Not really," Bill replied. "We've howdied but we ain't shook."

There, I thought, was the essence of the Great Plains — the human capacity for anger and resentment, but an inexorable nudging toward forgiveness and normalcy.

In much of the world, alas, this is not true. We see great civilizations soured almost beyond redemption by deep-seated hatreds based on what Librarian of Congress Daniel Boorstin calls "intergenerational bookkeeping." We see otherwise bright and talented people making hells out of their little corners of the earth by nursing old atrocities and passing down fear and fury.

Somehow, these evil flowers wither quickly in the winds of high, dry America. Without denying that there exist individual miscreants and paranoiacs, there is on the Great Plains a general air of toleration, generosity and friendliness that, in its width and scope, is almost unique. It is good-people country.

We are poorer because we do not know our ancestors. In ancient and medieval days, writers concerned themselves with princes and plunderers, while ignoring the common man. It is only in the last century that American literature has begun to pay much attention to ordinary people.

Sometimes these views were sardonic. Sinclair Lewis didn't like his mythical Gopher Prairie, Minnesota, nor Sherwood Anderson his imaginary Winesburg, Ohio. Edgar Lee Masters painted both the saints and sinners of Spoon River, and William Saroyan frankly loved his Armenian neighbors in the San Joaquin Valley. But all have added to the richness of the American image and will be treasured in future centuries.

John C. Dawson knows what an awed Coronado called a "sea of grass," and he looks upon it with an appraising but tolerant eye. Although his chief interest is centered on Dalhart, it ranges through the Panhandles of Texas and Oklahoma. Whether he is describing the near-catastrophe of the Dust Bowl or Nettie Rittenhouse's cozy little bawdy house, he has a feel for the land, for its inhabitants, and for the truths that, ironically, make up the American Legend.

Such reminiscenses are important to man's understanding of himself. If any of Dawson's pages should fall into the hands of thirtieth century scholars, none of the twentieth century people of the High Plains will be entirely dead.

Tulsa
March 1985

Jenkin Lloyd Jones has been the recipient of the William Allen White Award, Oklahoma Hall of Fame, Distinguished Service Awards: University of Wisconsin, University of Oklahoma, Oklahoma State University, and numerous journalistic awards. He once wrote:

". . . My theory that human history is like a point on the rim of a wheel — an endless series of downs and ups, accompanied by forward progress, has saved me from the cynicism, if not despair, characteristic of many journalists. The lesson of fallen civilizations is that all good things decay, and the lesson of nature is that out of decay new life springs."

Preface

The Dalhart High Plains area is perhaps best known as the coldest place in Texas. With "only a barbed wire fence between it and the North Pole," as the saying goes.

To some, it is famed for the great 3,000,000-area XIT Ranch, carved out of Texas Public Domain as payment for construction of the State Capitol building at Austin, pursuant to a contract let in 1882.

To others, it is famed for its annual XIT Ranch Roundup at which thousands gather from far and wide seeking to celebrate and keep alive their vision of life in the area as it was during the period 1885, to about 1906, the heyday of that ranch.

To many persons passing through the area en route to New Mexico or Colorado, it may appear an endless, uninteresting, dusty, and hot — or cold — flat country they are eager to get behind them so they can finally get to where they can begin to breathe the cool, refreshing air of the mountains.

But, to the more perceptive, this High Plains area has a very significant meaning.

Dalhart supplies and is supported by a wide area that may justly be called the Last American Frontier. This area, which includes the Texas Panhandle north of the Canadian River, and extends into Oklahoma and Kansas on the north, and into New Mexico and Colorado on the west, remained largely unsettled and unused Public Domain until the coming of the great ranches of the late nineteenth century.

Persons living in the area witnessed and took part in its transition from a purely cattle raising empire to a cattle and farming empire, particularly during the period 1901 to 1939.

Only venturesome, independent, and self-reliant people were sufficiently attracted by this new land to cast their fate with it.

When my father gave up his medical practice in Kentucky (for reasons of health) in 1907, and moved his family to the Dalhart area, I was four years of age. He settled first in Channing, thirty miles

John C. Dawson

south of Dalhart, but moved to Dalhart and resumed medical practice in 1909. I grew up in Dalhart and came to know the early settlers, and experienced the vicissitudes of climate that characterized the area, observing at firsthand the settlement of the High Plains in the Texas Panhandle.

In 1916, when I had reached the age of thirteen, my parents sent me to Northwestern Military and Naval Academy in Lake Geneva, Wisconsin. From then on and through college at the University of Wisconsin, and law school at Northwestern University and The University of Texas, I saw the area only on vacations.

It was my great good fortune while in the military academy and at the University of Wisconsin and Northwestern University, to come to know, and be accepted by, young men and women from leading families of the Chicago–Wisconsin area, an area that had long since passed the pioneer stage of the Texas High Plains, and had reached a highly elevated state of business and cultural maturity. Knowing these young men and women and visiting in their homes showed me a life in sharp contrast to that I had known in Texas.

The result was to give me a sense of perspective which made the peculiar character of the High Plains settlers stand out in clearer focus. Therefore, I would come away from each visit home more deeply impressed with the feeling that here on the raw, barren plains of Texas was being lived a kind of life that was different but virile and unique. I would feel that here I was seeing life as it may have been many years earlier in Wisconsin and Illinois — a life that was shaping, and being shaped by, the land. I would feel there was something close to the earth, something fundamental, going on here, something I yearned to better understand, and to help others understand.

My feeling of closeness to the High Plains area and its people, and my desire to better understand and convey to others their message, grew as my law practice carried me among business and professional leaders in burgeoning Houston, and sent me into the heart of the financial world of Wall Street and Washington.

It has now been nearly sixty years since I graduated from the University of Wisconsin and well over fifty years since I finished law school at Northwestern and Texas. All this time I have felt that some day I would try to record, and convey to others, the raw materials by which the lives of the settlers of this area may be assessed.

This is the reason for this effort, on which I have been engaged, as time permitted, since retirement about ten years ago.

Many times I have felt the task I have undertaken was beyond my capability and that I could not put together a work of any consistency, of any central theme, that would have any lasting interest to others or show them the picture I wanted to convey. Each time I came to the point of abandoning the effort, I shortly felt, and responded to, a nagging sense that here was a story that must be told, and that, perhaps, there was no one but me to tell it.

JOHN C. DAWSON, SR.

Houston, Texas, 1985

Acknowledgments

My grateful thanks to all those old-timers whose stories of what went on in the early days of the Dalhart High Plains area and the later Dust Bowl period made the book possible.

Trying to name them all would require many pages and then some would be inadvertently omitted. But a few must be named: Albert Law, veteran reporter and editor of the *Dalhart Texan*; Joe Scott and J. T. Mann; Zumie and C. C. Lucas and their daughter, Virginia, all of Dalhart; Jesse James of Colorado Springs, son of Walter James and nephew of Andy James; W. W. Steel of Dumas, Texas; Sam Wohlford of Stratford, Texas, and Mrs. E. R. Stewart of Dalhart, remembered for her lifetime of volunteer caring for the unfortunate. Also, Evelyn Jeanne Claytor of Amarillo, daughter of John McCarty, who took over as a guiding spirit to me after her father died, and the imaginative and indefatigable Jo Randel of Panhandle, Texas, on whom I have often leaned for words of encouragement.

To have Jenkin Lloyd Jones honor me with a Foreword to my book, brings a sense of gratification I am unable to express. I am appreciative.

Lastly, I thank the brilliant, dedicated and highly capable Shirley D. Ratisseau, Editor of Eakin Press. She gave professional polish and otherwise gave immeasurable help to me in my efforts to tell my story.

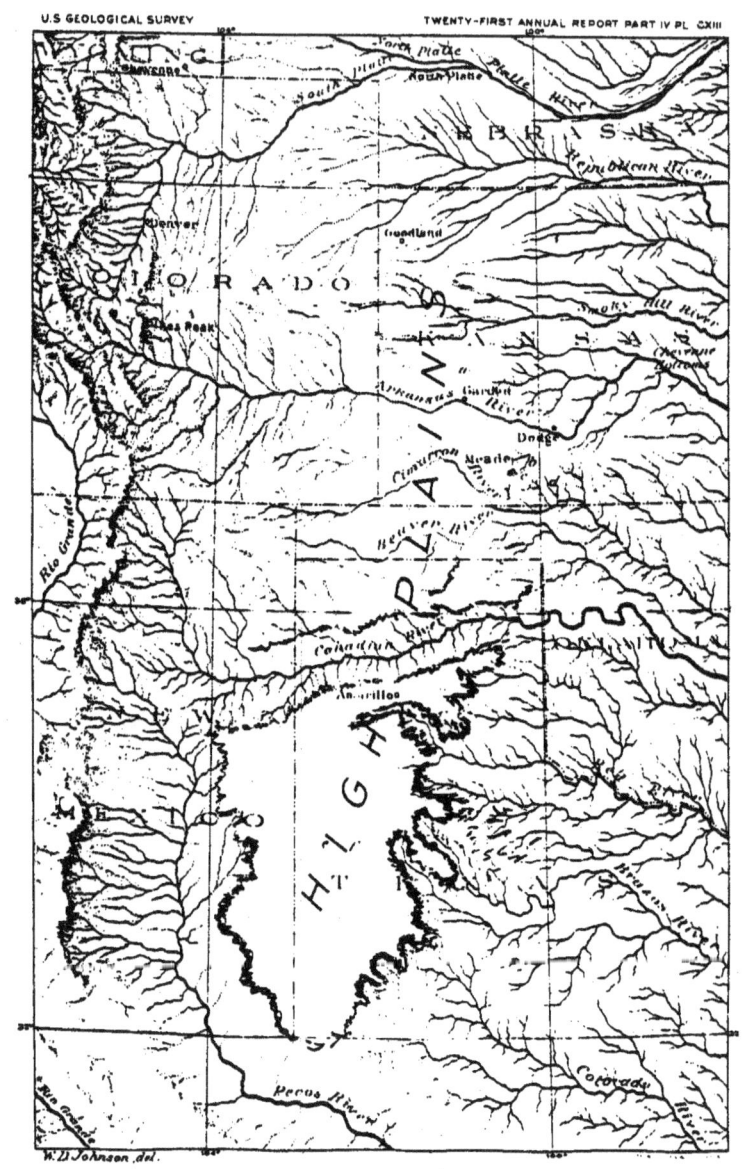

HIGH PLAINS
(Texas Caprock and New Mexico Mescalero Escarpments added)

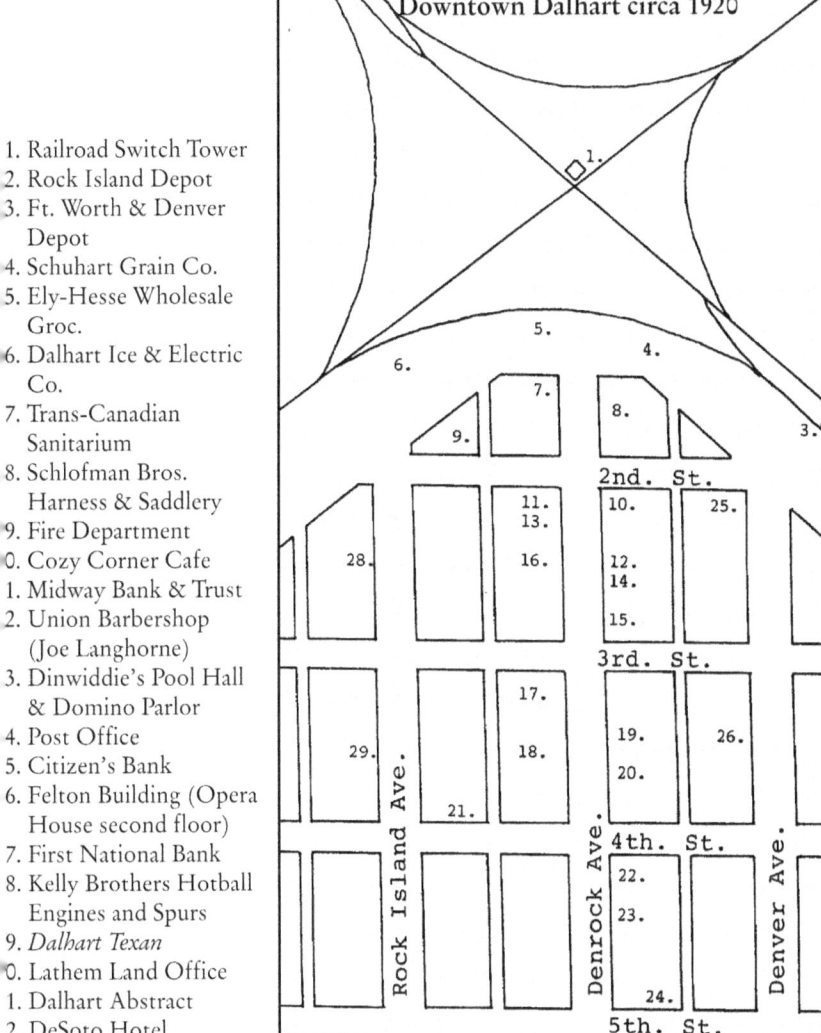

1. Railroad Switch Tower
2. Rock Island Depot
3. Ft. Worth & Denver Depot
4. Schuhart Grain Co.
5. Ely-Hesse Wholesale Groc.
6. Dalhart Ice & Electric Co.
7. Trans-Canadian Sanitarium
8. Schlofman Bros. Harness & Saddlery
9. Fire Department
10. Cozy Corner Cafe
11. Midway Bank & Trust
12. Union Barbershop (Joe Langhorne)
13. Dinwiddie's Pool Hall & Domino Parlor
14. Post Office
15. Citizen's Bank
16. Felton Building (Opera House second floor)
17. First National Bank
18. Kelly Brothers Hotball Engines and Spurs
19. *Dalhart Texan*
20. Lathem Land Office
21. Dalhart Abstract
22. DeSoto Hotel
23. Mission Theater
24. Dallam Co. Courthouse
25. Commercial Hotel
26. Galbraith-Foxworth Lumber Co.
27. Early water works
28. Dalhart Bottling Works
29. Blacksmith (Val Powell)

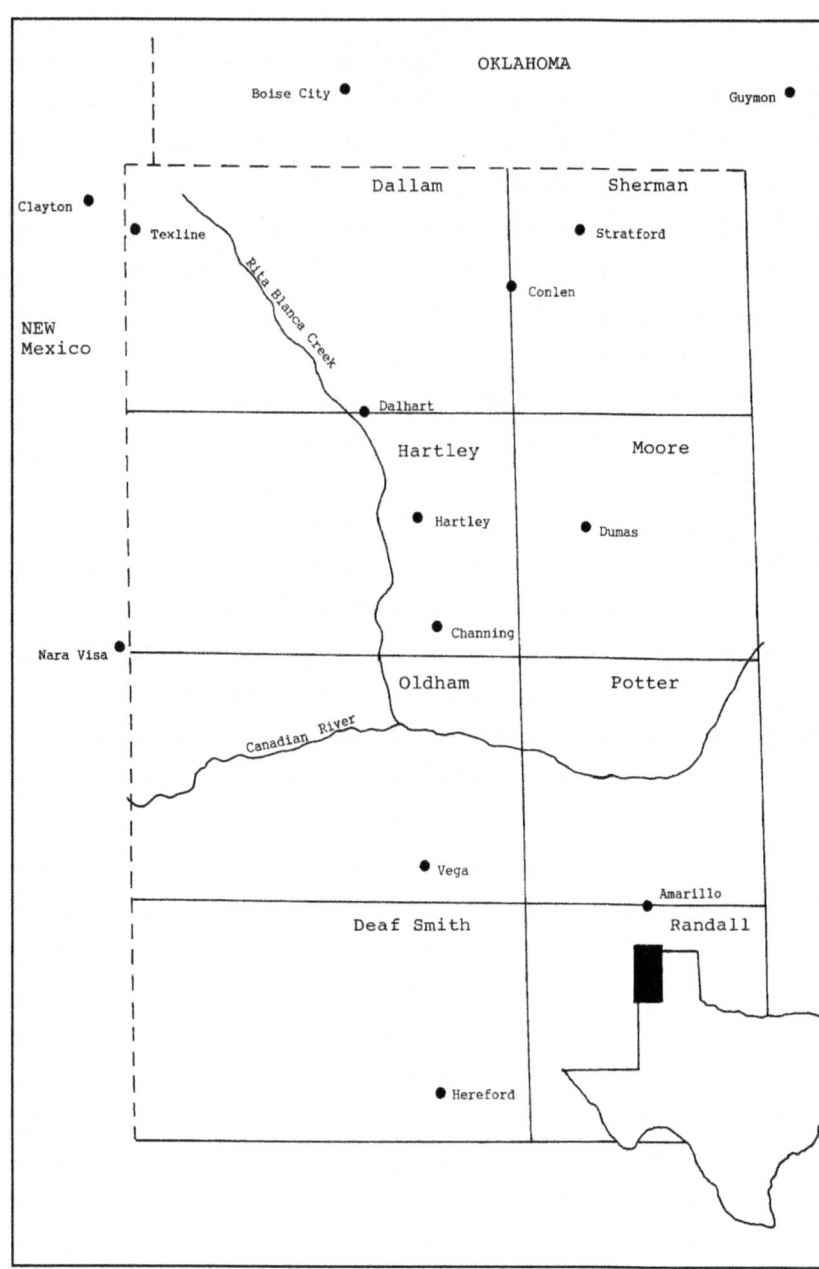

Channing, Texas circa 1900

Dalhart about 1910

Courtesy Jimmy Newby

XIT cowhands pulling a wagon across the Canadian River

Dallam County Courthouse constructed 1922

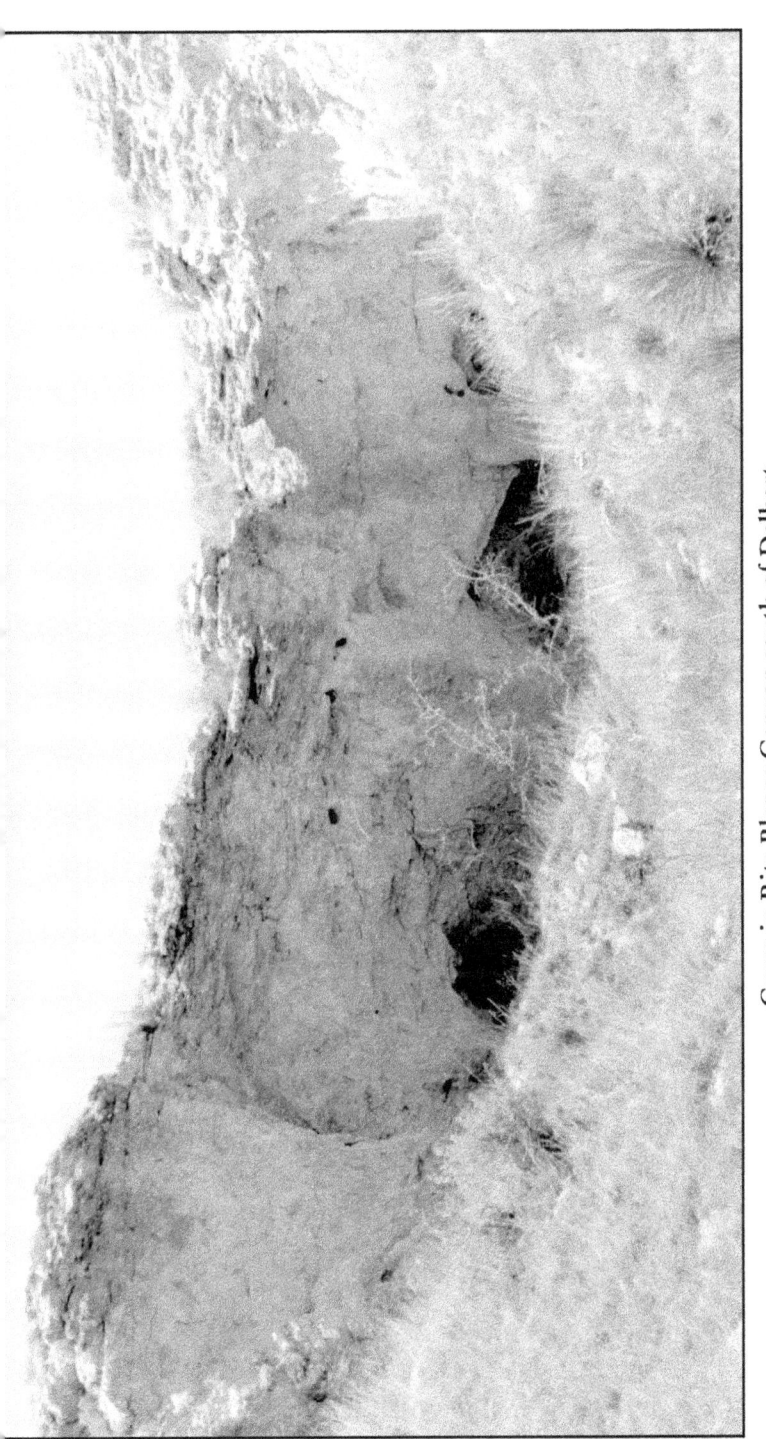

Caves in Rita Blanca Canyon south of Dalhart

Early Dalhart parade?

Courtesy Jimmy Newby

Dalhart Water Co. circa 1910

Courtesy Jimmy Newby

Felton Building, First National Bank. Circa 1915
Courtesy Jimmy Newby

The Trans-Canadian Sanitarium, Dalhart, Texas

Part One

The First Generation Settlers

> Like other parts of the Great Plains, the Panhandle suffered from the Great American Desert label which early nineteenth century American explorers had attached to the region. In 1820, Major Stephen Harriman Long who commanded the first United States military expedition along the Canadian River wrote: "In regard to this extensive section of the country, I do not hesitate in giving the opinion, that it is almost wholly unfit for cultivation, and of course uninhabitable by a people depending upon agriculture for their subsistence." Randolph B. Marcy re-enforced this notion after exploring the headwaters of the Red River by describing the Llano Estacado as a "... desolate waste of uninhabited solitude, which always has been, and must continue uninhabited forever..."
>
> — Garry L. Nall
> Panhandle-Plains
> Historical Review, 1972

INTRODUCTION

In 1900, a United States Geological Survey Report entitled, *The High Plains and their Utilization,* declared:

> . . . the High Plains continue to be the most alluring body of unoccupied land in the United States and they will remain such until the best means for their utilization shall have been worked out.

This statement applied with singular accuracy to the portion of the High Plains lying in Texas and Oklahoma west and north of the escarpment known as the Caprock. The Texas Caprock Escarpment forms a distinct, though irregular, dividing line between the flat, dry, treeless High Plains or Llano Estacado and the rolling, humid, wooded, areas to its east. The impact on settlement of the High Plains contributed by this physical barrier and division line is dramatically described by Frederick Rathjen in his book, *The Texas Panhandle Frontier,* by Bishop and Giles in their book, *Lots of Land,* and by Walter Prescott Webb in *The Great Plains.*

This area, comprised largely of the Texas and Oklahoma Panhandles, lies approximately in the center of the High Plains area. The City of Dalhart, founded in 1901, lies a bit north and west of the center of the Texas Panhandle.

The area around Dalhart may properly be characterized as the highest of the High Plains. It is one of the last areas of the United States, if not the last, to achieve permanent settlement.

Garry L. Nall, in the *1972 Panhandle Plains Historical Review,* says that even if there had been no Great American Desert concept to frighten pioneers from the Southern Plains, the presence of Indians would have delayed immediate settlement. For several generations nomadic Comanches, Kiowas, and Kiowa-Apaches had roamed the area stalking buffaloes for their livelihood. Although their leaders made an agreement with the Federal Government in 1867 to move onto a reservation in southwestern Oklahoma, most of the tribesmen continued to wander freely in the Panhandle until American and British buffalo hunters arrived in the early 1870s. Seeing the bison herds threatened for extinction, the Indians attacked the newly-established trading post site at Adobe Walls in June 1874, and raided so many hunters' camps that federal military troops converged upon the region and within a year drove the tribesmen back to their reservation.

Until about 1876, the Texas Panhandle remained practically uninhabited except for Indians, whose survival depended largely on the buffalo, and the Comancheros, Mexicans from New Mexico, who came to trade with the Indians. By 1876, the American hide hunters had destroyed most of the buffalo, greatly aiding the U.S. Army's efforts to drive the Indians out.

Historians appear to agree that the first permanent white settler to come to the Texas Panhandle was Charles Goodnight. Goodnight, in 1876, moved his herd of 1600 cattle from Colorado to a point in the Palo Duro Canyon a few miles south of present Amarillo. Here was permanent water and free grass (it would be many years before the cattleman found it necessary to purchase or lease the land on which he pastured his cattle). Others followed and by about 1880, cattlemen occupied most of the area where permanent water could be found. Even then, however, not even the cattlemen had moved to a great extent onto the plains areas not served by live water.

Significant movement of settlers, either cattlemen or farmers, onto these plains areas did not occur until barbed wire and the windmill became available to them. A successful barbed wire was invented in 1874. Although the windmill had been previously in common use in more settled and more humid areas, it was the barbed wire that invited its general use in the semiarid areas such as the High Plains. Both were widely available by about 1883. Barbed wire enabled the farmer to protect his growing crops from the roaming herds of cattle. And, of course, the windmil made it possible for the settler to subsist upon the vast areas of the plains where permanent surface water was unavailable.

Since it took both the windmill and the barbed wire to make these areas available for settlement, we may consider 1883 as the year in which significant settlement by permanent residents began on the Texas Panhandle portion of the High Plains, including the Dalhart area.

The year 1883 may seem a long time ago, but it seems a very recent date when one considers that seven years earlier Colorado had reached statehood, Kansas had been recognized as a state for twenty-two years, and east and south Texas had, since about 1850, been largely occupied by permanent settlers. And it had been about thirty-five years since the California gold rush had brought hordes of immigrants from southern and eastern United States to the Pacific coast.

As late as 1880, the United States Census showed zero population for four counties in the northwestern corner of the Texas Panhandle, namely Dallam, Sherman, Moore, and Carson. It was not until 1888 that transportation by rail became possible in the Dalhart area, the Fort Worth and Denver going into operation between Fort Worth, Texas, and Denver, Colorado, in May of that year. In 1901, the Chicago Rock Island and Pacific crossed the Fort Worth and Denver in Dallam County — the most northwesterly county in the Texas Panhandle — widely expanding the rail transportation available from the area. Dalhart, at the junction of the Rock Island and the Fort Worth and Denver, then came into being. Substantial settlement of the area then began, but both the cattleman and the farmer had much yet to learn about their new environment.

Historian Walter Prescott Webb, in his book, *The Great Plains,* has observed:

> Nowhere in the world, perhaps, has the wind done more effective work than in the Great Plains. As compared with the humid east, the Great Plains, particularly the High Plains, is a region of high wind velocity. The level surface and absence of trees give the air currents free play. On the whole, the wind blows harder and more constantly on the Plains than it does in any other portion of the United States, save on the seashore.

Any Dalhart area resident will proudly tell you that the wind blows harder and more consistently there than anywhere else in the world.

Professor Webb also observed:

> The five weather phenomena — hot winds and chinooks, northers, blizzards, and hailstorms — are all localized in the Great Plains country. Four of the five bring distress and economic ruin to man and beast and crop — they are a significant part of the unusual conditions which civilization had to meet and overcome in the Great Plains.

The Dalhart, Texas, area is in the highest portion of the High Plains, the altitude rising to 4,600 feet above sea level.

Introduction

The Dalhart area does not have Chinooks (hot, dry winds from the mountains), but for other hot winds, northers, blizzards and hailstorms, the Dalhart area can boast the biggest and the best.

What type of people would be attracted to this semiarid country and its apparently forbidding climatic conditions? For a number of reasons the early settlers of the Texas Panhandle were predominantly cattlemen. Nature had supplied the land with nutritious grasses and an abundant water supply available to the windmill. Moreover, the land system there was compatible with the cattleman's needs. The mistake, such as was made in New Mexico, Colorado, Oklahoma, and Kansas, of offering tracts of 160 to 320 acres of subagricultural land for settlement by homesteaders was never made in the Texas Panhandle. Texas kept its own Public Domain to which the Federal Homestead Laws did not apply, and under the law applicable to its public domain, areas of up to four 640-acre sections per person were available for purchase at about two dollars an acre with half a lifetime to pay.

The early Texas Panhandle cattlemen seemed to be a breed of people who could not stand being confined either to a strictly farming operation or to small tracts such as were common in older, more humid areas or offered to settlers under the Federal Homestead Laws.

Modern farming machinery and methods and modern ranching methods may have made both occupations acceptable or even desirable to people of the same outlook. But, to hear the old-timers tell it, the early day cattleman abhorred the plow.

Walter Prescott Webb has observed that the early settlement of the Great Plains was largely a movement westward of southerners from states such as Tennessee, Mississippi, Alabama, and Kentucky. This may account for one characteristic which always seemed to me to be fairly common among the early Dalhart area settlers. They seemed to have the ease, civility and charm of the Old South with, however, an added energy and industriousness infused into them by the higher altitude and the aridity of the High Plains. Moreover, these people had to have rare qualities of optimism and self-confidence and a high degree of individualism and desire to be beholden to no man for their survival. After all, they came of their own free will, giving up the people and the means of livelihood to which they had become accustomed, in order to take a gambling chance of finding a better life in this new and undeveloped land.

Despite the difficulties of survival presented by this new environment, the early settlers seemed to find the challenge stimulating. For the most part they stayed and became the most independent, individualistic, and altogether happy people that I have ever known.

Beale Queen and Childhood Memories

> *It used to be the greatest cow country in the world. We didn't have dust storms and tumbleweeds until the farmers came and plowed up all the grass.*
>
> — Beale Queen, old-time cowboy and wagon master

It was, in the spring of 1972, over sixty-five years since we had moved from Stanley, Kentucky, to Channing, Texas. It had been over sixty years since we had moved from Channing, Texas, to Dalhart, Texas. And it had been over fifty years since I had left Dalhart for school in the Midwest. For the past forty years of this period, I had been absorbed with a commercial law practice in Houston, Washington, and New York.

Now, as I had begun adjusting my life to withdrawal from active law practice, I gave release to a long felt urge to revisit the scenes of my early boyhood. I flew to Amarillo, rented a car and headed northwest over the high, flat, barren plains toward Channing, the town to which my father had brought us in 1907.

I drove into Channing and looked around. There was a well-preserved little Methodist church, an old red brick courthouse, a few business houses adjacent to the highway, obviously located there mainly to derive business from persons passing through by auto, an old stone building that once had housed a combined bank, post office, grocery and general merchandise store, and a few residences that looked as if they had been there forever. One would assume a population of about a hundred with hardly any stirring about.

I stopped the car and just sat there trying to remember something about life in Channing. Vaguely, I seemed to recall some fine horses father had brought down from Kentucky — something about a bunch of cowboys dashing on their ponies to a huge barrel of brooms set in front of the mercantile store, each grabbing a broom and dashing away — going to fight a prairie fire — that's what I remembered. Something about a little ranch father had started — a stone house there — and springs — somewhere near a canyon that had running water and quicksand — a canyon the Queen boys and my brothers and I used to expore on donkeys. Who on earth, besides me, would have the slightest recollection of these things?

I was on my way to Dalhart and was about five miles out of Channing when I saw a sign on a trail leading toward a ranch house half a mile off the road to the east. The sign said simply:

BEALE QUEEN

Instinctively, I slammed on my brakes, backed up, turned into the roadway, undid the barbed wire gate and headed down the trail toward the ranch house.

Well, it was Beale Queen all right, the same Beale Queen I had known in Channing sixty-five years before when Beale and my older brother, Artis, were about nine, his brother, Ralph, and my brother, G. W., about seven, and I the youngest of the lot.

Our lives had taken totally different courses. Beale had stayed close to the land, and essentially had remained a cowboy. At fifteen he had become a cowhand on the great Matador Ranch. And he had gone on to become wagon master at the great JA Ranch. Here from 1931 to 1935 he had held this position — going out on the range for as much as nine months at a time — working cattle with about twenty cowboys under his command, and a *remuda* of up to 200 horses. Now Beale was occupied with breeding, raising and marketing quarter horses.

Somehow the sixty-five years of our complete separation from one another — each occupied with pursuits and interests totally unrelated to those of the other — completely disappeared. Once more we were boys in Channing. We began testing one another's memory, and, to our amazement, found that we both clearly recalled much that had happened in that distant past — just as if it had happened yesterday.

We remembered how we would ride burros down to the Las Ruedas Canyon five miles west of town, my brothers and the two Queen boys each on his own burro and I hanging on behind Artis or G. W.

Beale Queen and Childhood Memories

We remembered the time one of the burros slipped off the bank of the little stream that ran down the Las Ruedas; he was in quicksand and there was a struggle getting him out.

We remembered how the XIT pasture we had to cross was full of black Angus cattle and the time Beale, Ralph, Artis, and G. W. put me on top of a twelve-by-twelve fence post while they went into the pasture and taunted the bulls. They had jumped down into a little wash-out when the bulls came at them — and one old bull had spied me and came over and butted the post I was perched upon.

Beale remembered the horses father had brought from Kentucky and the names of the two great stallions — Fezjlo (imported from Germany) and Major (a fine pacer). He said Fezjlo was the finest looking stallion he had ever seen. He remembered father's surrey and his gig and racing cart. And he remembered that the horses had all died after eating clover that had mold in it.

Beale remembered how we all used to love to go out in the street and "lie down" against the high winds. And he remembered the cockleburs, grassburs and goatheads we used to get into when we tried to go barefooted.

Beale corrected my pronunciation of Lăs Ruedas. "It's Lăs Ruădăhs, not Lasaratas," he said. It is a little canyon with a small stream in the bottom, fed by springs. It leads into the Rita Blanca which leads on into the Canadian. Los Ruedas means "the wheels." It was given that name because on its western bank there long remained iron rims from wagon wheels left there in about 1870, when Indians surprised and destroyed an army scouting party ranging out probably from Fort Bascom, in New Mexico. Beale told me that near the site of the battle was a portion of a dugout in which the remains of a Mexican sheepherder were buried. He had died of smallpox in about 1900, and there was such fear of infection from that disease that the cowboys simply left the body in the dugout, covered it by pushing in the walls and then set it afire.

Beale remembered the smallpox epidemic that hit Channing in 1908, and how my father had come out of medical retirement to treat those affected; and how he had become County Health Officer and imposed a quarantine making people stay indoors and put red flags in front of their houses if anyone in the family had smallpox.

Beale remembered prairie fires. He told of one which struck when his mother, his sister Thelma, and he were alone at their ranch house. He said his mother put him and his sister in the garden where the fire could not reach them and then went out with a broom to keep the flames from reaching the house. He also remembered the great fire of 1907, which was started near Channing by sparks from an engine pulling a freight train on the Fort Worth and Denver, and that had burned all the way up to the Cimarron River in Kansas.

Beale even remembered hearing my father tell Beale's father about the time we all spent a night out at the little rock house on father's place near the Las Aritas. He quoted father, speaking of my mother: "She was cooking breakfast," he said, "and a snake fell out of the dirt roof right onto the floor near her. And what do you think my Willie did? Why she just grabbed a broom, whacked that old snake dizzy and swept it right out the door!"

Beale admitted his dislike of farming. "I couldn't stand farming," he would say. He deplored what farmers had done to the country. "It used to be the greatest cow country in the world," he said. "We didn't have dust storms and tumbleweeds until the farmers came and plowed up all the grass."

Channing had been the headquarters of the three million-acre XIT Ranch when we moved there, with Colonel Boyce as manager. Since Channing was really on the XIT, Colonel Boyce ran the town, and he kept out all influences that might improperly distract his cowboys. His rules forbad liquor and dens of iniquity. Such distractions could, however, be found at Dalhart, thirty miles to the north.

About the XIT Ranch: In 1943, Albert Law of *The Dalhart Texan*, wrote a *Thumbnail History of the XIT Ranch*. This was for distribution at the annual XIT Reunion held in Dalhart each August, the attendance at which often reached over twenty-two thousand. Here are some excerpts.

> The XIT ranch in the 1880s was the largest range in the world under fence, and it all laid in the Texas Panhandle. Its three million acres sprawled from the old Yellow House headquarters near what is now Lubbock, Texas, northward to the Oklahoma Panhandle, in an irregular strip that was roughly about 30 miles wide.
>
> It covered portions of ten counties: Dallam, Hartley, Oldham, Deaf Smith, Parmer, Castro, Bailey, Lamb, Cochran and Hockley, which has apparently helped perpetuate the mis-belief that the brand — XIT — stands for "Ten in Texas." The brand, in fact, was originated to thwart rustlers; one of the two originators still lives and usually attends the Annual XIT Reunions.
>
> XIT history is a triangle of superlatives. The XIT range was

the largest in the world under fence. Texas, the biggest state in the union, used it to pay for its red granite capitol, still the biggest state capitol on the North American continent. The Austin structure after more than a half century, still houses the Lone Star state government, and as capitols go, is second in size only to the one at Washington, D.C. In one respect it is even bigger than the U.S. capitol. Its dome stands seven feet higher.

The long lasso of time must drop back to 1875. The Lone Star government was getting cramped in its old capitol, and the Texas Constitutional convention set aside three million Panhandle acres with which to get a new capitol.

Action dragged till fire destroyed the old capitol Nov. 9, 1881. Gov. Oran M. Roberts called a special legislative session. It struck a bargain with Charles B. and John V. Farwell, brothers of Chicago, under which they agreed to build a $3,000,000* capitol and accept the three million Panhandle acres in payment.

Ground for the capitol was broken in 1882. By ox-power and a specially-built railroad, Burnet county's famous red granite was transported to Austin for the historic structure.

The Farwells borrowed money in England to develop the ranch, and on this fact probably was hung the one-time myth that the ranch belonged to Englishmen. The debt was liquidated in 1909.

In 1885 the first cattle, long of leg and horn, rolled onto the XIT. Thousands of hoofs drummed along the trail, and the Longhorns were pushed on to the No. 1 division headquarters at Buffalo Springs, 32 miles north of Dalhart, now easily available by modern highway. Once the ranch ran 150,000 cattle.

The corrals, foreman's residence and bunk house had just been built at the Springs, and still stand, the oldest structures in Dallam County.

Ab Blocker, a South Texas trail driver, and B. H. (Barbecue) Campbell, first general manager of the ranch, who once ordered a carload of brown cigarette papers, squatted on their boot heels and in the corral dust at Buffalo Springs figured out a brand that could be run with a straight iron and that rustlers could not successfully burn over. Blocker ran the first 'XIT' then and there.

Rustlers could never entirely circumvent Blocker and Campbell, but they did learn to make XIT into a Star Cross if the "T" was crossed crooked.

For more than three decades the ranch has been slowly sell-

---

* [This is slightly misleading for the price or cost of the capitol was unknown at the time. J. Evetts Haley, in *The XIT Ranch of Texas* verifies that the materials and labor alone cost the builders $3,744,630.60.]

ing into smaller ranges and farms. But it was so vast that there still remains 350,000 acres, including the Buffalo Springs headquarters. These original holdings are in charge of the Capitol Freehold Land Trust, with Texas headquarters in Dalhart, and the general headquarters in Chicago, where heirs of the first owners are still in the saddle.

Roaming and living in the Southwest and many parts of the world, are old cowpokes who once pounded leather and smelled six-gun smoke on the XIT. It is to honor these men and their families that the annual XIT Reunion is held. Fort Worth started it in 1936. The second reunion came to Dalhart, and former XIT cowhands, comprising the XIT Association, voted Dalhart the permanent reunion home.

Two years after my father moved to Channing, intending to retire from medical practice, demands for his services coupled with certain financial reverses dictated a resumption of medical practice and a change of location. Thus, in 1909, we moved to Dalhart.

Pristine Channing

Robust and Rowdy Dalhart

Dalhart in 1909

I could never forget the town-awakening fire whistle at the icehouse, followed by the fire wagon, with bell clanging, and two giant dapple-gray Percheron horses leading. Slim Batis drove with obvious glee, and volunteer firemen rushed from their business places along Main Street, donning yellow slickers on the run and mounting the fire wagon as it rolled past. Then, fully loaded, Slim Batis urged the horses to a gallop . . . enjoying being watched by the many townspeople by now gathering along the street. Slim's handlebar whiskers flowed backward toward his ears as he sped along.

Only in memory does there seem something faintly theatrical about these people. Like actors in a comic opera, they were conscious always of the impressions they were making on others, and happily played their parts.

— John C. Dawson

My visit with Beale Queen carried me back to early boyhood and made me yearn to see again the Channing and Dalhart areas as I saw them in the infancy of their development.

After I left Beale Queen's place and drove along on the way to Dalhart looking at the open sky and the distant horizon, I saw occasionally, a ranch or a farmhouse I remembered from many years past. People I had known, events I had witnessed, yarns I had heard, came flowing back in a vague jumbled disorder.

Sandstorms that sometimes lasted for days, so that there was just no one out on the streets . . . the stores empty . . . people becoming nervous, edgy, short-tempered. Then the sudden clearing of the air . . . the beautiful, invigorating clean air!

The sudden deluges of rain and hail we had . . . again the sudden lifting of the storm, leaving the air washed and sweet smelling.

There were unbelievably flamboyant sunsets and sunrises, and clear, star-filled nights!

I remembered Ada Mae and Eula Swearingen in their elevated cage in Swearingen's Grocery Store handling the billings and cash transactions sent to their cage by little buckets propelled along wires strung from behind the counters. Sunday afternoons at the Swearingens, Eula playing the piano . . . everyone singing. Besides Eula and Ada Mae, there were Blondie Killen, Anna Lou Boyce, Agnes Carnes, Willa Griffith, Marcella Walker, Regina Tatum, and Doris Ford; all wonderful examples of feminine loveliness, but all too old for me except Marcella, Regina, and Doris — and they too smart.

Uncle Dick Coon . . . silent, crafty, a landowner, rancher, poker player, and unpretentious philanthropist . . . Lon McCrory, Orville Finch, and Lawrence Steel of the Citizens State Bank. Once Lawrence Steel pointed to my father's signature on a promissory note and said, *That name can have anything it wants at this bank.*

Joe Scott and J. T. Mann, aristocratic southern gentlemen from Tennessee, advertising their Scott Motor Company with tires hung on fence posts for miles along the highway reading:

SUDDEN SERVICE.

I recalled the colorful, legendary characters like Jess Jenkins, Eugene Cyclone Logan, Scandalous McCandless, and Andy James. Lovable people like Joe Langhorne, I. J. Gushwa, and Shorty No Legs.

I could never forget the town-awakening fire whistle at the icehouse, followed by the fire wagon, with bell clanging, and two giant dapple-gray Percheron horses leading. Slim Batis drove with obvious glee, and volunteer firemen rushed from their business places along Main Street, donning yellow slickers on the run and mounting the fire wagon as it rolled past. Then, fully loaded, Slim Batis urged the horses to a gallop . . . enjoying being watched by the many townspeople by now gathering along the street. Slim's handlebar whiskers flowed backward toward his ears as he sped along.

Only in memory does there seem something faintly theatrical about these people. Like actors in a comic opera, they were conscious always of the impressions they were making on others, and happily played their parts.

Dalhart in 1909

I drove on in to Dalhart and immediately remembered the impressions of it that I had had when we moved there in 1909.

Dalhart, having been formed in 1901 when the Rock Island crossed the Fort Worth and Denver, was only two years older than I was.

Even back then, it was a lot bigger than Channing. Father said there must be 3,000 people, what with all the folks coming out from the east to buy the cheap land, the railroads offering bargain fares and everything. He said this was just a ranching country now but with the land so rich and cheap, pretty soon there would be lots of farmers.

Dalhart was also a lot more modern than Channing, too. It had a business district nearly three blocks long — all on Main Street with boardwalks in front of the buildings. It had a picture show that ran every day except Sunday with a man who played a piano in the mood of the action in the shows. There was a new two-story brick building in the center of town that folk called the Felton Opera House. Across the street from our house was a big, black, eighty-foot silo-like tank, rising from the ground, which held the water supply. This delivered water right into every house. Dalhart had a "scavenger" who came down the alleys one night each week in a horse-drawn, open-bed wagon to clean up under the outhouses. By lanternlight he shoveled and drove.

A brand new yellow brick hotel called The De Soto was being built on Main Street near the movie house.

Dalhart had streetlights. They called them carbide arc lights. They were suspended over the places where Second, Third, Fourth and Fifth Streets crossed Main Street. A rope that was run through pulleys attached high up on two telephone poles, held up the lights. Every evening men would come along, untie the ropes that held the lights up and lower them down to where one could reach them from the ground. Then the men would light the wicks in the lights and pull them back up in the air. When daylight came the men dropped the lights again, put them out and pulled them again in place in the air.

On a dark night a great cone of light would be thrown on the street from these devices. In bug season, these cones of light would be filled with millions of illuminated moths or crickets or grasshoppers.

Dalhart had a sprinkler wagon that went up and down Main Street to keep the dust from blowing so bad. Despite the work of the water wagon, a cowboy trotting his horse down the street would usually send up a cloud of dust unless there had been a soaking rain. When that happened the wagons and buggies would cut deep ruts in the street. One day I saw a six-mule team straining to pull two well loaded ranch wagons through the mud right in front of our house.

I made friends right away with Henry Moore, Glen Lathem, Flossie Smith and C. R. Kendrick.

Henry's father was a lawyer and had come to Dalhart from East Texas. Glen's father sold real estate — he had just moved to Dalhart from Idaho. I don't know where Flossie came from, but C. R.'s father was in real estate, too, and he had moved to Dalhart from Missouri a year or so before we moved there.

One day, C. R. took me all over to show me the town. We went by the movie house. It was showing *Ben Hur*.

We saw Fatty Arterbury, a great tall man in a fine looking black suit with a gold watch chain on his vest. He had a huge paunch which hung out over his legs and C. R. said that Fatty's belly was so big he hadn't seen his tally-whacker in ten years.

Then we came upon a group of boys gathered around a little man with a derby hat and a cane. His face was red and he looked angry, but the boys were all laughing. Every now and then one of the boys would say something to the man, whereupon the man's face would turn crimson and he would hiss and strike at the boys with his cane. "That's Old Kid," said C. R. "He hates boys. They know he can't do any more than swing that cane at them so they gather around him and say things he won't like. Of course, the more they do that, the more Old Kid hisses and swings his cane at them, and the more he hisses and swings his cane the more the boys say things he won't like."

We saw Scandalous McCandless, the deputy sheriff, wearing his big black hat, cowboy boots, two big pistols and a big shiny star on his chest.

We went past Bowman's livery stable. I saw three or four covered wagons inside a high fence that ran around the back of the lot. C. R. said people would come in there in their wagons for a safe place to spend the night and they could board their horses in the stable.

We went by several saloons as we walked up Main Street. Between the boardwalk and the inside of each saloon, there were two swinging doors with about a foot of doorway space both above and below them. A strong smell of whiskey and beer came out to us as we passed by. One saloon had a sign in front that read "Jack Jesse's Place." On the boardwalk outside the saloon in a wheelchair was a

Dalhart in 1909   19

pleasant looking little man with a big belly and skinny little legs. "That's Jack Jesse, the owner," said C. R.

Across the street was a saloon called "The Cozy Corner." A number of horses were standing tied to hitching rails along the sides of the street near the edge of the boardwalks. These hitching rails were made by setting two poles in the ground extending up about four feet, holding up another pole laid on top of them. There were a lot of cowboys on the street, wearing big, flappy leather chaps, wide-brimmed hats, high-heeled boots, and fancy big spurs. The rowels on their spurs would jangle as they walked along the boardwalks.

C. R. said we ought to go out to Blair's Dam. "That's our swimming hole." He said it was about three miles out west of town. As we came to the Rock Island Railroad track on the edge of Dalhart, I noticed there were only two houses on the prairie west of the tracks. Both were at least a quarter of a mile from any other house. One was a nice looking two-story yellow house with little trees around it. The other was a very plain looking little house built like a square box with no trees or anything like that. C. R. pointed to the nice looking yellow house and said, "That's a cathouse." Then he pointed to the other one and said, "That's the pesthouse." I had to ask him what a pesthouse was.

C. R. told me that a man and his wife both caught smallpox the day they got married and had to spend their honeymoon in that pesthouse.

On the way to Blair's Dam, we passed Moreman's slaughterhouse and went in and watched a man shoot a cow in a little room that had a cement floor from which he could wash the blood. It made me kind of sick.

Blair's Dam turned out to be a great place. A Mr. Blair had built an earthen dam across the Rita Blanca Canyon at a place where the canyon was only about a quarter of a mile wide. He forgot to provide a proper spillway and when a gulley-washer came along one day, the dam broke. It left a nice swimming hole right in the bottom of the canyon with the broken sides of the dam rising on either side and making a great place from which to jump or dive into the muddy pool. We stripped off our clothes and splashed around in the shallow part of the pool a long time.

My brothers, Artis and G. W., made friends with "Rats" Smith, "Toots" Vineyard, "Chock" Dellinger, Joe Billy Stone and Weaver Moore. Weaver and G. W. hadn't known each other five minutes before they got in a big fistfight. After that, I think they had a fistfight every time they met. It was their way of enjoying themselves.

Father bought a nice horse and buggy to use making calls.

Mother joined the choir in the Methodist Church and also joined the Eastern Star.

So, altogether, Dalhart turned out to be a pretty interesting place to live.

John C. Dawson, age seven, on porch of Dalhart home in 1910

The Rita Blanca and

Lessons in History and Nature

Then we all sat down and picked off the grassburs, cockleburs, and devil's claws that had lodged in our clothing as we came down the canyon.

There was not a gymnasium, a swimming pool or a tennis court in Dalhart back in 1909 when we moved there. On the open ground in the block on which the four-story brick school building stood were the town's only public recreational facilities, consisting of a few swings, seesaws and parallel bars and some wooden basketball goals set on the bare ground. I should mention the fire escape that stood on the outside of one corner of the school building. It was just a three- and one-half story high, sheet-iron pipe about eight feet in diameter with a slick metal slide inside it that ran around and around like a corkscrew to an outlet about ground level. When school was out, the metal door on the fire escape's ground outlet would be closed and padlocked. We used to love to break that lock, climb up the slide inside the fire escape and then slide back down. This was one of the best recreational facilities in town.

The town had no organization devoted to youth such as the Y.M.C.A. or the Boy Scouts. Moreover, the land around Dalhart was a hilless, treeless plain. There were no rivers or streams; in fact, there was practically no surface water at all except for temporary ponds created by the occasional rains or earthen water reservoirs built for livestock and fed by windmills. One had to go about twenty miles south down the Rita Blanca Canyon or about fifty miles northeast to Adobe Walls to find a fishing hole. These were long distances in those days. We always heard there were some nice holes at Buffalo Springs about thirty miles northwest of town. But these were on the XIT Ranch North Division Headquarters and not open to the public.

So you might think life for the youngster in Dalhart would have been mighty uninteresting. But you would have been thinking wrong, at least so far as I and my brothers, Artis and G. W. and a few of our friends were concerned. For we had great areas of the plains, mostly unfenced, on which we could roam and hunt. We'd crawl up on cattle tanks or prairie ponds to shoot ducks or doves, or walk up cottontails or jackrabbits or quail and prairie chickens. Sometimes we would get a shot at a coyote, a badger or an antelope. We had the marvelous sky-paintings of the prairie sunrises and sunsets and the nights in which the stars shone through the thin, dry air with a magic brightness.

And we had the Rita Blanca Canyon.

The canyon originates only a few miles above the old Blair's dam, which was about three miles southwest of Dalhart, so it was not a very big canyon at that point, maybe three-quarters of a mile from caprock to caprock and maybe a hundred feet deep at the very center. My brothers and I loved to explore the canyon. I think we went somewhere in it almost every weekend. Sometimes we would go horseback but we went on foot most of the time because we liked to walk along close to the caprock which necessarily led us in and around the draws. The "caprock" was the strip of cliff-like limestone (or caliche) which marked the boundary between the prairie and the canyon. At Blair's Dam the caprock was only about ten feet thick, but by the time one reached Schroeder's Well, eight or nine miles below the dam, the caprock was, in places, a thirty or forty foot cliff. The "draws" were breaks in the sides of the canyon made by concentrations of water directed into the canyon by swales in the prairie. Where the draws began there was generally a very sharp drop, or cliff, made by the water falling into the draw from the prairie. Water holes were frequently formed by such falling water and the water would sometimes stand in these holes long after the rain had ceased. The result was that the draws often had nice stands of scrub oak, cottonwood, willow, mesquite or hackberry trees in them. And the caprock where a draw originated was usually thicker and more cliff-like than elsewhere in the canyon.

The caprocks, with their many little caves and depressions and the draws with their trees and occasional water would attract most

The Rita Blanca and Lessons in History and Nature

forms of the canyon's animal life, which probably sought both food and shelter. Aside from many types of native birds that nested in the trees or rocks, we would find migratory birds like doves and red-winged blackbirds, tiny bluebirds and finches. We found predators such as a variety of hawks and great horned owls — skunks and whole nests of snakes and once in awhile, a bobcat or a bobcat's tracks.

I think my brothers and I, joined from time to time by various friends, explored every foot of that canyon within walking distance of town. All the caprock between town and a point about twelve miles down the canyon was examined for pockets of sandy soil that could be dug out and enlarged into caves. We dug out five or six nice caves this way. We would carry shovels and pickaxes down into that canyon and back — to use for digging caves. We often would take blankets or bedrolls along and stay overnight. And always we would take canteens of water and knapsacks crammed with bread, bacon, salt and pepper, coffee, several cans of pork and beans and sardines and maybe an apple or two. We would depend on getting cottontails or doves or quail or prairie chickens which we would cook over a cowchip fire on green forked sticks. Occasionally we would try a prairie dog or a meadow lark, if necessary, to fill out a meal.

I remember particularly well one of our trips to the Rita Blanca when my brother Artis gave us a lecture on the history of the country thereabout.

We had planned to spend the night camping out and had picked a spot in a draw on the west side of the canyon in a grove of hackberry trees.

We had finished supper and were just sitting there watching the glowing cowchips we had used for our fire. Stars began to sparkle in the cloudless sky and shortly a bright, full moon rose above the eastern caprock of the canyon. It made the hackberry trees cast long, soft, eerie shadows.

It was late in August, and while the afternoon had been blisteringly hot, when the sun went down, the customary cool breeze from the southwest sprang up.

We donned our jackets.

We just kept sitting there saying nothing for a long time, just looking at the fading embers of the fire, at the sky, the stars, the moonlight, and the shadows. Finally Artis (who was always the scholar in our family), broke the silence. I cannot now recall the exact words my fourteen-year-old brother used all those years ago. But the story he told was about as follows:

Have you ever tried to picture what this country was like about fifty years ago before the white man came? You learn a lot, reading about it. There were no towns, no windmills, no fences, no farms, just open prairie with great herds of buffalo and lots of wild mustangs, antelope, turkeys, and lobo wolves. There were Indians — mostly Comanches and Kiowas who lived here because of the buffalo. They depended on buffalo meat for their food and used the skins for clothing and tents. For hundreds of years the Indians did not travel far from the few places where there was always water, like the Punta de Agua, the Agua Fria, and Las Ruedas. The reason they didn't travel far from the watering places was because they could travel only on foot — horses had not yet been brought here. It was Coronado, the Spanish explorer, who brought horses to this land in about 1541. He and his party came right up through the Dalhart country looking for a city of gold. They traveled on horses they had brought from Spain. They failed to find the city of gold but some of their horses stayed and multiplied. These were called mustangs.

The Indians learned to tame and ride the mustangs and then they began to range far from the water holes. In rainy seasons they would go far out onto the plains and camp on high spots near places where the rainfall would collect in ponds.

Mexicans had settled in New Mexico two or three hundred years ago, and when the horse came, parties of these Mexicans began coming onto the high plains to hunt buffalo and to trade with the Indians. These Mexican traders were called Comancheros. They began coming across the plains to trade with the Indians about 1770, with clumsy wooden-wheeled carts, called *carretas,* drawn by oxen and loaded with beads, mirrors, knives and hard bread. And later on they brought guns, ammunition, alcoholic spirits and other miscellanies. At first the principal trade with the Indians was for buffalo robes. But the Indians learned they could range as far away from home as Mexico and a trade sprang up by which the Indians would raid the Mexican haciendas for cattle and horses, bring them back up onto the high plains and trade them to the Comancheros. Later, along in the 1870s when the white ranchers like Charles Goodnight began to come to this area and raise herds of cattle on the free range, the Indians turned to stealing cattle and horses from these early ranchers and trading them to the Comancheros.

Then there were the Ciboleros. These were Mexican buffalo

hunters. They would sometimes come in parties with ox-drawn *carretas* to carry the meat back to their homes in New Mexico and would sometimes stay for weeks hunting buffalo on the plains. The Ciboleros were great horsemen. They had highly-spirited, swift horses. Sometimes they hunted with bow and arrow but mostly they hunted with lances about eight feet long, tipped with a steel blade about fourteen inches long. When they spotted a herd of buffalo they would strip to their waists, straddle their ponies bareback and with brightly colored cloth tassels streaming from their heads and from the ends of their lances, would ride down upon the grazing herd. Before the buffalo could get away, each Cibolero might kill as many as six. Their horses were much faster than the buffalo and they could ride up alongside one of these lumbering beasts, thrust the lance into its shoulder and into a vital organ, and then as the buffalo would fall, would pull the lance out, dash on to catch up with another, kill it and dash on.

The American buffalo hunters, equipped with their long rifles, began to slaughter buffalo in these parts for their hides in about 1860, and had killed nearly all of them by 1882. Without the buffalo there was little here on the plains for the Indian to live on and so the Indian went away. Comancheros ceased to come on the plains to trade and Ciboleros ceased to come.

The main things that remain to prove that the Comancheros and Ciboleros traveled and plied their trade around here are the names they gave to the high plains and the creeks, canyons, arroyos and water holes as they traveled back and forth across them.

It was not easy for anyone to find his way from the Mexican's home in the mountains of New Mexico out across the high plains. Apparently to keep from getting lost, they built mounds of rock or earth by which they could find their way. It is believed this is the reason they came to call the Texas High Plains El Llano Estacado, which means the "staked plains."

They named this canyon the Rita Blanca, which means the "white river." The watering hole up by Buffalo Springs they named Agua Fria, which means "cold water." The canyon down by Nara Visa they named La Punta de Agua, which means the "point of water." The little canyon near Channing that we used to go down to with Beale and Ralph Queen, was named Las Ruedas, which means "the wheels."

Down near Lubbock there is a canyon where the caprock is a yellowish color and there are cliffs there that look like Indian pueblos. This the Mexicans named Las Casas Amarillas, which means "the yellow houses."

I don't know how it was that the Mexicans gave all these places these names, or why the names have stayed with them. I suspect the Mexicans must have made maps that carried these names and when the white settlers came they simply used the names that were already there.

The Indians must have had their own names for many of these places too, but whatever names they had for them have been forgotten. About all there is now to prove that the Indians were once here are the arrowhead fields like the one down by Schroeder's Well where we hunt arrowheads. I have read that there are lots of arrowhead fields up on the plains on high places near where the ponds formed in the rainy season. The Indians would camp on these high places so they could see a long distance and not be surprised by some enemy. Most of these old campgrounds are covered with grass now so you don't find the arrowheads there very easily except when somebody plows through one of them or the grass gets killed out some other way.

I remember well that after I had spread my blanket on the ground and rolled up in it, I lay awake a long time thinking about the things Artis had told us. I would look at the shadows of the hackberry trees made by the moonlight and would imagine I could see Indians creeping among them. I could see parties of Mexicans coming across the staked plains in their wooden *carretas* and could see gatherings of Indians and Comancheros meeting to trade with one another. I could see Ciboleros riding bareback and racing their ponies into a surprised herd of buffalo and yelling as they sped among them killing buffalo after buffalo with their lances.

When I fell asleep I was trying to roll over on my tongue words such as *Ah-mah-rhēēl-yo, Pūnta day ah-gwah, Lăs Ruā-dăhs, Rhēē-oh frēē-oh* . . .

Over the years, my brothers and I developed a wild birds' egg collection and on our trips to the canyon we were always on the lookout for the egg of some bird that we had not been able to find before. From time to time we had seen a pair of great Mexican eagles near the Schroeder well about nine miles down the canyon from Dalhart. One spring we noticed that those eagles were carrying sticks to build a nest in a depression in the caprock at the spot where it made a cliff about thirty feet high. The place they had chosen for their nest was about midway up that cliff, totally inaccessible to any animal that did not fly.

Artis and G. W., who were then respectively about fourteen and ten, were determined to get one of those eagles' eggs for our collection. They figured we could get to the nest by lowering one of us down over the face of the cliff. I was eager to take part, though I didn't have much voice in the matter. After all, at that point in time, I was just a skinny little runt about seven years old and pretty much in the way in the eyes of my big brothers.

They talked it over and decided that G. W. was to go down the cliff and look for the egg. They decided we needed about fifty feet of one-inch hemp rope and some extra manpower which had to be enlisted from among my brothers' friends, "Rats" Smith, "Toots" Vineyard, "Chock" Dellinger and Joe Billy Stone. As it turned out, Rats and Chock were the ones who joined us.

We all had an early breakfast and left our house for the canyon at dawn. It was only about a mile from our house to the edge of the canyon. When we reached that point, we looked to the east and marveled at the flamboyancy of the sunrise.

After a bit we came upon a buffalo wallow that had about six inches of water left in it from the last time enough water had fallen to make a continuous stream down the canyon. In such a flow, fish are believed to sometimes swim upstream and we were told this explained the presence of fish in buffalo wallows in our part of the canyon. Anyway, there were a lot of catfish crowded into the tiny puddle of water remaining in this wallow and somebody said we ought to come back down in a day or so and get those catfish before the water dried up and let the air drown them.

We came upon a school of kangaroo rats. These beautiful little tan-colored varmits, about the size of a ground squirrel, have the bodily shape, leg proportions and heads very similar to kangaroos, and they can make prodigious leaps. They live in little clusters of burrows much as prairie dogs do.

Before we got to Schroeder's Well and the eagles' nest, G. W. had shot a nice cottontail, Artis had downed a lone mallard drake that had risen from one of the buffalo wallows, and Chock had shot a quail out of a covey that rose from a bunch of sagebrush, so we had some nice food for lunch. We decided to stop by a cave we had dug in the caprock near the well and rest awhile and have lunch before we went after the eagle egg.

On the way to the cave we picked up a horned toad, examined

him carefully and then turned him loose. And we came upon a water dog. Artis held it down on the ground a while with the butt of his gun and we watched it wiggle. It ran away when Artis lifted his gun. A water dog is a salamander. This one was about ten inches long, and had a slick skin of a yellow greenish color with large blotches of a very dark brown.

There was a huge, hairy black tarantula on the floor of the cave when we got there. He was a frightful looking thing, with a body about the shape and size of a bantam egg and legs about two inches long. One of us took a gun butt and knocked the tarantula out of the cave and down the cliff. Then we all sat down and picked off the grassburs, cockleburs, and devil's claws that had lodged in our clothing as we came down the canyon. The cave smelled as if a skunk had been living there in our absence. But someone went around into a nearby draw and got an armful of dry tree branches and several nice, dry cowchips and we started a fire. The smell of the fire drove out the skunk smell and made the place seem homey. We got out a gallon bucket we had stashed away in the cave, filled it about half full of water, dumped some ground coffee in the water and put this on to boil. We skinned and cleaned the rabbit and picked and cleaned the birds. We washed all the meat with water from our canteens and cut it into small pieces. We went around into the nearby draw and cut some small green tree branches from which we each fashioned a forked stick to cook with. Pretty soon we were all cooking that fresh wild game over the open fire. Game cooked this way, with a little salt and pepper on it, together with a plate of Van Camp's Pork and Beans and a cup of coffee makes a meal that is hard to beat.

After lunch Artis and I climbed up the cliff and out onto the prairie above the canyon to have a look around. We had only a few feet of caprock to climb and there were little ledges and holes in the rock that made the climbing easy. However, before we started up, Artis cautioned me always to be careful not to reach over a ledge in a cliff unless I was sure I wouldn't put my hand on a snake or a scorpion.

There was a prairie dog town up on the prairie above the caprock and several of those pudgy, tan, nervous little fellows were sitting up on their haunches on the edges of their burrows and looking at us. Two or three prairie dog owls were out there with them. All the prairie dogs and the owls scuttled down into the prairie dog holes when we started walking toward them.

We jumped a chaparral or roadrunner while we were up there. I chased him awhile. This long-legged, short-winged bird is colored a lot like a guinea, but it has a long neck and long legs that are made for running. It cannot fly far off the ground and depends on its running ability to protect it from its enemies.

We examined two or three kinds of cactus growing up there on the prairie. The flat-leafed prickly pear cactus and the spiney pincushion shaped cactus were showing their lovely yellow and red blooms. And there was a yucca plant nearby sending its shaft of waxy white flowers up from the center of its sword-like, green, spiked branches.

It was past midday and the sun had passed the zenith and was in the western part of the sky. We looked back across the plains to the east and marveled at a great mirage we could see there. What we saw was sunlight reflecting from the surface of a layer of air lying in a slight depression in the prairie, but it looked exactly like a lake of water, wavelets, reflections and all, except that a cow or a horse standing in it appeared to be upside down.

Everybody but Chock Dellinger had gathered some cedar bark when we climbed through a barbed wire fence and after Artis and I got back to the cave they rolled the cedar bark in newspaper and began smoking it. Chock bit off a chew of Climax chewing tobacco. I had a package of Cubebs and I smoked one of these. The rest of the boys thought my Cubebs were sissy but I had tried Chock's Climax and it made me sick and I hadn't yet learned how to endure either cedar bark or tobacco smoke. Everybody agreed that all the smokes must be put out before we left the cave in obedience to the rule of the plains that everyone must use care not to set a grass fire, because grass fires could quickly become raging prairie fires.

Finally, it was decided we should go ahead and get the eagle egg. The eagle's nest was high up in the cliff on the same side of the canyon that our cave was on. The Schroeder windmill was in the bottom of the canyon about a quarter of a mile from the nest. It was decided that Artis and G. W. and Rats and Chock would get up on the top of the caprock and walk to the spot above the nest, from which point they would lower G. W. down to the nest on the rope. I was to go down in the canyon and point out to them where to stop and be above the nest. Then I was to get under the windmill tower and stay there. Artis said that eagle might be pretty mad and might come after me. I guess they thought they were too big for the eagle to attack them or maybe they planned to ward off any eagle attack with their guns. Anyway, Chock, Rats and Artis tied the rope around G. W.'s waist, put a knapsack filled with hay on his back for him to put the egg in and let him over the cliff. He found two beautiful eagle eggs in the nest, took one of them and put it in his knapsack and Chock and Rats and Artis pulled him back up to the top of the cliff. I was watching these operations and wondering if I would ever grow up to be big like my brothers, when I noticed one of the eagles flying madly back and forth above the nest. Evidently it was the mother eagle who had returned and found her nest disturbed. Suddenly she spotted me, made a great circle in the air and then seemed to dive downward and straight at me. I cringed down behind the six-by-six base post on the well tower and the eagle ended her dive and soared back upward and out of sight.

Rats and Chock and Artis and G. W. came on down to the windmill and we got out the eagle egg and looked at it. It was about three and a half inches long and about two and a half inches wide in the middle. It was basically white, but nearly covered with hundreds of beautiful little brownish and reddish spots. We put it back in the knapsack, carefully tucked in the hay.

Then we all went out into the old Indian campground that lay just below the Schroeder Well and hunted arrowheads until we had each found some good specimens. Then we started the trek home. Artis and G. W. and I said we planned to put our arrowheads in our arrowhead collection.

It was still early in the afternoon when we started back and we felt we didn't have to hurry home, so as we walked toward town we went back into a lot of the draws and stayed up along the caprock a lot of the time.

Toward evening we saw several of those black and white bullbats flying in their clumsy zigzag way out of the draws. Great flocks of martins were seen returning to their mud nests on the wall of one of the cliffs. And a number of ordinary bats began floating out of their caves to start their night of flying and feeding. Turtle doves which had come to roost in the trees in the draws began their peculiarly mournful calls.

The sun set in a blaze of glory in the west.

Val Powell's Blacksmith Shop and Joe Langhorne's Barbershop

When the bellows was worked it made a Whoosh-whoosh sound, and sent up showers of sparks when the coal was fired up.

For my part, I thought Val Powell's Blacksmith Shop was about the most interesting place in town. I would go there lots of times during summer vacations and also I might get to do it on a Saturday during the school term if my brothers and I didn't go hunting in the canyon.

On the way to Val's shop I might stop by the fire station and look at the harness suspended above the fire wagon's tongue, ready to be dropped in place on the great Percheron fire horses should there be a fire alarm. Or I might go a block out of the way so as to pass Lewis's Livery Stable so I could find out whether they were going to breed a mare.

The shop was in a one-story corrugated iron building one block off Main Street but near the business section of town. The building was about thirty feet wide. At its front were two huge doors opening from the center and reaching up high enough to permit a prairie schooner to be driven into the shop. Because of that big door and those thin walls, you could hear Val banging on his anvil a couple of blocks before you got there.

I think the floor of the shop was the earth, but it may have been cement. It was always covered with something soft, black and sooty, possibly dust mixed with ashes from the bellows-activated open furnace.

The furnace was really an open space about four feet above the floor atop a large solid platform or fire bed built of red fire brick. It was on the righthand side of the shop as one entered from the street. About three feet above the fire bed there was suspended a tin smokestack, the lower part or mouth of which was spread out about even with the top edge of the fireplace.

The first thing you noticed was the smell. It was a mixture of the odor of coal dust, smoke, exploding sparks and fresh horse manure.

A huge bellows was affixed above one end of the furnace platform and there were pipes attached to the bellows through which air could be forced upward through the granulated coal that would be piled in the center of the fireplace.

When the bellows was worked it made a *Whoosh-whoosh* sound, and sent up showers of sparks when the coal was fired up.

In front of the fireplace was a great anvil, bolted to a huge, round-topped wooden block. A wooden bucket containing perhaps five gallons of water was set on the floor to one side of the anvil and between it and the fireplace. Red hot iron would be plunged sizzling into this water for the purpose of cooling and tempering it.

All along the dark wall of the shop opposite the fireplace there were hung a great variety of pieces of iron such as long strips of various widths that could be bent and molded into rims for wagon or buggy wheels, round rods and square rods that could be fashioned into branding irons, and pieces of sheet iron which could be cut and melted and reshaped for a great variety of uses. And, of course, there were barrels of horseshoe forms of various sizes.

Val seemed always to be smiling and to have his face and arms and clothing smudged with ashes or soot. He always greeted me with a hearty: "Hi, son, come in and set a spell." He was a huge man with heavily muscled and hairy arms, neck and chest. He usually wore a cotton shirt with open collar and the sleeves cut off almost to the shoulder. He would have on a leather apron which could shed sparks coming from the fire or the anvil.

I was always particularly intrigued with his horseshoeing. He had a rasp and a heavy curved knife which he used for the purpose of trimming and shaping the horses' hoofs to make them ready for shoeing. He would position himself beside a horse's leg, facing to the rear, then reach down, and, grabbing the horse by the hock a few inches above the hoof would lift backward the lower part of the leg. This way the hoof could be lifted about eighteen inches off the ground and laid across Val's knee. He would first remove the old shoe if there was one, clipping the old nails off at the sides of the hoof and prying the shoe loose. Then he would cut and file the bottom of the hoof to prepare it for the new shoe and, before releasing the hoof, would try a new shoe form for size, holding the shoe with a pair of iron tongs.

He would let the horse's hoof go back to the ground and thrust the iron form into the bed of coals atop the fire platform. With his left hand he would then grasp the handle on the bellows and pump it a few times. The air would rush through the coals on the fire platform with that *whoosh-whooshing* sound, the sparks would fly up umbrella-like from the coal and soon the fire bed would be a great heap of brightly glowing, burning coal.

When the shoe form had become red hot, Val would take it from the fire bed with his tongs, holding them with his left hand, lay the shoe on its side or flat on the anvil, and, seizing his great hammer in his right hand, would strike the shoe several mighty blows, shaping and bending it as he saw fit.

Then again lifting the horse's hoof with one hand and holding the red hot shoe by means of the tongs held in the other, he would test it for shape by pressing it lightly against the hoof.

After that he would plunge the hot shoe sizzling into that bucket of water, then reheat it in the fire box and again hammer on it and test it for shape on the horse's hoof until he was satisfied that it would fit. Then he would again heat the shoe red hot and, with a hammer and punch would drive holes through it as needed for nailing it to the hoof.

After cooling the shoe, he would again take the horse's hoof across his knee and attach the shoe by driving nails through it and out the sides of the hoof. The sharp ends of the nails would then be cut off or hammered down flat along the side of the hoof and the shoe job for that foot would be done.

I could stand and watch Val go through these procedures for hours at a time. When I would leave and wander toward home, I would remember the sight of that fire casting bright red umbrella-like showers of sparks as Val would work the bellows with that *whoosh-whooshing* sound. I would hear the joyous *clang-clang* of Val's hammer striking the anvil and the *sizzle* of the hot iron being thrust into the bucket of water. I would smell the coal dust, ashes and fresh manure and would hear the soft *smack-smacking* sound of the nails being driven through the horse's hoofs and bradded down.

And I would think that Val Powell must be the happiest man

one could imagine, and that blacksmithing must be one of the best occupations a man could have.

The westbound Fort Worth and Denver train which pulled in to Dalhart on May 8, 1908, bore a man from Mineral Wells who had decided to move further west. He was ticketed to Clayton, New Mexico, but when the train stopped at Dalhart, he looked out to see a baseball game between the Boston Bloomer Girls and the Dalhart Texans in progress.

The passenger, one Joe Langhorne, an avid baseball fan, left the train, watched the baseball game and decided, mayhap, it was Dalhart, not Clayton, that he was looking for.

What he wanted was a new place in which to ply his trade of barbering.

Next morning he walked into Charlie Hill's Barbershop which was across Main Street from Dinwiddie's Pool Hall and Domino Parlor and Jack Jesse's Saloon. Charlie was busy shaving a patron. "Who owns this place?" asked Joe. Charlie looked up and said, "I do." "How much do you want for it?" asked Joe. Charlie paused, then said, "Four hundred dollars." Joe said, "I'll take it," and pulled $400.00 in currency from his pocket and handed it to Charlie. Charlie said, "When do you want to take over?" Joe said, "I want to finish shaving that fellow you're working on." Charlie handed Joe his razor, and Joe, the new owner, finished shaving Charlie's patron, who, Joe learned when the job was finished and the last of the hot towels applied, was Jess Jenkins.

Thus began a lifelong friendship between a man who loved life and made friends with everyone and a stoic, reserved, mysterious figure whom few knew but about whom everyone in Dalhart had a very positive opinion.

Everyone knew Jess Jenkins had come to Dalhart in 1905, and promptly became owner of the 101 Ranch, one of the north Panhandle's larger spreads. Jess was a tall, stately man and apparently a wealthy one but one who kept the story of his life and his business very much to himself. The source of his wealth was what seemed to intrigue most people.

Jenkins had lived in Old Mobeetie, and in Old Tascosa, the two earliest (and perhaps wildest) towns in the north Panhandle. He was believed to have once been the boss of "Hogtown," a portion of Tascosa devoted primarily to saloons and brothels. Characters such as the killer, Billy the Kid, and the silver tongued lawyer, Temple

Houston, were said to have patronized his establishments. Jess Jenkins was said to have been involved in some of the more spectacular shoot-outs that occurred there, providing several occupants for Tascosa's famed Boot Hill Cemetery.

Jenkins may have been a champion of the nester and small cowman in the early-day life and death fight between them and the cattle kingdom.

Mobeetie and Tascosa both fell prey to progress when the rail transportation supplanted trail drives as the means of moving cattle to market. Jenkins had come to the Dalhart area when Tascosa died.

Joe Langhorne was as different from Jess Jenkins as a man could be. Joe loved everybody, and was completely open, frank and uninhibited. His inward happiness and easy adjustment to life was infectious.

One of Dalhart's favorite people was the man who shined shoes and boots at Joe's Barbershop. He was John Burke, better known as "Shorty No Legs." Shorty said he had come to Dalhart on a freight train in 1901. His legs had been cut off a few inches below the knees in some accident. If asked, he would say, "A steamboat ran over me." He got about very well on canvas pads. His conviviality and good humor made him a legendary figure. He was a natural counterpart for Joe Langhorne.

Joe's friendliness and enthusiasm accompanied by the Irish banter of Shorty No Legs and the ready wit of Joe's partner (and fellow member of the town's baseball team) Joe Bass, made Joe Langhorne's Barbershop at once a "melting pot" and meeting place where the townspeople talked, laughed, and told jokes and news. It was the focal point for the comings and goings of many.

Here each morning if court was not in session, Frank Tatum, the irrepressible lawyer, began his daily shopping tour for the latest gossip. Next stop, to see I. J. Gushwa, manager of the De Soto Hotel. Next to see W. H. Lathem, the land dealer (who would likely repeat his view that the Dalhart area could produce more but promise less and promise more and produce less than any other area in the country). On up Main Street, Frank would go by *The Dalhart Texan* office to see W. H. Walker, editor and owner; by Guy McGee's and Shorty Wolf's drugstores; by Dinwiddie's Pool Hall and Domino Parlor (if open), by Stedman, the crippled jeweler; by Charles Summers and Sons to see E. R. Stewart and by T. L. Swearingen's Grocery Store to see T. L., and watch the little baskets be shot up to the cage where Ada Mae and Eula sat and kept account of the business. He might even step over to the fire station for a word with Slim Batis, the Fire Chief. When he would reach his office in the Midway Bank and Trust Company Building, Frank Tatum would be always fortified with the latest news.

Back when there was no radio or television and the roads were such as not to beckon one to travel far from home, the town's baseball team was a great source of entertainment. Joe Langhorne usually played second base, Shorty Wolf left field, Joe Bass first base and Chuck Dellinger, pitcher. Joe Langhorne was a kind of cheerleader, keeping up a lively chatter throughout each game. When the umpire would make a call he didn't like, he would chant, "Mighty close, Mistah Umpiah, mighty close."

Shorty No Legs would be there adding his part. He would station himself in front of the grandstand and near home plate. When the Dalhart team would make a good play, he would often get excited and race up to third base on his stumps, bringing himself to a halt by upending himself onto his hands.

Every regular customer at Joe's Barbershop had his own shaving mug in the shaving mug case. My father would get by some time early every day for his steam towels and his shave.

Old Al Dalton, the man said to have headed a trail drive of cattle from near Vernon, Texas, to Oregon ("longest trail drive on record," some said), would drop in occasionally.

In fact, almost everybody in town patronized Joe's shop except Eugene Logan — the uncommunicative ex-ranger and man of law. He avoided Joe's because he might meet Jess Jenkins there. Whenever either of these men came close to the other, those present sensed the possibility of a shooting. For some reason known only to them, each of these men had an abiding hatred of the other. No direct confrontation ever developed but as long as both men lived, those about them felt that some day they would have it out.

Legendary Eugene Logan

Numerous times men were hired to kill him. Two were hired once at Tucumcari. Though bolstered by whiskey, the men quailed when Logan, cool and steady, got off the train with his fire-eating six-guns at his side . . .

— The Dalhart Texan

Whether he was sitting in his rocking chair on the porch of his home on the north side of town, making his weekly rounds collecting rent from his tenants or presiding at a meeting of the City Council, Eugene (Dad) (Cyclone) Logan was an impressive figure.

During his tenure as mayor of Dalhart, one could often see the giant figure of Eugene Logan ambling along down Main Street on his way from his northside home to the Dallam County Courthouse.

He would come from across the point where the Fort Worth and Denver and the Rock Island Railroads intersected, then proceed southward past the Ely–Hesse Wholesale Grocery, the Schuhart Feed Store, the Trans-Canadian Sanitarium, Art Schlofman's Boot and Saddlery Shop and Joe Scott's Ford dealership, on past the Midway Bank and Trust Company, the Cozy Corner Cafe, Dinwiddie's Pool Hall and Domino Parlor, Joe Langhorne's Barbershop, and Guy McGee's Drugstore, on past the Citizen's State Bank, the *Dalhart Texan* office and the Felton Opera House, on past W. H. Lathem's Land Office, Jim Pigman's Abstract Company, the De Soto Hotel and the Mission Theater. Here, turning left, he would enter the courthouse.

He was a big man, well over six feet tall, broad shouldered and erect, giving the impression of immense physical strength which seemed little diminished even at age seventy-two, when he became mayor of Dalhart in 1924. He was impressive in his costume, too. He always wore a baggy black suit, a huge broad-brimmed black Stetson hat and had an unlighted, crooked cheroot protruding from his mouth. But it was not these physical attributes alone that made Eugene Logan such an impressive figure. There was something about his demeanor and the way he looked at you that made him appear at once forbidding, mysterious and commanding. He seemed self-contained, aloof, and vastly silent. There was something about him that made one wonder what past experiences had helped mold him into the strong, silent, imperturbable character he exhibited. Yet, while everyone seemed to know him, he was always uncommunicative and guarded, and few were close enough to him to learn details of his past.

There was embodied in his life much early Texas history. As was true of many Texans, he came from Tennessee. The occasion of his coming, however, was extraordinary according to his account confided to Joe Scott and revealed after his death. The story, consistent with and perhaps explaining other legends about him was this: Following the end of the Civil War, Logan, as a lad of nineteen, was working as an expressman on a mail car carrying a load of gold bullion then commonly used in the transfer of funds. Carpetbaggers were then flooding the South, sometimes with ill intent. A group believed to be carpetbaggers undertook to hold up Logan's express car and rob him of the gold. Logan pretended to be opening the safe, then drew his pistol, turned about and killed three of the robbers. The others fled. Fearing reprisal, Logan immediately fled from Tennessee, heading toward Texas.

That was in 1865. He first settled in Hill County where he married and accumulated a small herd of cattle. About 1879, he moved his family and his livestock to a point near the intersection of Boggy Creek and the Brazos River in Young County. For a number of years after that he served as an inspector for the Texas Cattlemen's Association assigned to Doan's Crossing, a point on the Red River a few miles north of the present site of Vernon. Here cattle herds, following the Chisholm Trail en route to Dodge City, Kansas, converged to cross the Red. His functions as such an inspector were primarily that of finding, rounding up, and returning to their owners, cattle that strayed from their own herds.

In 1889, the entire community in which Logan lived was bit-

The Legends of Eugene Logan

terly excited, torn and divided by an episode known as the Young County Massacre, the facts of which are unclear to this day. Insofar as the affair may have involved Logan, it could be called the Eugene Logan Mystery. There were those then, and there are those today, who believe that Logan's part in that affair was an heroic one, in which he was severely wounded in gunfire occurring while he was undertaking to guard prisoners in his custody. However, there were then, and there are today, those who believe that Logan was a villain of the episode, acting in concert with, or as a part of, a mob attempting to seize and kill prisoners in the custody of a U.S. Marshal.

So far as this sketch of Eugene Logan is concerned, it is not important which of these versions was true. All that is important is that the affair occurred and, regardless of the true role played by Logan, it left persons at large who were his mortal enemies.

Much has been written about the Young County Massacre and of Eugene Logan's probable part in it. Perhaps the most impartial version is that given by Justice Gray of the Supreme Court of the United States, in his 1892 opinion in the case that grew out of the affair, namely, *Eugene Logan, et al v. United States, 263 U.S. 310.* Other facts which appear reliable are related in the book, *History of Young County, Texas,* by Cary J. Crouch.

From the court opinion and Crouch's account, the affair may be summarized as follows: In the fall of 1888, four brothers named Marlow, charged with horse and cattle theft in the Oklahoma Indian Territory, had been brought to the U.S. jail at Graham, Texas. After being released on bail they were working at the Denson farm near Graham. There a fifth brother — Boone Marlow, who had been charged with murder in the Indian Territory, and who was a fugitive — joined the four others. The sheriff of Young County, Marion D. Wallace, and his deputy, one Tom Collier, went to the farm for the purpose of arresting Boone. Boone Marlow shot and killed Sheriff Wallace and disappeared. The remaining four brothers were returned to the Graham jail. Feelings against the Marlow brothers became intense, and after an unsuccessful attempt by a masked and armed mob to take the brothers from the jail, a deputy U.S. Marshal named Ed Johnson was ordered to move the prisoners to Weatherford, Texas, for safekeeping.

Meantime, Collier had been appointed sheriff in place of the slain Wallace, and Collier had appointed Marion A. Wallace (nephew of the slain sheriff) as deputy, Sam D. Waggoner as constable for Graham, and Eugene Logan as constable for Belknap.

After dark on the night of January 19, 1889, two hacks and a buggy left Graham, ostensibly to carry out the order of U.S. Deputy Johnson to move the Marlows to Weatherford. One of the hacks was driven by P. A. Martin the county attorney. It contained the four Marlow boys, who, Justice Gray declared, "were shackled together two and two by irons riveted around one leg of each and connected by a chain." One of the hacks contained the U.S. Deputy Johnson and Deputy Wallace. In the buggy was Samuel Waggoner and another man.

A few miles out of Graham, the entourage was met and stopped by about forty masked and armed men who opened fire upon the prisoners. Then, said Justice Gray: "The four Marlows, in spite of their shackles, immediately dropped out of the hack and wrested firearms, either from the guards or from their assailants, with which they defended themselves, killed two of the mob, wounded others, and finally put the rest to flight. Johnson (the U.S. Deputy) was wounded, and he and all the guards fled."

When the shooting ceased, Alfred and Epp Marlow lay dead. Charles and George Marlow, though severely wounded, survived but each remained shackled to a dead brother. Cary Crouch, in her book, *History of Young County, Texas,* says Charles and George Marlow freed themselves by severing the ankles of their dead brothers. The hack which had brought them to the spot was still there. Charles and George Marlow boarded the hack and drove to the Denson farm. Here they surrendered to federal authorities. They were later tried on the larceny charges against them and acquitted.

Eugene Logan was present at the scene of this shoot-out and was severely wounded, but it is not clear what role he played. A July 1969 letter from Logan's daughter Kate, to Logan's granddaughter Mrs. Roy Stout of Dalhart, says her father told her he was riding a horse beside the hack and was one of the guards. The surviving Marlows claimed the guards were in league with the attacking mob and had seen Logan shoot at them. After an investigation by a deputy U.S. Marshal a federal grand jury issued indictments against Logan, Waggoner and Wallace charging them, "together with diverse other evil-disposed persons whose names to the grand jurors are unknown," with conspiracy to oppress citizens while in the custody of a U.S. Marshal and with murder.

At the trial, the only evidence the U.S. Attorney was able to produce to connect Logan and the others with the alleged crimes, was testimony of what certain persons said they heard other persons say. Thus, certain persons testified that U.S. Deputy Johnson, (who had given a newspaper account that Logan was one of the guards) had later told them that Logan was not such a guard and must have tipped off the mobsters.

Others testified that they had heard Collier, Hollis and others say on the night of the assault that Logan had been present at the fight but not as a guard.

The two surviving Marlows were permitted to testify that while escaping in the hack after the assault, Charles Marlow had said he believed that Logan was the man at whom he had shot and who shot at him during the fight.

In April 1891, a jury found Logan, Waggoner and Wallace guilty of conspiracy but not guilty of murder. All other defendants were found not guilty.

The court rendered judgment, fining Logan, Waggoner, and Wallace $5000 each, and ordering that they should thereafter "be ineligible for any office or place of honor, profit or trust, created by the Constitution or laws of the United States."

On April 4, 1892, the Supreme Court of the United States, in an exhaustive opinion, reversed the trial court decision, after which the charges against all who had been indicted were dropped.

Logan then began his career as a Texas Ranger, having been appointed by the governor of Texas with a roving assignment entitling him to function throughout the northern Panhandle. At some point an appointment as Deputy U.S. Marshal extended his roving authority to the Oklahoma Panhandle and northeastern New Mexico.

He achieved a reputation as a fearless and feared peace officer. Legends about his exploits abounded. Some of these were recounted in his obituary appearing in the May 9, 1935, *Dalhart Texan*:

> Violence leered at Colonel Logan many, many times. But the color never drained from the old peace officer's face, his hand never wavered, and the many foul plots laid by bad men, who hated him because of his fearless enforcement of the law, never struck.
>
> Numerous times men were hired to kill him. Two were hired once at Tucumcari. Though bolstered by whiskey, the men quailed when Logan, cool, and steady, got off the train with his fire-eating six-guns at his side and his saddle gun, that would shoot two miles on the level, in the crook of his arm.

One other time Colonel Logan was retained by town authorities to break the grip of terror and vice in Dalhart. A hired killer, with several killings to his credit, was hired to stop Logan. A friend tipped Logan off. With his guns swinging loosely in their worn leather holsters, Logan started looking for the hired assassin, who, learning of it, left and never returned. In 1900, Colonel Logan guarded the personnel and property of the Rock Island Railroad employed in its building the bridge across the Canadian River near Tucumcari. The town of Logan at the point of the crossing was named for him.

Because of his reputation as a fearless lawman, Colonel Logan was known to many as "Cyclone." I knew him at a later period and by then the nickname most commonly given him was "Dad." So I think of Colonel Logan as Dad Logan.

Dad Logan lived in Dalhart from its inception in 1901. He became a substantial property owner possessed of a hotel and numerous rent properties.

While he continued to be remembered for his early exploits as a peace officer, he seemed to mellow and became an affable and even lovable character as time wore on.

He was a highly respected citizen of the town and was elected mayor in 1924, a position he held continuously until voluntarily giving up the position in 1931, on condition that Orville Finch be elected to replace him.

Once during his tenure as mayor, my brother Artis, then a doctor in Dalhart, asked me to approach Dad Logan on the subject of having the City Council adopt an ordinance requiring the pasteurization of all milk sold in the town. I did so and Dad Logan responded: "Well, that's a right pregnant idee." Shortly thereafter the ordinance was adopted.

Folks in Dalhart still like to tell the story on Dad Logan about when he went to collect his rent on his rent houses, and the renter would tell him he could not pay and needed time to get the money. Dad Logan would take off his big black Stetson, remove his twisted cheroot from his mouth and very gently say: "Well, that's just all right, I can understand and of course I'll give you time — any time *today* — will be just fine."

Andy James and

The James Brothers' Ranch

— Part One

Then at dawn on April 9, out of the north came a howling blizzard. The snow, wet and sticky at first, clung to the cattle's hides and filled their nostrils. Then, as the temperature plunged to seventeen below zero, the snow froze. When the wet snow that filled the cattle's nostrils froze, they died, for cattle cannot breathe through their mouths.

As a boy I had always admired Andy James. To me he typified the old-time bronc riding cowboy. He was a rugged, rough-and-ready appearing man, powerful looking with a windblown and sun-tanned, leathery-looking complexion. He was noted for his independence and individuality and was respected by everybody.

One story about a tooth pulling episode seems characteristic of this man. It was said that in his old age Andy was rapidly losing his teeth. His dentist examined him and said the teeth next to the last bridge installed had become too loose to hold and that he should go ahead and pull all of Andy's remaining teeth. Andy told the dentist to have at it then and there. But when the dentist started to insert a hypodermic needle, Andy balked, went down the street and returned with a pint of whiskey. Andy took a good drink and told the dentist to proceed. After each tooth was extracted, Andy would get out of the dentist's chair and dance around a bit holding his jaw in his hands. Then he would take another swig, get back in the dentist's chair and tell the dentist to proceed. This kept up until all his teeth were pulled, all without any anesthetic.

He was one of Dalhart's most prominent early-day citizens, and had once owned principal interest in the Midway Bank. The James

Brothers Ranch owned by him and his brother, Walter, was the biggest ranch in the area next to the XIT. The story of the James Brothers Ranch explains a lot about the opportunities and the problems presented in the early days.

In 1871, six years after returning from service in the Confederate Army, Andy's father (Captain Andy) gave up trying to rebuild his Virginia plantation and moved his family to a spot near Altus, Oklahoma, where he established a ranching operation on land leased from the Chickasaw Indian Nation. The land was a few miles north of Doan's Crossing where, during the previous ten years or so, trail herds en route to Dodge City, Kansas, had converged to cross the Red River. Here he built a herd of about five hundred cattle and horses and began raising his family, consisting of his wife Sue and twelve children. Andy, Jr., (Andy Marmaduke) was born in 1882, his brother, Walter, was then four years old.

When Captain James first came to the Altus, Oklahoma area, the Texas Panhandle was still buffalo and Indian country. When, in about 1880, the buffalo and the Indians were pretty well cleared out, white settlers began coming in and settling where there was live water such as along the Canadian and the Palo Duro.

On the vast plains without live water there was little settlement until after about 1883, when barbed wire and windmills became generally available.

The Federal Homestead Act of 1862 which had drawn many farming oriented settlers into areas such as those in the Oklahoma and New Mexico Territories — persons of a type who could be happy with the opportunity to acquire, free of charge, small tracts such as 160 acres — was never extended into Texas.

Perhaps borrowing from Mexico's experience proving that semiarid areas such as those in the north Texas Panhandle could best be used either exclusively for stock raising or for stock raising in combination with farming, the state of Texas, by an act adopted in 1895, had provided for the state's school lands in the Texas Panhandle to be placed on the market in tracts of up to four 640-acre sections, the pasturelands at not less than one dollar an acre and all other lands at not less than two dollars an acre, payable over forty years. While the amount of such lands that any one man could buy was restricted to four sections, each member of his family could acquire a similar amount, or a man could add to his holdings through the device of having the purchase made in the name of a nominee. Lands conveyed by the state to railroads for constructing their lines or to surveyors for their services were open to unrestricted sale. So there was land available in tracts large enough to interest the cattleman.

In 1898, Captain James journeyed to Texline, Texas, then the county seat of the Panhandle's most northwesterly county of Dallam. From there he traveled out upon the Texas Panhandle prairies, east of Texline. He found a vast, unoccupied area covered by waist-high bluestem, interspersed with rich gramma and buffalo grass. He concluded that this land was too sandy, the rainfall too sparse, and the markets too remote, for it ever to be occupied by dirt farmers. He marked the approximate location of this land on a map.

Filled with enthusiasm, Captain James returned to his Altus, Oklahoma ranch, and began planning to move his operations to this new land, where, he opined to his family, "The land will never be plowed."

Captain James died in 1900, but, following his advice, his widow and sons Walter and Andy journeyed in 1901, to Texline, where they hired a team of mules and a buggy, drove out over the prairie and found the general area marked on Captain James's map. They made the down payment on four sections of that land. The tract chosen was about ten miles north of the present site of Dalhart, Texas. The purchase price was $1.25 an acre. Walter joined Mother James in signing the note. Andy did not, for he was only nineteen years of age.

Andy built a two-room dugout, put down a well (drawing water at 420 feet), built a small barn for storing feed and riding equipment, and a corral and pasture for saddle horses. Walter went back to the family ranch in Oklahoma, and soon began moving the family's livestock from that ranch to the new one in the Texas Panhandle.

Thus began the fabulous James Brothers Ranch, which, phenomenally, by 1914, comprised over 400 sections of land or over 250,000 acres, extending from near Tucumcari, New Mexico, into Cimarron County, Oklahoma, with about 17,000 head of cattle (mostly steers) bearing either the Locked J brand (ᗡ) (the first brand chosen by Mother James) or the Diamond brand (◊) later adopted.

Unlike the Panhandle areas with live water, on the high, flat expanses on which the James brothers launched their enterprise in 1901, "water rights" were held only by those possessing the right to water produced by a water well powered by a windmill.

From about 1900 to 1910, a man need own only the tract on which his well was situated in order to have the free use of all the grass to which his cattle would go from the well.

"A big old steer could easy range at least four miles from the well," Jesse James, Andy's nephew told me. "Moreover, there was no need for fencing during the first ten years or so of the ranch because no one else was using the land. All we needed was a kind of fence of men, just a few cowboys out on the range to see the cow critters didn't wander too far over yonder."

So it was possible for a man to buy or lease a quarter section (or less) put down a well, build a dugout, a feed and saddle shed and a horse corral, man the camp with a few cowboys and have the use of all the grass within a circular area having a radius of about four miles. That's an area equal to about fifty sections of 640 acres each or about 32,000 acres. While with only one well he could water only up to about 200 "cow critters," he would have available enough grass for about 1,000, at twenty a section. Most of the Texas part or the "South Ranch" was put together this way. Then, in 1906, Walter and Andy bought from a man named "Daddy" Bull, six forty-acre "water right" tracts and a 160-acre homestead tract in Cimarron County, Oklahoma. These tracts had been originally assembled by the Carawaka Cattle Company (the 3Cs). The purchase price was $19.20 an acre, or $7,680. Ownership of these 400 acres gave them control of grazing rights on about 60,000 acres. This property they called the "North Ranch."

"Beginning about 1910, we started being troubled by settlers," said James. "But usually where we saw signs some landowner intended to put down a well, we could go to him and make a deal to lease his land for a year's grazing for about twenty-five cents an acre. Sometimes we had to buy the land, or enough of it to control the water rights.

"As time went on and we got to having more and more neighbors, we had to lease or buy more and more land, drill more and more wells and build more and more fences.

"By about 1917, the water right method of holding land was all gone; we had a well for about every four- and one-half sections (about sixty-four wells) and the ranch was all fenced on the outside and big pastures were fenced — twenty to forty sections to a pasture."

Nineteen sixteen, 1917, and 1918, were the finest years for the James Brothers Ranch. It then owned or held under lease nearly 500,000 acres of fine grassland on which it was running about 20,000 head of cattle.

Late in 1918, about 3,000 head of cattle were sent to market, and the ranch went into the winter with about 17,000 head.

Then, on December 22, it began to snow — a blowing snow at first, then just a steady fall that covered the whole ranch about three feet deep except on the hilly part of the North Ranch. In many places

Andy James and The James Brothers Ranch — Part One

there were snowdrifts twenty feet deep. The snow covered all the grass on the South Ranch and most of it on the North Ranch. From then on until late the following April, the ranch remained snowbound. There would be slight thaws, leaving the ground an almost impassable mud; then more snow. So, from December 1918, until late in April 1919, the James Brothers were using all the men and all the equipment they had or could get, trying to get cottonseed cake and fodder (maize, kaffir, and sorghum stalks) to the cattle to keep them from starving.

They bought all the fodder they could from nearby farmers like the Crabtrees and the Lucases but getting it to the cattle was rough going. The snow most of the time was too deep for ordinary wagons, so the farmers built and used sleds. Even then about all they could do was haul the feed to the James ranch fence lines and throw it over. There would be little relief even when the snow would let up and there would be a thaw. For then the mud would be too deep to allow hauling, even by wagon. The James Brothers managed to pull most of the cattle through January, February, and March 1919, but they were thin and weak. Andy and Walter knew that unless the weather cleared they were in for a disaster. That disaster came on April 9, in the form of a blowing blizzard.

Letters from Andy to the Interstate National Bank of Kansas City in the winter of 1918, and spring of 1919, (preserved by Andy's daughter, Mrs. Priestly of Dalhart), give a vivid account of that fateful period of the ranch's life.

In his letter of December 31, 1918, to R. M. Cook, vice-president of the bank, Andy wrote:

> We are still having severe weather here, been snowing a little yesterday and today, but is clearing off now and looks like the storm might be over. The snow hasn't gone very much since I wrote you last, and everything is having to be fed, more or less roughage, as the grass is still covered till cattle are not getting any of it. There hasn't been any losses here to speak of so far, but if this continues, it is going to get cattle in condition that they will not be able to stand any very severe storms later on.

In a letter of January 9, 1919, to Cook:

> There is still lots of snow on the range and cattle are not able to get any grass yet except in the sand hills. They are able to get sage brush and a little of the long grass. We have gone through this storm a great deal better than I thought possible for us to get through a week ago. We had several days that the thermometer went below zero; it

went seventeen below one night, but we had no wind with our severest cold, consequently we don't have as many frozen footed cattle as we had from our severe storm last January.

We will get through this storm in good shape if we can just have a few warm days now before we get another storm. If we should get another snow before this is all gone, it will certainly make it hard on every one. We still have some roughage left, but have fed up the biggest part of it . . .

This storm is going to make our winter expenses a great deal more than I had figured on, but don't believe it pays to cut down expenses and lose the cattle. We are going to have to ask you for an advancement of something like $25,000 at this time. If you feel that you can let us have this amount, please prepare the papers for our signatures.

In a January 13, 1919, letter to Cook:

I enclose you herewith note and mortgage which you sent us, properly signed and acknowledged.

Note what you say in regard to the losses we have sustained in this country from the very severe storm which we have had, and which we are still having. We have something like twelve inches of snow all over this country yet and are having to feed everything roughage as they are not getting any grass yet except in the sand hills.

Our cattle look considerably better now than they did a week ago, but we are not out of danger yet by any means. If we have decent weather, and can get rid of the snow that is now on the ground, we will not have any losses to speak of, but if we have another storm on top of this. it is going to be bad, as roughage is getting scarcer every day . . .

We had about thirty inches of snow fall between the 16th of December and Christmas, and it is remarkable, indeed, that the losses have not been any heavier than they have. Our feed bill is going to be something enormous. We have already fed as much feed as we had expected to feed for the entire winter. We still have some cake on hand, but it is getting almost impossible to get cake for immediate shipment. I have 500 tons of Louisiana cake bought, which they are promising me to begin loading out immediately, but have had no definite advice on any of it having been loaded yet. If we keep plenty of cake, with the hulls we have on hand now, I believe we will be able to get through in fairly good shape.

On January 27, Andy wrote David T. Beals, cashier of the bank:

I have your favor of January 24th, and was very glad to know that you were relieved from Army duty and back at your old station again.

We have had the worst storm in the country that the oldest settlers here have ever known. We have had thirty inches of snow on the level, and it has been on the ground six weeks today. We have a little grass showing in the sandhills now, and cattle are getting a place to lay down, but conditions are still very serious with us. If we can only get rid of this snow before we get another one, we will get through in better shape than we had any hopes for a few weeks ago, but if we should get another storm, it is going to be the worst we have ever seen. I have just written to Mr. Cook fully, and you can see what I have to say to him in regard to conditions generally.

There were a few warming days in March and early April. Patches of new grass began appearing where the snow had melted, and were quickly devoured by the hungry cattle. The James Brothers' trucks and tractors were now moving a good deal of roughage to the cattle. Losses had so far totaled about 3000 cattle. Andy and Walter felt the worst was over.

Then at dawn on April 9, out of the north came a howling blizzard. The snow, wet and sticky at first, clung to the cattle's hides and filled their nostrils. Then, as the temperature plunged to seventeen below zero, the snow froze. When the wet snow that filled the cattle's nostrils froze, they died, for cattle cannot breathe through their mouths.

The storm lasted only about thirty hours, but in that thirty hours, thousands of the already weakened cattle were smothered or simply perished from freezing and exhaustion.

It was several days before the cowboys could get out over the ranch to assess the losses. When they did, they learned that on that *one-day* blizzard about 5000 of the James Brothers' remaining herd of 14,000 had died.

The expenses had been enormous. For example, cottonseed cake had become so scarce it went up from a dollar a sack to a hundred dollars a sack. "The feed bill alone averaged over a thousand dollars a day for one hundred days," said Jesse James.

"We owed the Interstate Bank of Kansas City about $1,500,000, which was a lot of money, but only about two dollars fifty cents an acre on all the land in the ranch. We thought we could pull through, but the bank moved in to take control and by 1923, the ranch was no more.

"In the storm in 1912, we lost about 1200 head of Herefords, and there had been other bad storms but we had been able to survive these. But this one proved to be one calamity too many."

Andy James and
The James Brothers' Ranch
— Part Two

> *Crossing the Canadian was always dangerous whether there was water in it or not. If there was flowing water there was a risk of having the wagon turned over, so two or three cowboys would go along upstream from the wagon with ropes tied to the wagon and hitched to their saddle horns.*
>
> — Jesse James

In the summer of 1979, Jesse James, Andy's nephew (then living in Colorado Springs), told much about how the ranch was put together, how it ran, the character of the cowboys who did the work and the problems which had to be faced:

"My father used to tell me about bringing the livestock from the ranch near Altus, Oklahoma, to the new ranch in Texas. This was 1902 to 1910.

"All the while they kept adding to the herd at Altus, and then moving 200 to 500 at a time to the new ranch.

"My father and Uncle Bob headed up most of the drives. If everything went well they could make about twelve to twenty miles a day. Sometimes steers would get sore feet and they were hard to drive and they would lose weight if you drove them too far. It was about three hundred miles, so it would usually take at least two weeks to make the trip.

"They would have three or four cowboys along, one to drive a wagon loaded with food, water and camping equipment, the others on horseback. They would go up through Wellington, and White Deer, and Tascosa. Tascosa was the best place for crossing the Canadian River.

"Crossing the Canadian was always dangerous whether there was water in it or not. If there was flowing water there was a risk of having the wagon turned over, so two or three cowboys would go along upstream from the wagon with ropes tied to the wagon and hitched to their saddle horns.

"When the river was up, the extra horses would be put in the lead to get the cattle to enter the water, and there would be cowboys on either side of the herd to keep the cattle strung out. The wagon would be the last to cross.

"When the river looked dry they had to be especially careful. It could look dry and even crusted on the surface, but there might be quicksand or a red slough just below. The slough was the most dangerous, [a place of deep mud or mire]. So, even when the river was dry, one man would be sent across ahead of all the rest to test the footing. He would go across on a pacer. At that gait the horse was not likely to sink in quicksand or break through the crust. The surface would buckle or wave from the horse's weight and if he traveled at a fox trot there was more danger of his breaking through the crust or sinking.

"In the spring of 1910, we made the permanent move from the ranch near Altus to the new ranch headquarters north of Dalhart. My mother drove a buggy with two mules all the way. I was six years old then and I was in the buggy along with my mother and my two brothers, Walter, Jr., two and one-half years old and little Andy who was just three months old.

"There had been a rain just before we came to the Canadian, and the river was up. But with the help of two cowboys upstream with ropes to the buggy, we made it across.

"From the time we bought the North Ranch in 1906, until we sold it after the big 1918–1919 storm, my father lived on the North Ranch headquarters and was in charge of the North Ranch. Uncle Andy ran the South Ranch. The North Ranch headquarters was about nineteen miles southeast of Boise City, about twenty-seven miles from Texhoma, and about twenty-two miles from Stratford, which was really the closest of anything. We were thirty-five miles north of Dalhart.

"My father was a quiet, family type man. He always liked to stay pretty close to the actual, every day operations, didn't like to move around too much and was calm and steady, and I guess it was a good thing he was that way because Andy was just the opposite. Andy was a restless, in-a-hurry sort of fellow, and loved to take chances. Rube Johnson, who was our foreman on the North Ranch most of the time, used to say that Andy always thought he could do anything — and he damn near could.

"Andy and Rube Johnson were both bronc riders and there wasn't anything too wild or too mean for Andy to get on.

"My father, Uncle Andy and Uncle Joe Taylor used to go to Arizona and round up wild horses. Having a bunch of wild horses to tame was a heyday for Uncle Andy and after him and Rube would get the herd tamed to where you could sell or ride them for saddle horses, my father and Uncle Andy and Uncle Bob would trade them for cattle.

"In 1903, they brought two freight cars full of wild horses to Trinidad, and after Andy and Rube had broke them they took them to Altus. My Uncle Bob took twenty horses to Arkansas, and came back with 400 head of yellow-back cattle. They was just old scrubs but after a year or so on our grass, they brought a pretty good price on the market.

"The North Ranch was way easier to run and way safer than the South Ranch," said James, "because the Beaver River ran through it and this gave protection for cattle in wintertime that the flatlands of the South Ranch couldn't provide. Also, because the North Ranch was a little hilly, there'd usually be sage or grass on the hilltops even when we had a heavy snow. Besides, we only had to go about seventy-five feet for water. A seventy-five foot well is a lot cheaper to drill, and easier to keep up than wells 250 and 400 feet deep like they were on the South Ranch.

"My grandma, Sue Cole James, (that's my father and Uncle Andy's mother) was some lady. We called her 'Mother James.' She was a hard worker and expected everyone else to work, us kids and all the men. One time we were dipping at the ranch and the dipping vat had sprung a leak that let the creosote drain out. My wife's grandfather, Dr. Robinson, was a state cattle inspector and what you did when the state inspector came around was to put him up in the bunkhouse and feed him until he got through. It took several days to fix the dipping vat and fill it with creosote, so Dr. Robinson was living in the bunkhouse and eating on us for quite a while. Grandma James went out to the bunkhouse one day where Doc Robinson was sitting around drinking coffee and eating with the cook. 'Doc,' she said, 'you can eat more, stay longer and do less than any man that was ever on the Diamond Ranch.' That was the way grandma talked to everyone.

"In about 1910, she dropped a churn on her foot. That was the first time we ever saw Dr. Dawson.

"Nineteen ten was the worst lightning year there ever was. Started lots of prairie fires here and there. Not much rain, but lots of lightning. One day Malcolm Stewart's brother, Walter, and about ten other cowboys were working cattle in the Matlock country to bring them back to the headquarters of the South Ranch. The boy (he was only about sixteen years old, like a lot of other cowboys in those days) was riding a gray horse. Cowboys used to believe a blue or gray horse attracted lightning. Anyway, they were about a half-mile southwest of the Gable well when a storm came up and a bolt of lightning came down and hit Malcolm's brother in the head and came on to his belt and saddle horn. He died right there. It was near sundown when John Woods got to the ranch and told Mother James and everybody. That's the only time anybody got killed by lightning on the ranch.

"In the camps the men mostly lived on sowbelly and beans and biscuits. We would have lots of beans and 'taters and bacon or salt-pork for breakfast with molasses and biscuits. For supper maybe they would have stewed tomatoes and corn. In the north camp they had goats and in the fall and during the winter months they would kill a kid every Saturday, put it in a tarpaulin and keep it on the windmill. They would keep coffee on boil all day.

"Except in extreme snows and so forth, such as in 1918–1919, when we would have to bring in bundle feed for roughage, we depended almost entirely on range grass and cottonseed cake to maintain the cattle. Sometimes our cattle could go through the whole winter just on the range grass.

"We always tried to raise a little maize and kaffircorn to feed the cattle and horses but cowboys don't like to farm and we raised more sand than feed. We mostly depended on farmers like the Crabtrees and the Lucases for roughage.

"Along about in 1916, we put in a telephone at the North Ranch — mostly by using the wires on the barbed wire fences. But every time there came a little lightning it was knocked out. Better off without it. Of course, we didn't have any radios or television, but we had lots of fun. Like after supper sitting around telling different things that happened through the day or maybe somebody would have met some fella and heard a new joke.

"I think we had the first Gramophone in the country, and after my daddy got sick in 'thirty-four he got a radio and I think it was the first radio. Our closest neighbors, the Haversticks, had a player piano.

"We usually had seven camps for the whole ranch. The number of cowboys in each camp varied. At some, we would get by with one or two. On others, like the north camp, we'd have up to eight. We would keep about four saddle horses available for each cowboy at all times. During roundup or branding, we would add about seven cutting and roping horses for each cowboy. Each camp would consist of a small house built of adobe or lumber, a water well, a corral and a small shed in which to keep saddles and other riding gear and feed for the horses.

"We worked 365 days a year. A lot of good men who had worked for big companies like the XIT or the Matador weren't used to working like we wanted them to. Some of them would do about half as much as we would expect of them. So it was hard to keep all the men on the ranch that we needed. Some people said Uncle Andy worked three crews, one a comin', one a goin', and one a workin'. It was easier to keep men on the North Ranch. It was nicer work, a little nicer country to work in, more breaks along the river, more protection and things like that.

"Usually each of our cowboys would take off a day or two about once a month and go to town for a shave and a haircut and a little entertainment. Usually they'd go to Dalhart, but in the fall, if they'd saved enough money they might go to Kansas City. That was the big deal.

"The big go until about 1919, was steers. We always had a few heifers and raised a few calves but mostly ours was a steer operation. We would buy yearling steers and keep some up until they were four or five years old before sending them to market. Steers can forage for themselves tougher than heifers can, and require less handling. But there is a bigger risk of loss with steers than with heifers when the market drops. If you have heifers you can keep them and get calves and wait for better markets.

"The windmiller was really the most important man on the ranch. After the big 1919 storm, Mr. Beall of the Interstate Bank came down and took charge of the South Ranch. He didn't understand the importance of the windmiller. He hired a ranch manager from Santa Rosa, New Mexico, which is a live water country. Well, he ran it like he would a live water ranch — didn't watch the wells and keep them fixed and so forth. In two weeks 500 baby calves and one hundred colts died for lack of water.

"In 1917, my dad and Uncle Andy leased the YT Ranch and threw it in to the James Brothers Ranch. It was owned by the Wyatt Cattle Company out of Denver. It was about halfway between Texline and Coldwater. We leased it and subleased all of it except one pasture — about thirty sections — and we bought 1100 cows and run them on this thirty sections. It had living water on the Rita Blanca there north of Perico. But there was one old deep well in that pasture, over 400 feet deep — you may know where it was, about a mile and a half north of Smokey Bonner's — but I started to tell you, we had those 1100 cows there. Uncle Andy tried to look after them by himself, tried to do it. That was the year the war started and we couldn't get help to brand or nothin' hardly. Well, two boys named Moore got on the place and stole twenty head of our unbranded calves. The north camp was eighteen miles away. They drove the calves there and sold them to Rube Johnson, foreman of the North James Brothers' Ranch. Well, Uncle Andy and Billy Gibbs just happened to go up the next day and counted those twenty head of cows that had had calves jerked off of them. So Billy, he just followed them calves' tracks right to the north camp — and there they was in the lot. Rube had bought them, *bought our own calves.* Those two boys got four years apiece in the pen.

"Uncle Andy used to like to put a new man on a spoil horse [a mean, outlaw horse]. He'd tell the new man that my father's little boys rode that horse.

"Uncle Andy used to like to tell about how him and John Polecat Woods could drive out sixteen miles from headquarters in a buggy, build two miles of three-wire fence using posthole diggers and then drive back to headquarters, all in one day.

"I'll tell you one thing about Uncle Andy that's real funny. Him and Rube broke some old horses, went over to Arizona, and got some big old buggy-type horses. And Uncle Andy broke one. He was a pretty thing.

"One time his girl friend, Miss Letts, was visiting us. (She worked for Doc Dawson for awhile). Well, she and mama and my two brothers were setting out on the front porch when Uncle Andy come in on that horse from the southeast end of the water lot. Well, Uncle Andy rode out about fifty yards, and I'm sure he goosed that horse to show off for his girl and, man, he throwed him just as high as his bridle reins would reach. Like Rube Johnson would say, Andy thought he could do anything, and he could just damn near get 'er done. That's the way Uncle Andy was. He thought he could do anything and he could *nearly* get it done — but not quite. Uncle Andy would try anything. It didn't make any difference what. Old DeWitt Reynolds, he had a little bay horse — Punkin was his name — and he could slip the bridle off of him and cut cattle on him. Somebody come along and told Uncle Andy, well, I forget who it was, what they wanted, and they just mentioned that DeWitt's best cutting horse — he could pull the bridle off. Uncle Andy said, 'Hell, I can too,' so he slipped the bridle off of his horse and that pony throwed him as high as a mountain. That's just the way . . . the kind of fella he was. Now his horse was Sweetheart, and was a full brother to the horse Malcolm Stewart's brother was killed on."

Symbols of Change and I. J. Gushwa

> *I miss Dalhart hotels. We were in Hot Springs, Arkansas two weeks. We managed three trips to the races, bet $11.00 and won $15.40, the winning being sufficient to cover the attendance expense . . . We went thru the lobby of the Arlington Hotel, one of the finest in the South, but we were a little afraid to draw a good breath for fear they would charge us for it. They think it is the finest thing ever, because it has 600 rooms, but shooey, I have put up at the Stevens in Chicago and it has 3,000 rooms.*
>
> — Willie Catherine Dawson
> Letter, April 3, 1935

During the first years we were in Dalhart, many of the passenger trains, especially those coming west on the Rock Island, would have a lot of landseekers aboard, sometimes whole carloads of them.

All the lands thereabout had been owned by the state and it had conveyed vast portions to the railroads to get them to build their lines. Much of it had been conveyed to surveyors as compensation. The XIT had received its three million acres for building the state capitol. Alternate sections had been reserved for the public school funds. There was a big movement by all these landowners to sell their lands, hoping to bring in new settlers.

Prospective landowners, arriving by train, would be worn out from their long ride, which was a hot one in summertime. The smoke and cinders from the coal-burning engines would have added to their discomfort. So they would be greatly relieved on arriving in Dalhart and seeing the big sign on the Commercial Hotel:
STEAM HEAT — HOT BATHS

The Commercial Hotel, 1903

The Commercial was opened in 1903. It stood south of the Rock Island, and Fort Worth and Denver tracks. Of course there were other hotels, including some in the older section of town north of the railroad tracks. But, until the coming of the De Soto in 1910, the Commercial was the most prominent hostelry in the town.

While the traveler could get a hot bath and a good meal at the Commercial, there was little to be found in Dalhart in the way of evening entertainment. Or, to be more specific, entertainment of a character to which a man could take his wife and children.

This void was to some extent filled in 1908, when a man named Felton opened, at the corner of Main and Second Streets, the Felton Opera House.

It was not at all like what today one might expect an Opera House to be. It was a two-story brick building, the first floor of which was intended for rental as stores or business offices. Access to the second floor was by means of two stairways, a narrow one leading from Main Street and a great, wide one, leading from Second Street. Both stairways led to a hallway running the length of the

The Felton Opera House, 1908

building and from this, one entered a room, also extending the length of the building, at the front of which was a stage with huge canvas curtains that could be lowered or raised by means of man-operated pulleys. In front of the stage was an orchestra pit. Balconies ran along both walls and here, as well as near the stage below the balconies, were boxes where the more opulent and discriminating could see and be seen better. The chairs available for the audience were movable, so the place could be converted into a ballroom.

Here lecturers or candidates for office appeared occasionally. Annual high school graduation exercises were staged, chautauquas were presented and theatrical groups traveling between Denver and Fort Worth, or between Kansas City and California, would sometimes stop for overnight appearances.

A 1908 ad in *The Dalhart Texan* disclosed certain difficulties the Opera House met, both in obtaining quality entertainment and in teaching some elements of Dalhart society certain niceties to be observed in such places of culture.

The ad announced a double bill of *Canal Boat Sal* and *A Quiet*

Boardinghouse. It reminded the public that families bringing babies must also bring nurse girls to look after the babies should they threaten to disturb the audience. Moreover, said the ad, *Spitting tobacco juice on the floor is strictly forbidden!*

The railroads not only brought many new settlers to the north Panhandle in the early 1900s, they also took many north Panhandle residents to places like Kansas City and Chicago, previously very difficult for them to reach. They vastly improved the markets for what the people had for sale — particularly cattle. The area, already very attractive to the cattle ranchers, became much more attractive to them; and their numbers and activities increased. Dalhart soon became an active cattle shipping point and cattle trading center.

The total result was substantial stimulus and added prosperity to the business community. Merchants, cattlemen and professional men all began to travel more and learn more about how others lived. It became popular for the more prosperous families to send their children away to school; daughters to Ward Belmont, Hockaday, and the like, and sons to Culver, Wentworth, Northwestern Military and Naval Academy, or others of like reputation.

In short, people in Dalhart were becoming more knowledgeable about how others lived, more worldly and more discriminating in their tastes.

In about 1908, one C. R. Woods looked over the situation and decided the time had come for Dalhart to have a new and better hotel — one, indeed, that could cater to even the most erudite, traveled and demanding. So he bought a quarter of a block at the corner of Third and Main Streets in Dalhart and announced that here he would build the finest hotel in Texas; not the biggest, but the finest. The finest accommodations, the finest service, the finest food.

Construction began in 1909. By now hot water and baths could not only be made available, every room could and would have a full bathroom — hot water, commode, bathtub, and all. And every room would have a telephone — an amenity rarely found in that day. Every door on every room would be of solid walnut. The door fixtures would be of solid brass and the bathroom fixtures the best obtainable. There would be uniformed bellhops promptly available at the guests' beck and call. There would be a horse-drawn hack, manned by a uniformed driver, which would meet every incoming train and carry guests and their baggage to the hotel and return them to the depot at the time of their departure. The hotel would provide in-the-house quarters (and meals) for all employees.

The De Soto Hotel, 1910

The dining room (equipped with fine linen tableclothes and napkins, and impressive silverware), would accommodate up to forty-eight people at twelve pure walnut tables.

Woods decided to name his hotel The De Soto after Hernando De Soto, the Spanish captain and explorer credited with discovery of the Mississippi River. In keeping with this choice of name, Woods had terra-cotta duplicates of De Soto's coat of arms made and these he had embedded prominently in the brickwork about the hotel entrance. The hotel opened for business in 1910.

Shortly after the hotel opened, Woods imported from Ohio a famed greeter and hotel operator named I. J. Gushwa and an equally famed cook and dining room manager, I. J. Gushwa's wife, Phoebe Anna.

The Gushwas promptly got to know, and be loved by, the people of Dalhart and thereabout, and I. J.'s fame as a greeter and Phoebe Anna's fame for the meals served in the dining room soon spread widely. For many years the hotel was deservedly known as one of the finest to be found.

The Gushwas were of Dutch extraction — a fact which perhaps explained the spic-and-span starched cleanliness and freshness of their dress and physical appearance. Mrs. Gushwa was seen mostly in the dining room where she would occasionally appear in order to enjoy the guests' compliments on her fine food and to make sure the waitresses were meeting her high standards for table service.

She had beautiful gray hair, a light complexion and blue eyes. Always dressed in starched cleanliness and exuding boundless energy and friendliness, she was a truly beautiful woman.

On one's left-hand side, as he entered the hotel lobby, was the admissions desk. Here, usually, one would find I. J. Surely this man should rank as one of the greatest greeters of all time.

He had a light, reddish-brown shock of hair and a huge moustache of the same color. He seemed always to be beaming with love of life, enthusiasm and puckishness. He had pale blue, mischievously twinkling eyes, and a ruddy complexion which would quickly redden when he would turn on his charm on greeting a guest or when he burst into laughter, as he often did.

Mrs. Gushwa was credited with seeing to it that I. J. was always wearing a freshly starched, stiff-fronted white or blue shirt topped by a monstrous detachable white collar out of which protruded an equally monstrous, stiffly-starched, bow tie of the same material and color as the shirt. John McCarty, formerly the editor of the *Dalhart Texan,* told me that "I. J. always looked like he had just stepped out of a well-starched bandbox."

I. J. had a disarming way of turning away complaints. For example, it is said that once he purchased a large stock of cigars that turned out to be less than popular with his customers. One customer came up to I. J., complained of his cigar and demanded his money back. "Why," said I. J., "what are you complaining about? You have only one of them and I have a thousand!"

One arriving in Dalhart by train would find the De Soto's horse-drawn hack with uniformed driver readily available to take him to the hotel. He would be met at the hotel by at least one uniformed bellboy waiting at curbside to take his bags and lead him into the hotel. Entering the hotel he would first pass through a sort of sub-lobby — a small room separated from the lobby proper in a manner designed to insulate the lobby from hot winds, northers or sandstorms.

The lobby was a square shaped room about sixty-by-sixty feet, with a ceiling which rose perhaps ten feet from the floor. The floor was of hand-set colored tile. Richly colored throw rugs were spaced about between and in front of the sturdy solid walnut lounge chairs, each upholstered with fine, tan-colored leather. Alongside the chairs were large brightly polished brass spittoons and ashtrays. Decorative fixtures overhead and along the walls provided the lighting at night. Several sets of well-polished mounted horns from early-day longhorn steers could also be found along the lobby walls. A wide, two-tiered stairway led to the second floor where the guest rooms were located.

In other words, the lobby reflected the opulence and worldliness of many of the early-day cattlemen.

Much of the time each day the center of the lobby would be occupied by a gathering of men readily identifiable as cattlemen by their Stetson hats, polished cowboy boots and easy carefree demeanor. They would appear to be simply whiling away their time in conviviality. Here, however, much of their business of buying, trading or marketing cattle was done. There was a Western Union desk in the lobby, placed there largely for convenience of the cattlemen, much of whose dealings with banks, feeders or other stockmen was handled by telegram. Several cattle merchants had trading desks in or near the lobby and one old-timer claims that "if one had a dime for every steer handled by these merchants he could build a Houston skyscraper."

Southward down the hall from the lobby one could enter the De Soto Hotel Barbershop. Here was indeed one of the most popular meeting places in the town. Joe Langhorne and Joe Bass barbering and Shorty No Legs shining boots and shoes! What a happy, warm-hearted, loquacious and gregarious trio!

The hotel's dining room compared in decor and opulence with the lobby. Under Mrs. Gushwa's direction it enjoyed widespread fame for fine food. Luncheon clubs vied for the opportunity to meet there and it was easily the town's most popular place for "dining out" in the evenings.

On occasion the tables and chairs would be removed from the dining room. Many a lavish dance was held here with orchestras imported from Fort Worth or Denver.

Once, when a blizzard stranded in Dalhart both the Rock Island and the Fort Worth and Denver for several days, the passengers were put up at the De Soto. The local people, with an impromptu orchestra featuring Al Morris and his fiddle, entertained the visitors with dancing in the De Soto's ballroom.

Widely respected for its fine accommodations, its good management and its food, the De Soto Hotel did much to improve the public image of Dalhart, and it provided a place for decent sociability among the citizenry. It clearly reflected the halcyon days of the High Plains cattleman and of the era when most travel was by means of the passenger train.

Dalhart Life and Lore and Shorty No Legs

When Tennessee was arraigned before Judge Reese Tatum, the Judge said, "Tennessee, I see you don't have a lawyer. Don't you want me to appoint one for you?" And Tennessee said, "No, Your Honor, if you don't mind, I'd rather not have a lawyer — I want to get out of this mess."

— Sid Johnson

In the wintertime in Dalhart there usually was much less wind than in the spring and summer, and we would have lots of beautiful, cool, clear days.

On those beautiful, clear wintry days the stores would be quiet and there just didn't seem to be much that anybody had to do other than gossip and enjoy the weather.

The cattlemen, plutocrats of the High Plains, that well-dressed, well-heeled, high-spirited gambling breed, seemed to spend all their time gathering in the De Soto Hotel lobby, talking cattle, making trades and spinning yarns.

With next year's wheat crop planted, the farmers would have time on their hands waiting for spring planting of their maize or kaffir or other row crops. So, especially on Saturdays, one could usually see thirty or forty overall-clad farmers warming themselves against the south side of the Citizens State Bank building, drinking in the clean fresh air and the sunlight and whittling, spitting tobacco juice and spinning yarns.

Before the auto replaced the passenger train as the customary means of travel, the coming and going of the Fort Worth and Denver and the Rock Island passenger trains punctuated life in Dalhart. Their steam powered whistles would be blown just before entering town and could be heard for miles. Everyone seemed to know just when each passenger train was due and would listen for it.

People also knew about how long it would take after the train's arrival for the mail to reach the post office, be sorted and made ready for distribution. A crowd of people would always gather at the post office about the time they thought the mail would be ready. It was a kind of social gathering.

On Sunday afternoons, back when the roads were mostly just trails worn in the prairie, almost everybody who had a car would load his family in it and get out on Main Street for an outing, assuming there was no baseball game on. The long string of autos would move slowly, and in single file, up and down the street, going north to near the Fort Worth and Denver tracks, and making a U-turn. They'd return, going back south about five blocks to just past the De Soto Hotel, then making another U-turn and repeating the performance. This would go on for hours, with everybody going one way smiling and waving at those going the other way.

In such a setting, any event that was out of the ordinary was a big event that everybody would love to tell about over and over. A lot of legends developed this way and grew richer and spicier with time. Here are a few of these:

★ ★ ★ ★ ★

Shorty No Legs, while standing on his stumps shining shoes in Joe Langhorne's Barbershop, was said to have told this yarn about W. L. Peeples, the undertaker. Peeples was a tall, gaunt man with a big Adam's apple, who walked kind of stooped over and wore a loose fitting, black suit. He actually had a kind of funereal air about him. Shorty claimed that for years every time he came back to his job after a big toot, Peeples would walk up and down the sidewalk in front of the barbershop watching Shorty real close to see if he was going to die.

"Finally," Shorty would say, "I went down to the Peeples Funeral Home and made a down payment on a funeral. I figgered that this way Bill would know he was going to get me when I died and would quit hanging around the barbershop waiting for me to do it."

Shorty was a scrappy little Irishman. Sid Johnson likes to tell about the time Shorty and Pete Adams got into a fistfight out in the dusty street in front of Jack Jesse's saloon. Shorty couldn't reach Pete swinging at him so he tackled Pete around the legs, threw him down and got on top of him. Shorty was getting the best of Pete when Tennessee Combs showed up. Tennessee was a part-time night watchman who lived in a room above Jack Jesse's saloon. He decided to stop the fight, so he pulled Shorty off of Pete.

Then Pete got up and started in after Tennessee and gave Tennessee a good beating. Tennessee went up to his room and in a few minutes came back on the scene carrying his Luger. Pete was standing on the boardwalk in front of the saloon, and when he saw Tennessee he broke and ran down First Street toward Mitchell's Saloon — the one that used to be in the old Commercial Hotel. Tennessee leveled down and fired. The bullet hit Pete in the crotch and castrated him.

When Tennessee was arraigned before Judge Reese Tatum, the Judge said, "Tennessee, I see you don't have a lawyer. Don't you want me to appoint one for you?" And Tennessee said, "No, Your Honor, if you don't mind, I'd rather *not* have a lawyer — I want to get out of this mess."

The story is that Tennessee served ten months of a one-year sentence and when he returned he went back to shaking down doors at night for the merchants. This authorized him to carry a gun and he made use of it to meet freight trains and relieve the hobos of their knives and watches. This enabled him to do a lively secondhand business.

★ ★ ★ ★ ★

People up in Clayton, New Mexico, liked to tell about old Dr. Fruth. Clayton was about fifty miles northwest of Dalhart where the foothills leading to the Sangre de Cristo Mountains began. It had come into being back around 1875, during the first great rush of white settlers to the High Plains.

It seems that this Dr. Fruth came to Clayton with a mining company in about 1880. He gave up practicing medicine and opened a drugstore. He was quite a drinker. Once he got hold of some bad bootleg whiskey and got to seeing snakes. So he put a sign in the drugstore window that said, SNAKE SHOW INSIDE — ADMISSION 50¢. Some patrons paid the admission but found no snakes, so they reported the doctor to the local sheriff. The sheriff came down to the drugstore to investigate. Dr. Fruth proceeded to get the sheriff to take a few drinks of his whiskey and before the sheriff left, Dr. Fruth had sold him a half interest in the snake show for $500.00.

★ ★ ★ ★ ★

A lot of the stories concern, or emanate from, one Earl Ross, an amiable, happy-go-lucky fellow who did a lot of odd jobs for people so long as the work didn't interfere too much with his loafing around Dinwiddie's Pool Hall and Domino Parlor.

One story has it that during Prohibition, Earl set up a still down near Nara Visa, New Mexico, and got to doing a lively business peddling bootleg whiskey.

One time he loaded up his Model T with whiskey and drove up to Dalhart, parking his car behind Dinwiddie's Pool Hall and Domino Parlor. He was inside making some sales when he looked out and saw Sheriff Rube Wharton examining his car. Earl headed for the front door, walked down to the Rock Island depot and caught a train for Nara Visa. When he got to Nara Visa, he called Rube Wharton on the phone, described his car and said somebody had stolen it the night before from his garage.

Rube Wharton then told Earl that he had found Earl's car; that it had been parked behind Dinwiddie's Pool Hall and Domino Parlor, and evidently had been stolen by some bootleggers because it was loaded with whiskey.

Earl then caught the next train back to Dalhart, got his car back and talked Rube Wharton into letting him keep the whiskey to help pay for the damage the bootleggers had done to it.

★ ★ ★ ★ ★

Everybody, including my father, loved the Earl Ross story about my father the doctor, and Ross's father's diabetic leg.

Earl would tell it about this way:

"Did I ever tell you about Doc Dawson and my dad's diabetic leg?

"Well, my dad had diabetes and it settled in his right foot. He was having lots of trouble with it, so he went down to see Doc Dawson. While Doc Dawson was examining my dad's foot, my dad told the Doc that he had $10,000 in the bank. Right away Doc Dawson said he would have to operate. So Doc Dawson cut off a part of my dad's foot.

"Right after my dad paid his bill to Doc Dawson and got over the operation, Doc Dawson told him the diabetes had moved up and he was going to have to cut some more of my dad's foot off. Then, when my dad had paid that bill and about got well, Doc Dawson told him the diabetes had moved still farther up my dad's leg and he was going to have to operate again.

"Well, this kept on with my dad's leg getting shorter and his bank account getting smaller, until finally Doc Dawson had cut my dad's leg off clear up to the hip. By then Doc Dawson had all of my dad's $10,000.

"It's a good thing my dad didn't have any more money for Doc Dawson to cut for."

★ ★ ★ ★ ★

Frank Tatum, father's longtime friend and the lawyer who helped him out of many of his scrapes, used to love to tell his theory as to how my father won his reputation as a great doctor.

"I can tell you how Doc Dawson makes everybody think he is so great," he would say.

"Well, he does it this way — when you get around to calling him or going to his office, he examines you and tells you you have a good chance of dying and should have called him sooner.

"If you die, he explains that this was because you didn't get to him soon enough.

"But if you live, why then, Doc Dawson has just performed another miracle."

★ ★ ★ ★ ★

Another legend about father that is still going around is that after Black Jack Ketchum was shot in the shoulder during his attempted train robbery, arrested and sentenced to be hanged, he was brought in to father's sanitarium at Dalhart suffering from gangrene around his wound. This was on the day before Black Jack was to be hanged at Clayton. Father found out that Black Jack had a little money on him so the next morning, just a few hours before Black Jack was to be hanged, he amputated Black Jack's arm and collected his bill for the operation. As soon as the operation was over, Black Jack was taken back to Clayton and hanged that afternoon.

The main trouble with this yarn is that Black Jack was hanged in Clayton in 1901, over six years before father had left Kentucky, and over ten years before he had a sanitarium.

★ ★ ★ ★ ★

One story concerned one Martin Kovarik and his problems with women. Martin was a member of a sect headquartered in the midwest somewhere. It was a closely-knit sect that believed the needs of male members for wives should be met only out of the membership of the sect.

After some years living alone in a remote dugout on the plains, Martin Kovarik wrote the sect's management asking that it send him a woman. It did, and the two hit it off quite well for a few years. But then the lady got sick and died.

Martin sent for another and the sect complied. After a few weeks, however, Martin decided this one was not suitable. Martin shipped her home.

He then requested a third. This one was reasonably acceptable but within a few years she, too, became ill. Martin brought her in to the sanitarium but, on arrival, she was found to have expired on the way to town.

Martin was now totally disgusted with his efforts to find a suitable mate. He took the deceased lady to Peeples Funeral Home, arranged for embalming and a casket, then shipped her back to the sect with a sight draft on the sect for the total cost of the casket, the embalming and the ticket home on the railroad. "By Gott," said Martin, "I'm through with women."

★ ★ ★ ★ ★

Shorty Wolf, the druggist, said that one night after he had closed up and gone home he had a call from a Dalhart man wanting him to go back to the drugstore and sell him some medicine. The man said he had just come home unexpectedly from a trip to find his wife in bed with a severe headache. "She wouldn't even let me turn on the lights," he said. "Couldn't stand the glare. After I'd undressed and gotten in bed, she begged me to call you and see if you would come back to the store so I could get some medicine."

"When he went to pay," said Shorty, "he pulled a pocketbook out of his hip pocket, looked at it and said, 'This isn't *my* pocketbook.' Then he looked down at his trousers and said: '*My God, these aren't my pants!*' "

★ ★ ★ ★ ★

The old crowbar-hole story is still told to newcomers. One asks the newcomer whether his house has a crowbar hole. When asked what it is, one replies: Every house out here on the High Plains should have a crowbar-hole so's you can know whether it's safe to go outside when there's a high wind. You poke the crowbar out through the hole and pull it back in. If it isn't bent, it's safe to go outside.

★ ★ ★ ★ ★

Then there is the story about Webb Wharton's killing a man he thought was stealing his wife's affections and his resultant bouts with the law. There are a lot of versions, some which are more interesting than others. I will try to relate the one I like best.

There are just a few things that I really know about Webb. I know that he had a cattle ranch near Dalhart and that in about

1920, he and his wife bought the biggest house in town and came there to live. And I know they had a stuffed cow in the sun parlor.

Joe Scott, the Dalhart Ford man, tells me that Webb got in financial straits during the Depression of the 1930s. Prohibition was still in effect, and Webb imported a whiskey maker from Kentucky and made and sold bootleg whiskey until he had made $100,000. Then he closed the still and bought his whiskey maker a nice home in Amarillo.

Webb was very jealous of his wife, Minnie, and he became suspicious of one particular man. So suspicious that one night he came home and thought this man was hiding under Minnie's bed. Webb had a bad back that made it hard for him to lean over and get his head near enough to the floor to have a look, so he just leaned over far enough to poke his six-shooter under the bed and spray bullets all over the suspected area.

Webb and my father were good friends and Webb kept coming down to father's office at night to tell father about his suspicions. Many a time after such visits father would say to me, "There's going to be a killing, son, there's going to be a killing."

One day, a woman Webb thought was Minnie took the train up to Texhoma, which is about fifty miles northeast of Dalhart. Webb suspected that this was Minnie going up there to meet this man, so he got aboard on a different car, and arrived at Texhoma at the same time the woman did.

Then he saw the woman meet a man and start walking into town with him. Well, it so happens that the boundary between Texas and Oklahoma runs down the middle of Main Street of Texhoma, and just as this woman and this man were crossing this line into Oklahoma, Webb came up from behind and shot the man dead.

Father was terribly upset. "Those Yankees in Oklahoma don't respect the unwritten law the way we do in Texas," he said. "Confound it, I *told* Webb not to kill that man in Oklahoma!"

Webb was indicted for murder in Oklahoma, and was tried in Guymon. It is said that at the trial, he proved that he was in Texas when he did the killing and got an instructed verdict of not guilty; then was indicted for murder in Texas, and at that trial proved that he was in Oklahoma when he did the killing, and got another instructed verdict of not guilty.

Pioneer Doctor:

G. W. Dawson

> . . . *His practicing territory covered an area from Spearman, west to Nara Visa, New Mexico, and from Tascosa, north to Boise City, Oklahoma. A portion of the XIT Ranch, then in its final years, was included in this area. The county was sparsely settled; roads were impossible in bad weather. The chief mode of transportation was the covered wagon. Operations were performed in dugouts by dim candlelight . . .*
>
> — Sign by G. W. Dawson's
> Surgical Instruments
> XIT Museum at Dalhart

My father, George Waller Dawson, was born in 1871, in Kentucky, the son of a Baptist minister serving a number of rural areas in the state. He apparently was blessed from the beginning with an inherent ability to win favor with others, and a conviction that he could readily make a living at any enterprise he might undertake. Also he plainly had a fierce determination to be forever free of the poverty in which his father had lived.

He taught himself to be a veterinarian doctor, and when still a lad, began collecting fees for treating injured or diseased livestock. He put himself through medical school at the University of Louisville largely with funds derived from a stint at teaching school, trading horses in the Indiana hills in summers, and performing dissection assignments for more affluent students. He could tell hair-raising (and unverifiable) stories of robbing graves for bodies sold to the school for use as cadavers.

He was immobilized by infantile paralysis when about ten, los-

G. W. Dawson, M.D.
. . . Father of the author

ing for a time the use of his legs. While he largely overcame this handicap through power of will and constant massages given by his mother, he remained throughout life a person of frail physique and seemed always a prey to respiratory and other diseases.

On finishing medical school he quickly built a thriving medical practice in the Thruston, Kentucky, area. At age twenty-five he persuaded the beauteous and talented Willie Catherine Mitchell, daughter of a Kentucky planter, to become his wife. By this move he acquired a steadying and sustaining force that offset — and many times forgave — weaknesses and temptations that often beset him.

The conflict between father's respiratory problems and the heavy physical demands of his rural medical practice forced a decision, in about 1907, to seek a change both in climate and in occupation. Relief from the respiratory problems, it was thought, might be found in the high, dry atmosphere of the newly developing area of the north Texas Panhandle. Here — that is to Channing, Texas, (headquarters of the great XIT Ranch) — father moved his family. The challenge presented by this newly developing area probably contributed much to his decision to move there.

In Kentucky, he had acquired two great stallions: one called Fezjlo (an import from Germany), and the other called Major, a fine pacer that had won fame on the racetracks. He brought these and a fine group of mares to Channing, bought a pretty tract of land on the bank of a nearby canyon, and planned to make a business of breeding and raising fine horses. However, shortly after the horses arrived, the entire herd died from eating clover that, unknown to him, had mold in it. Added to this came the failure of a bank in Kentucky in which he had invested. By 1909, he had exhausted his financial resources and his planned change of occupation had failed. However, there was heavy demand by the citizenry for his services as a doctor. He then borrowed train fare at a Channing bank, went to Dalhart, and let it be known that he was back in practice. Shortly, he again had a thriving medical practice, this one serving people in the north Panhandle of Texas, and nearby areas in Oklahoma, Kansas, and New Mexico.

Despite his frail physique, he acquired a reputation as a man of enormous stamina, capable of keeping on the go without sleep for days on end. This he did by disciplining himself to completely relax and rest at will, using ten minute- to half-hour pauses throughout the day (or night) and thereby maintaining a high level of energy.

He seemed able to survive almost any physical adversity: infantile paralysis, Bright's disease, tuberculosis, asthma; and even a heart attack. This was brought on by a headstrong and reckless trip in a blizzard in an effort to comfort an impecunious drunken barber friend suffering from delirium tremens. Finally, however, his ability to survive came to an end when, at age seventy-one, he died of a brain hemorrhage.

Except for the absence of a great shock of black hair, carefully roached, and a Kentucky Colonel type moustache and goatee, the model for Sir Luke Field's famous portrait, *The Doctor,* could well have been my father.

The painting shows the doctor sitting at his patient's bedside, exuding a sense of personal concern, professional self-confidence, pride and charm, and a complete insensitivity to the passage of time. It depicts the doctor of the era when people stayed at home with their pains and expected the doctor to come to them. Also it suggests the doctor in the role of general practitioner functioning long before the age of specialization.

In the XIT Museum in Dalhart, there is a sign by a display of some of my father's surgical instruments. It reads in part,

> Dr. G. W. Dawson, Sr., one of the Panhandle's Grand old Medicine Men, died in Dalhart, September 29, 1942, at the age of 71. Born 1871. Was a Kentuckian, coming to the area (Channing in 1907), seeking his health for an asthmatic condition.
>
> The panic of 1909 brought financial havoc to many, but to thousands of the High Plains residents it indirectly brought health and often life.
>
> When Dr. Dawson came to Channing in 1907, after 13 years of active practice in Kentucky, he was in bad health and planned to retire to a ranch. Two years later the financial panic affected his investments in Kentucky, and Dr. Dawson was forced to resume his practice.
>
> The pioneer physician then came to Dalhart to form a partnership with Dr. Hedrick, one of the thirteen doctors in the town. His practicing territory covered an area from Spearman, west to Nara Visa, New Mexico, and from Tascosa, north to Boise City, Oklahoma. A portion of the XIT Ranch, then in its final years, was included in this area. The county was sparsely settled; roads were impossible in bad weather. The chief mode of transportation was the covered wagon. Operations were performed in dugouts by dim candlelight — conditions called for a hospital.
>
> In 1912, Dr. Dawson opened the Trans-Canadian Sanitarium — the name meaning "North of the Canadian River" — with

Mrs. Dawson as anesthetist and matron in charge. From that time until Loretto Hospital opened in Dalhart in 1929, over 2000 major operations were performed at the Sanitarium. During one month, with the help of Mrs. Dawson as an assistant, Dr. Dawson performed 63 operations.

In early days of the Sanitarium, patients came in covered wagons from as far away as Colorado, New Mexico and Oklahoma. Their families usually accompanied them, as the illness and the long trip meant a lengthy stay. Cowboys rode miles on horseback to visit sick friends at the Sanitarium, remaining to join convalescent patients in talk, games of forty-two and other diversions.

The Sanitarium was well-equipped for such a pioneer institution, including an X-ray machine, the first in the Panhandle. It was brought from Kentucky for the institution.

The need for a place in Dalhart where the seriously ill could be housed and receive around-the-clock medical and nursing care was painfully apparent to my father from the very beginning of his practice there in 1909.

The nearest hospital was in Amarillo, eighty-seven miles to the southeast, and there was no hospital within a hundred miles in any other direction. For awhile, father rented some rooms upstairs in a downtown wooden building and rendered hospital-type care there. Then in 1912, he bought a two-story brick, steam-heated building on the north end of Main Street and converted it into a hospital. This he called The Trans-Canadian Sanitarium (a name it deserved, being the only hospital in Texas north of the Canadian River). The Sanitarium served as the Dalhart area's only hospital facility from its opening in 1912, until the Catholic Sisters opened the Loretto Hospital in Dalhart in 1929.

On the second floor, a large, well-lighted northeast corner room was painted all white inside and made into an operating room. The rooms in the center of that floor were made into a supply room, a sterilization room and an X-ray room. This left twelve rooms for patient care.

The building had no elevator. Instead, the second floor could be reached by means of a wide stairway leading up from twin doors opening on Main Street. Patients who could not negotiate the stairs would be carried up or down in a sturdy chair reserved for the purpose.

The first floor of the building had been divided into two huge rooms with ceilings about twenty feet high. Father had wooden partitions built to subdivide these huge spaces. These partitions extended upward from the floor about halfway to the ceiling and were painted white. One of the downstairs spaces was thus made into a reception room, several doctors' offices, a kitchen, and a dining room. Part of the other downstairs space was made into rooms for use as nurses' quarters and the rest of it was left open for use as a storeroom.

On a balcony overlooking the reception room were desks for mother and Bill Bennett. Here mother acted as receptionist, bookkeeper, purchase agent and anesthetist and otherwise helped run the place. Bill Bennett handled collections and acted as a general handyman for father.

There was a florid linoleum rug on the reception room floor, in the center of which there was a big oak table stacked with magazines and newspapers. Under the table there sat a large brass spittoon about eighteen inches high, and scattered about the room were several chairs and sofas. On the walls were a few pictures, including a huge picture of Fezjlo, the great stallion father had imported from Germany and brought to Texas. A picture frame holding his medical diploma from the University of Louisville also hung in a prominent place. In a corner there stood a heavy, black, iron safe.

When a person moved from the reception room down the hallway leading to the doctors' offices, he would pass a small room that was known to only a few — it was father's specimen room. Here, preserved in formaldehyde-filled bottles, were many specimens of human appendixes, hearts, livers, fetuses, tumors, goiters, gallstones, and so on, which father had removed during operations or postmortem examinations. I remember particularly Jack Jesse's liver. Jack had been a longtime saloon-keeper in Dalhart. He had been confined to a wheelchair most of his life, but evidently had consumed a lot of alcohol. After Jack died, father preserved his liver to show the effect a sedentary life and too much whiskey could have. The liver was several times the normal size and it was colored a gray-green. It had a chalky, brittle look.

On the north side of the building there was painted, in huge letters, the name of a land company that had previously occupied the second floor of the building and engaged in the business of selling out XIT ranchlands to smaller ranchers and prospective farmers. Also, on the north side of the building there was painted a giant red and white bull advertising Bull Durham Smoking Tobacco. That

The Trans-Canadian Sanitarium, Dalhart, Texas. 1912

bull was over a story high and of course his presence was inappropriate, to put it mildly, for a hospital building. Father had the outside of the building painted and thereby eliminated the real estate company's sign. But the paint on the bull kept peeling off and the bull kept reappearing. Finally father had the building covered with a beige stucco that dressed it up a lot and eliminated that pesky bull.

In the street on the north side of the building there was a large cement public water trough. The families of patients would often camp in that street in their covered wagons, using the watering trough to water their horses.

Until my brother, Artis, and Dr. Carl Pieratt, came in about 1924, it seemed to me that most of father's associate doctors at the hospital were always on the move, none staying very long with the exception of Dr. Lovell.

Father had better luck with nurses, however. He had four of them who were exceptionally competent and faithful and who stayed on with him and the hospital for many years. These were Grace Selby, Charlotte Steinle, Geneva Lofgren and Fay Pendleton.

Wondrous things happened at the hospital.

While practicing medicine in Kentucky before he came to Texas, father had bought an X-ray machine. He had it shipped to Dalhart and installed in the sanitarium. "The first X-ray north of the Canadian River," he would often say.

Sometimes he would let me help him use the machine. The walls of the X-ray room were painted black and the cracks around the door and the overhead transoms were covered, so as to prevent the entrance of any light from outside. We would all go into the X-ray room and take our proper places. I would sit on a chair at one end of the X-ray machine where I could operate the crank. Father would place the patient between him and an unshielded X-ray tube which was a large glass bulb shaped like a tadpole with two tails, one on either end. It was suspended from the ceiling by wires. Also, the X-ray tube had wires attached at either end running to it from two big glass bottles, one on either side of the floor.

The electric light in the room would be turned off and then, in the pitch darkness, I would begin to turn the crank. At this, two great glass wheels, each about one- and one-half inches thick and about a yard in diameter, would begin to whirl inside a glass encased box about five feet high and about four feet wide. Inside this box was the X-ray machine itself. Myriad little blue sparks would begin to dance from brushes set against the glass wheels. Shortly a blue light would fill each of the two large glass bottles sitting on the floor and a blue-white, acrid vapor would arise from the bottles and permeate the room. Suddenly a much brighter light would fill the X-ray tube. Father would then reach up and pull down before his eyes a device which was suspended from the ceiling and which looked like a piece of darkened glass encased in a wooden frame about eighteen inches long and about a foot wide. It was a fluoroscopic screen. Father would examine the patient's body by looking through this screen, through the patient's body and toward the now lighted X-ray tube. X-ray photographs could not be made with this machine but the bones in the body were clearly revealed by it.

Even after father opened the Trans-Canadian Sanitarium in 1912, he kept right on making lots of house calls. He used his buggy drawn by his old mare, Betsy, until in about 1916, when he acquired his first automobile. After he started using the automobile, he made calls over a much wider area than before.

On many of his trips out of town he would take me along either as a chauffeur or just as a companion. I would always jump at the opportunity of going with him. Many times we would drive to some farmhouse or ranch home forty or fifty miles from Dalhart where father, if he thought necessary, would perform an appendectomy or other operation on the spot. Often the kitchen table was the operating table and water boiled on the stove was used to sterilize the surgical instruments.

On trips to neighboring towns such as Stratford or Texline (each about twenty-five miles from Dalhart), or to Dumas or Boise City (each about forty miles), it seemed we would scarcely get there before people would begin to gather around to ask for his attention. I might be parked at a patient's home or stopped in town when running an errand to the drugstore when people would come up and say something like, "I heard Doc Dawson was in town, please have him come by our house and see my wife."

The whole town would seem to become alerted, once father had arrived. And he would be kept there until late that evening, calling on people who asked for his services. They seemed to actually save their pains for him.

The confidence the people had in him always amazed me. He relished their confidence and worked hard at gaining and keeping it. He held the respect of other doctors, too. For example, Mrs. E. R. Stewart told me that after a trip to the Mayo Clinic in Rochester, Minnesota, on father's recommendation, Dr. Charles Mayo had said, "We can always rely on Dr. Dawson's diagnoses."

Father was very proud of his skill with the surgeon's knife. And he often let me watch him operate. I watched one that brought home to me the awesome decisions the surgeon must sometimes make. A young boy was brought to the Sanitarium by his parents with a brain damage his parents thought may have been caused by his fall from a hayloft into a wagon bed, driving a nail into his skull.

Father said that if the nail had ruptured a blood vessel in the boy's brain the damage could not be repaired, but if the damage had been caused by a tumor, perhaps it could be removed and the boy might be restored to normalcy. He said the only way to find out was to open the skull.

Using a little circular saw, he made a hole in the skull about the size of a quarter. Then, with a little hammer, he tapped on the bone until it came loose and was removed. The opening revealed a white membrane which seemed to protrude from the surface of the brain.

Father then turned to the parents and said, "This may be a tumor. If it is, I think I can remove it and he will live. If it is not a tumor, but a ruptured blood vessel, I can do nothing for him. I can find out only by cutting into this membrane. If I do that and find a tumor, he may get well, but if I do it and find a ruptured blood vessel, he will die tonight. Of course, I can simply close this hole without cutting the membrane and he will go on living in his present condition. Shall I cut the membrane?"

The parents nodded their assent. Father touched his knife to the membrane, whereupon a thin stream of blood shot out several feet. The parents silently left the operating room. The boy died that night.

His ministry to the people was by no means confined to performing surgical operations and prescribing medicines. He was a sort of father-confessor to the town. Often of evenings after supper he would go down to his office and stay for hours. Some came to him in these hours for physical medical treatment. But many came to pour out to him their personal troubles and to seek his advice. He loved these confidential sessions and through them, perhaps, he was rendering treatment for ills which could not be reached by the surgeon's knife or the apothecary's pills.

He used to tell me that illnesses produced by people's minds were often more painful and harder to cure than actual physical ailments. These he would treat with prescriptions born of a deep sympathy for persons in distress and knowledge of human nature.

For example, another operation (which did not involve the use of the knife) served to illustrate father's understanding of human nature and the compassion he felt for people whose frailties, pride, desires and notions motivated their conduct. It also illustrated the Solomon-like wisdom he could exhibit in helping people solve their problems, whether real or imagined. As this was a most confidential matter, I did not learn of it until after father's death and until after some of those requiring the protection of confidentiality had themselves made the facts public.

This involved a prominent teenage girl involved in an unwanted pregnancy and a prominent citizen's wife who had long tried, but failed, to become pregnant.

The young lady was in a state of panic when she brought her problem to father. She was pregnant all right, and there was nothing to be done for her but let her go through with the pregnancy and the birth of the child. However, she convinced father that the situation involving the man who had made her pregnant was such that marriage was an impossibility, and that the known attitudes of her parents demanded that the fact of the pregnancy be kept from them.

Father was moved to try to help the girl find a solution to her problem. There was that other patient — the longtime patient who had been trying for years, but unsuccessfully, to have a child. He called her in, explained the situation and proposed that she and her husband plan to adopt the young girl's unwanted child. But these efforts failed, first because the matron's husband wouldn't hear of going through adoption proceedings and secondly because the matron herself adamantly refused to even think of having her friends learn that she had been unable to bear a child of her own.

Father's solution: He would try to arrange things so that the fact of this young girl's pregnancy would be kept from her parents and the childless matron would so conduct herself that, to the outside world, the baby would appear to have been born to her.

This he accomplished by having the young girl visit a cooperative aunt living in a mountain cabin in New Mexico, until brought to the Sanitarium when birth of the child became imminent. At this point in time, he had the matron come into the Sanitarium and be booked for a child delivery.

This done, several days passed with the young girl behind the closed door of her room and the childless matron in another room with the door open, a roomful of flowers and her gay, fussy, friends crowding about, talking about the problems of childbirth, asking about the pains and nausea and so forth.

When the baby came, the nurses at once moved it into the childless matron's bed and to all but father, the matron herself and her husband, the girl and her aunt and the three nurses father had put on the job and sworn to secrecy, the child was, and hopefully would continue thereafter to be, thought the natural born offspring of the matron and her husband.

Father disliked attending public meetings and was shy, retiring, and ill at ease at social functions. But he was gracious, warm and even loguacious when in privacy. Joe Scott used to say he was the best salesman he had ever known. He always seemed to do and say things in a polite and dignified manner, even when what he did or said was such that, if done or said by most of us, might not qualify as either polite or dignified.

For example, at the supper table he would usually remove his coat, drop his suspenders and maybe unbutton the top button on his trousers. Then, taking his fly swatter firmly in his left hand, he would shoo flies from the butter and when one lit in an open space on the tablecloth, would smash it with a loud *Splat!* Then flip it off the table to the floor.

And often he would receive calls from patients while supper was in progress. He would go to the phone which was on the wall near his chair and proceed with anatomical questions designed to elicit information about the patient's condition. Frequently (almost always, it seemed) he would inquire in an almost unctuously polite and dignified manner something like: "And how are her bowels?"

He always had a particular sympathy for the unfortunate or downtrodden. Marie Gibney of *The Dalhart Texan* said he always looked for some redeeming feature, some good quality, in men or women who had run afoul of the law. He could not pass up a beggar. It was, perhaps, these qualities that caused him to create and operate during the Depression what became known as the Dalhart Haven. It was a sort of impromptu free soup kitchen where destitute transients could get a plate of beans, a slice of stale bread and a hot cup of coffee.

Until about 1916, father made all of his calls by horse and buggy. Until then the roads weren't very reliable. You had to follow trails that might wrench your steering wheel right out of your hands and turn you over if you weren't careful to stay in the center of them. Besides, you could pull a tire right off the rim if you hit a rut the wrong way, the tires were easily punctured, you would have to carry gasoline and water if you went any distance, and not infrequently a fellow would get his arm broken when his motor would backfire while he was trying to crank it.

So for several years after we had moved to Dalhart, father relied on old Betsy to get him around. Old Betsy was a plump, gentle, bay mare. She got to know the routes father would generally take around town so well that she could make them unattended, making the right stops and all. Once in awhile father would let us boys saddle up Old Betsy and ride her down into the canyon. This was a chore she did not like. As long as we were going in a direction away from home it was difficult to get her out of a slow walk, and when we would get her to break into a trot or a gallop she would do so with her legs held so stiffly she would shake us to pieces. But when we turned around and started her in the direction of home, she would go into an easy canter so smooth that it made the rider feel he was gliding.

In about 1913, one of father's old Kentucky admirers sent him a beautiful Dalmation puppy that we named Prince.

Prince took up with Old Betsy right away and except on occasions when she would follow us boys on our trips into the canyon, Prince would spend most of every day in the company of Old Betsy, following behind the buggy as father would make his calls and then lying down on the ground in front of Old Betsy when she would be tethered near a patient's home or waiting behind the Sanitarium for father to call her into use. My older brother, Artis, went off to college and medical school in Chicago, and my next brother, G. W., went off to Wentworth Military Academy. While they were gone, Prince and I became great companions.

But in 1916, father decided it was time to start using an automobile. He bought a black Maxwell touring car and he gave Old Betsy and his buggy to E. R. Stewart, another Kentuckian who had come to Texas, and who was father's close friend. Father said he felt that E. R. would take good care of Old Betsy and treat her right. Shortly after that, I went off to military school in Wisconsin so Prince's way of life was vastly changed. He began staying over with Old Betsy most of the time.

Finally Old Betsy died, and in some way Prince became the companion of a man who ran the railroad watering station at Conlen, about fifteen miles north of Dalhart. Later I came home for summer vacation and one morning father had me drive him up to Stratford. As usual we spent the whole day there with word traveling ahead that he was in town, the result of which was that we stayed and made calls until late in the evening.

It was dark when we reached Conlen on the way home. I asked father if we couldn't stop and see Prince. This we did and when we left Prince insisted on following. Father had brought a patient who was lying on the back seat of the car so we couldn't put Prince in the car. We tried to get Prince to go back to the watering station but he would not. We would have to go through gates and each time we would stop, Prince would race up and catch up to us, his eyes gleaming in the darkness.

In this way he followed us all the way into Dalhart.

I think Prince stayed at our home after that. In any event I remember that one time after he had grown old he lost his temper and bit a child in the jaw when the child tried to pet him. When that happened, father said we would have to get rid of the dog.

G. W. then took the car and his .30-30 rifle and drove out on the prairie with Prince. He set Prince to chasing a rabbit and while he was racing along fifty to sixty yards away G. W. leveled down with his .30-30 and with regret, shot Prince through the heart.

Father sent Prince's body up to a taxidermist in Pueblo, who mounted him in a reclining position with the right front paw over the left and his head turned to one side looking much the way he did when he used to lie on the ground in front of Old Betsy.

Father then had a little platform built on the wall of the reception room of his Sanitarium next to the one that held a great horned owl. He put Prince on that platform. Here he stayed as long as that reception room was used, greeting everyone who came in.

Father loved trees and flowers and never gave up trying to raise Kentucky bluegrass in his yard. He kept all the trees about the house whitewashed up to the first spreading branches. He often would stand in the yard watering trees and plants, smoking his pipe and meditating until two or three in the morning.

It may be that it was his knowledge of human nature and sympathy for those in distress as much as his skill as a surgeon and capability as a man of medicine that won him his reputation as a doctor capable of marvelous cures. He somehow had a way of holding his patients' confidence — of making them want to get well for *him*.

On his seventieth birthday he received a great, spontaneous outpouring of congratulatory messages and gifts of fruit, home cured bacon and hams and carloads of flowers. These came from many people throughout the High Plains area and beyond.

I wrote and asked him for an explanation of this demonstration of love and respect from the people. He replied as follows, signing the letter formally, as he always did, with his full name.

May 26, 1941

Jno. C. Dawson, Atty.
Houston, Texas

Dear Son:

Your letter received. It is strange to me how news gets around, but probably from the grapevine way. Speaking of friends, I had a long distance telephone [call] from Stanley, Kentucky, which is 1300 miles, from old Ben Pate. When I knew him, he was as poor as a church mouse. He must have paid some two or three dollars to call me by phone and congratulate me. When I answered the phone, he immediately said, "Yes, that is our Dr. Dawson who did our practice forty years ago." He said he just wanted to hear my voice and he paid dearly for it. Someone there, or the *Messenger,* must have carried the story about my birthday. Now this is genuine friendship. My footprints must be on the sands of time. I am still getting four decked cakes, strawberry preserves, and many birthday cards. One this morning from California, from people whom I don't know. Of course I appreciate them and they still come. The Wilbanks children, some four or five, also wrote stating that I had treated them, delivered some of them and operated the others. Mr. Wilbanks, as you may know, is the Sheriff of his county who became locally famous recently in tracing down the hammer murderer of the woman that was found over there beside the highway. The only mark of identification was a trademark in her shoe which she had evidently purchased in St. Louis. He took this trademark and followed up until he finally located and arrested the murderer.

You asked me if there is any special formula for making friends. I don't know, but it seems that I have been a trouble shooter for some 50 years, listening to peoples' troubles and trying to show them a different slant on life. I spent thirty minutes with a lady yesterday. She had been phoning me for a number of days for an appointment. I was sure it was something of that nature so put her off until yesterday. I think that she went away more reconciled over her domestic troubles, and probably diverted divorce proceedings. Of course this is taking shingles off of the lawyers roof, but I do think many divorces could be estopped if some one could talk to them in the proper manner.

Tell Johnny that I am too old to play baseball but would enjoy seeing him throwing curves. I am glad Lucille is doing so well. Mother is not too well but up and about part of each day.

With love to Johnny, I am,

Yours truly,
G. Waller Dawson, M.D.

GWD:LF

My father was good about mentioning his grandchildren in letters. In 1938, after our second son was born, he wrote this:

Dear J.C.

Recevd. the boy's pictures and have decided that he will do to save, so would advise branding him to throw him in the Herd.

He always knew his friends and admirers were out there, but in his declining years his inability to serve them seemed to greatly weaken his will to live.

There remained, however, his faith in the land. In the years when income from his medical practice had been abundant, he had invested in farmlands. In 1929, determined that in the long run the land would prove his financial salvation, he had three sections, previously undeveloped, put into cultivation. He kept trying, unsuccessfully, to grow crops on these — and on the sections previously farmed — year after year during the drouth years.

On May 3, 1938, after he had gone to his office and found the entrance door had been blown open by a furious, dust-laden wind, he wrote me.

> . . . people are leaving here constantly, and we are having a real "Duster" most every day. Sat. eve came to the office, both doors blown open and I swept [an] even one peck of dust from the reception room and hall. Dan Spencer helped to measure the dust and carry it out. Aside from the amt in offices.
>
> We are all so discouraged and ready to go. Today people from Stratford, could not see to drive, and Bennett could not drive in from the farm.

By then — 1938 — ill health, weather, and Depression economics had wrought many changes. Most of those patients he could care for, were not able to pay their bills. My father's faith in his land as a final sustaining resource had been shattered by drouth, grasshoppers, dust storms, or blizzards. His will to hang on reached a near breaking point. By 1939, the eight-year crop failure had stripped my parents of funds needed for necessities.

Yet in 1942, after he had died, I found in his wallet, this card.

OLD LOCO'S
LAST MAN CLUB
. DALHART, TEXAS

This certifies that *Dr. H. W. Dawson*
Is a member of Old Loco's Last Man Club, and affixes his signature to the following pledge:

"Barring Acts of God or unforeseen personal tragedy or family illness, I pledge myself to be the Last Man to leave this country, to always be loyal to it, and to do my best to cooperate with other members of the Last Man Club in the years ahead."

I understand my name is to be placed on the roll of immortals in Old Loco's private scroll of heroic citizens.

Certified by *John L. McCarty*

Old Loco   Member
Date 4-25-25   4

Old Loco's LAST MAN CLUB

Pioneer Doctor's Wife:

Willie Catherine

> *Darndest weather I ever saw,*
> *Snowed in till the April thaw,*
> *Hens won't lay, the pump's all friz,*
> *All our folks got rheumatiz,*
> *Car wont go, and the old mare's lame,*
> *But Happy New Year just the same.*
>
> — Willie Catherine Dawson
> To Grandson
> Letter, January 23, 1941

When father spoke *to* her, he called her "Willie," when he spoke *of* her, he called her "My Willie." When we boys spoke to or of her, we just called her "Mother."

It seemed just part of life to know that mother was always there, keeping the home on an even keel, seeing that meals were ready when they were supposed to be, appearing always cheerful and always sympathetic and understanding when I would get hurt, emotionally or otherwise. She was a paragon of femininity and always dressed and looked like a lady. In 1923, she won a diamond ring prize as the most beautiful woman at a huge Fourth of July celebration and parade. She played the guitar and was a steady soprano in the Methodist Church Choir. She kept interested in everything that was going on, and was ever busy studying some literary work preparing reports for her Literary Society.

Actually, she had to endure a lot of heartaches and embarrassments, what with the various transgressions, excesses and so on of father and us boys. We would know when she was hurt by what we

*Willie Catherine Dawson
. . . Mother of the author*

did but she would seem to pretend she didn't know. She knew we knew, and we knew she knew and this fact did a lot to help us go straighter than we might have otherwise.

Surely no mother ever had a better influence on her home. Yet she was an indispensable business partner to father in his profession.

At a desk on a platform overlooking the reception room in father's Trans-Canadian Sanitarium, one would most generally find mother. She acted as receptionist. She kept the books. She gave the anesthetics during operations. She could pinch-hit as a nurse. She supervised the kitchen and all purchasing of food and supplies. In fact, it was she who made the Sanitarium run. When, in about 1916, father bought a more modern X-ray machine, mother went to Fort Worth and learned how to take, and develop X-ray pictures. Thereafter these functions were added to her duties. Father was very dependent upon her, though this he would rarely admit. Sometimes his love and concern for mother would surface in odd ways.

One time mother took a day off from the office and spent it at the country club attending a party put on by her bridge group.

To get to the Dalhart Country Club you drove out to the west of town past the steam laundry and took the dirt road running southerly alongside the Rock Island Railroad tracks. Then you drove south about two miles, crossing the Rita Blanca Canyon, and, having done so, turned off to the west across the railroad to the clubhouse.

It had been raining and word was getting around that the canyon had a bit of water trickling down it, and that it might go on a "rise." The canyon was normally bone dry. However, even with a slight rain, enough mud might form at the very bottom to bog down an automobile. To protect against this normal hazard, the highway people had laid a slab of concrete at the lowest point of the canyon crossing. It was about two feet thick, ten or twelve feet wide and about thirty feet long. It dipped downward at the center. One could expect to cross the canyon in one's auto by means of this concrete slab — unless the water was running deep enough to drown out the motor.

Although, normally, there was little or no water in the canyon, it drained a very wide plains area, and therefore was called upon to carry a tremendous load of water on those rare occasions when there was a heavy general rain or a water spout. When this happened, this little dry creek bed could suddenly become a raging torrent. People had been known to look up just as they reached the bottom of such a canyon and see a veritable wall of water eight to ten feet high come charging down upon them. Wagons and automobiles had been washed away by such sudden freshets and lives had been lost this way.

So, since it was raining a bit and mother would have to cross the Rita Blanca when she came home from the club, one could work up a worry about her if he was a mind to.

I did not feel any sense of concern about mother's safety. But father didn't see things my way. Maybe it was his sense of dependence on mother that was brought to the surface by her absence from the office. Maybe it was a kind of jealousy at her devoting the day to the bridge club. Or maybe he was really concerned for her safety. Probably he was moved by *all* of these emotions. Anyway, he began to fret about mother and the canyon the minute she stepped into a neighbor's car and thus set sail for the club.

About an hour after mother left for the club father called me from the office. I was at home working on our wild birds' egg collection. "Son," he said, "I'm afraid the canyon is going on a rise. Don't you think you should go out to the club and bring mother to town?" I said I didn't think we need worry but would go take a look. Which I did. I drove out to the canyon and looked around and came back and told father I thought mother would be okay. I said I'd go back out in a couple of hours and have another look.

In less than an hour he called again. "Your mother is still out with that bridge club. I've called her three times and she is calm as a cucumber and won't listen to reason," he said. "I think you must go out and get her." I kept trying to reassure him and get him to leave mother alone. But as the day wore on father's excitement, as well as his impatience with me, mounted higher and higher. And I think he was taking a little nip now and then, just for protection against the inclement weather and to keep his nerves calm. Needless to say this didn't help to allay his mounting sense of frustration. In another hour or so he took to driving home about every thirty minutes, pretending he had forgotten something. And each time he would look hard at the skies from under the porch roof and say to me, "It looks bad, it looks bad!" I felt every time he did this he was really trying to sway me over to plucking mother from the club. But I pretended I didn't get the idea and made not a move.

About midafternoon I got in mother's four door robin's-egg blue Chandler and drove out to inspect the canyon. It had a little stream of muddy water in it, just about big enough to cover the concrete slab I have described. I would guess it was a foot deep at the center of that slab. I felt reassured that mother would be okay and father was excited about nothing — so I drove back home.

On the north side of our house, there was a single lane driveway leading from the street and under a porte cochere from which one could step onto the porch. The driveway led on to the garage. There was an alley back of the garage and one could drive through the garage and into the alley. On my way home the rain had picked up and by the time I entered the driveway it was pouring down. Father's car was standing in the driveway under the porte cochere and he was at the wheel. When he heard me drive up behind him he mistakenly assumed I had mother with me so decided to drive ahead and through the garage so that I would drive up and let mother out under the porte cochere. Father had a Dodge coupe, the doors of which opened from the front. As I came up from behind, he gunned his motor and headed for the garage. But just before he got to it his left door swung open, the door jamb on the garage caught the car door squarely in the middle, and when the car emerged into the alley back of the garage its left door lay on the ground at the garage entrance.

This wouldn't have been so bad if I had really had mother with me. But when father came back around in the driveway and found it was only me, he was near in a rage. And, as I said, he had been having a little nip or two now and then just to calm his nerves. Heatedly, he said, "It's all your fault! You can just forget about your mother and let me take care of the whole matter!" With that, he went in the house and put on his great, fine, black Stetson hat, then got back in his doorless Dodge and roared away.

About sundown I heard a car drive up to the house and I looked out and saw it was father's Dodge. It was caked with mud. At the wheel was a fellow we called "Shorty," who worked regularly for father doing odd jobs and occasionally going along to help drive on bad trips. Father told Shorty to take the car down to Joe Scott's Ford place and have it cleaned up. Then he plunged into the house, looking neither left nor right. His clothes were soaking wet and rumpled from head to foot. And he was hatless. His usually beautifully roached great shock of hair looked as if it had been caught in a whirlwind and a waterfall. And his usually carefully brushed moustache and goatee were drooping and unkempt. He headed for the bedroom where he could bathe and get on some dry clothes. But on the way he caught me in his eye and, with whiskers aquiver and eyes flashing he said, "I could have drowned, I wrecked my car and I lost my hat. And it was all your fault! It all wouldn't have happened if you had the proper respect for your mother!"

I lit out for town and ran down Shorty to find out what had happened.

"Well," he said, "your dad called me about four o'clock and said he wanted me to drive him out to the Country Club to get your ma. We went out there and your dad went in the Club but pretty soon he came out and he was in a dither. He said your ma thought more of her bridge game and a bunch o' silly wimmen than she did of him and her family. He said your ma said she could come home over the railroad trestle if the canyon got on a rise. Anyway, she wouldn't come home with your dad. So we started back to town, with your dad at the wheel. He was hoppin' mad and when we drove down into the canyon he was a barrellin' it. He hit the water on that little cement slab with a big splash and the water came up in the engine and drowned it out. He hadn't aimed the car straight, so the right front wheel went over the side and the axle went down on the slab and we was stranded there in the bottom of the canyon on that slab with the muddy water rushin' in through the busted door on your dad's side of the car.

"You know what a finicky dresser your dad is and he didn't want to get out and wade to shore. So I got out and went around to his side of the car. He was a-holdin' his feet up off the running board so's to keep 'em out of the water. When I got around by him, he squooged around and got onto my back. He's pretty heavy, you know, but we started out, me a-holdin' your dad's legs and him a-holdin' me 'round the neck. When I got him to the edge of the slab he and I got our signals mixed up and he turned loose of my neck, but I was still a-holdin' his legs. So he fell over backwards, full length into that muddy water. And when he scrambled out we saw his big black Stetson hat float away. Purty soon a man with a pickup and a tow chain came along and he pulled us off the slab and onto the road.

"Your dad was mighty mad at you, and he didn't seem particularly pleased with your ma, either."

When I got back home father had gotten on some dry clothes, roached his hair and gotten his goatee and moustache adjusted back in place. He was slouched in his easy chair in the living room smoking his pipe and pretending to be absorbed in his Owensboro, Kentucky, *Messenger*. That's the way he would do sometimes when his feelings were hurt.

Mother came bouncing in, perfectly groomed, sweet, calm and beautiful as ever and began bubbling about what a jolly time she and the gals had had at the bridge party. Father barely looked up and mother saw right away that something was good and wrong.

Then I told mother what had happened and she and I could barely keep from laughing out loud, thinking about father losing his dignity in the canyon water and mud that way, but we didn't let on we knew. Mother said she thought father might feel better when he'd had a good supper. So then she got into a housedress and began rattling dishes in the kitchen and singing some of father's favorite songs like *Amazing Grace*, and *Abide With Me*, in her nice soprano voice that drifted through the house.

Mother put a clean tablecloth on the dining table and went out in the yard and picked a big bunch of sweet pea blooms and put them in a big cut glass bowl in the center of the table.

Supper began with potato soup, made of diced potatoes and onions — one of father's favorite dishes. Then she brought out a huge rump roast she had put in the oven the night before, cooked somehow so every slice seemed juicy and just rare enough. And succotash, the real kind, made with fresh string beans and fresh corn off the cob and salt pork, and mashed potatoes with thick, creamy, meat gravy. And hotwater cornbread, that only she knew how to fix. Hotwater cornbread! That was always a way to father's heart! And we had apple dumplings and coffee to finish off.

Well, father ate his way silently through the entire meal. And, needless to say, mother and I didn't say anything either.

But finally father let his eyes dwell a moment on mother and mother gave him that sweet, gentle understanding smile of hers and father began to laugh. And so did mother and I and we all laughed and laughed until our sides ached.

Then father, kind of sheepishly, reached in his pocket and pulled out a somewhat beaten and damp little package, and handed it across the table to mother. Sometime, during his many trips between the office and home that day, he had stopped at Coleman's Jewelry Store and bought mother a beautiful new diamond ring.

Over a number of years, my mother's letters gave an insight into her personality, as well as the Panhandle area, and what was happening there. She mentioned many people who lived in that area. She expressed herself well, for the most part, and her woman's eye view of those years is interesting from a historical standpoint.

December 5, 1929 [After the stock market crashed.]

Am enclosing bank statement as per your request, and you will see why I have not sent it sooner — Because the bank did not render a statement for Sept., Oct., separately, but made only one the first of this month.

The deposits on same represent our share of all the grain that has been disposed of so far. We have had the biggest, coldest, snow ever seen here in Nov. About 14 inches on a level, no drifts, and cold as Greenland for nearly four weeks. Consequently, all grain that was in the fields at the time the snow fell, remained there during that long spell of zero weather. Mr. Wilkerson has nearly all his crop yet to market; i.e. the crop he bought from Stovall, so our part of that will be coming in soon, and the corn is not yet gathered. Of course it is not damaged, and there must be a good deal of it to sell.

Mr. Bennett was out thru the Boise City country yesterday,

and the snow is still so heavy out there that farmers have done nothing, but we have had three days of sunshine and somewhat warmer here, and things are beginning to move a little.

. . . I like to know that I am on the safe side, and have a fund that I can get my hands on in case of emergency. As soon as the grain etc. begins to move, I think I shall invest that fund in town lots. I believe there is money in Dalhart property in the near future. We are talking strong of a Junior College, The Catholics are going to build a school, and hope to have it under headway next year, and there seems to be no end to the new business projects that are being considered, so I feel like all the money that we do not need to spend right now, can be safely invested in city property.

. . . And all along we have kept a kind of hold on the human side of life. I had one dinner party the first of Nov., consisting of fried chicken principally, with such things as usually accompany that edible, and to help eat we had as guests, Mr. & Mrs. Lane, Mr. & Mrs. Greenough, Mr. & Mrs. Killen. Of course Artis and Harriett. Had a lively party and everybody had a raring good time until late bed time. Then I had another one, and this time I cooked wild ducks, and venison. This time we just had the T. C. Clinic, Dr. & Mrs. Scott, Dr. & Mrs. Pieratt, Miss Selby, Artis & Harriett. How they did enjoy the ducks, and venison. Some of them had never tasted either before and were glad of the chance to find how good they were. Then I have attended two or three dinner parties that were very enjoyable.

I worked a whole heap in that Chrysanthemum Carnival that we Business women put over, and it surely went over "Big." Had the weather been pleasant instead of so terrible there is no telling what we might have done. But our first night we had such a blizzard one could scarcely keep ones feet on the ground, and it seemed the whole world was frozen over during the whole time the event was going on. Any how it showed us what we might be able to do if we only work and pull together.

April 3, 1935

Well at last — a letter from you. I had about concluded you had lost all interest in us as well as the whole country. And such a country!! Still no rain, and sand and dirt storms worse than ever. . . . nothing but dirt and sand dunes to be seen anywhere.

People who know, tell us that Kansas and Colorado are in much worse condition than we are. That is hard to believe, but when we see one of those monster storms coming from the North E. it looks like all of Colorado and Kansas was in the air, and falling upon us in great heaps. If we could just have the old time sand storms, the kind you remember, just throwing our nice clean sand in your face, we could take it much more philosophically, but when all that fine dirty dirt comes from the other states, well it is beyond your most vivid imagination, and far beyond description.

Last week 100 families in Baca Co. and Lewis Co. applied to the Govt. to move them into new territory. Four years of continued drouth, with this stifling dust choking them down daily, has proven more than they can withstand. They must give up all property and move out. They report deaths from dust pneumonia, and children strangling — trying to get to school.

In Kansas trains are delayed and often are compelled to stop, the dust is so dense. Your father went to Rochester last week. Said his train was 1 hr. 45 min. late getting out of KC. and they had to slow down, and stop, time and again and the passengers were almost suffocated. And those trains are air conditioned, too. If there was any prospect for a change it would help some, even tho it proved futile, but there is no such prospect, and the dry erosion territory is increasing by leaps and bounds, daily.

I had five college boys in our upstairs for a month. They are sent here by the Govt. to assist in land erosion control etc., tree planting and all that. Only have two boys now, out of the five. They get paid only when they work, and the wind and sand have been so terrible that they only get a day or two each week, and are not making expenses. Two of them are batching to save expenses. One other thought he was about to commit matrimony and had a chance to rent an apartment so he took that, for fear he would not find a place when he brought his bride here.

These boys, along with about 20 others were supposed to survey the tree planting belts, get the lay of the land, water sheds etc. and teach the farmers the art of terracing to conserve moisture. They have a tremendous undertaking and it will not amount to a thing on earth unless we get rain.

April 13, 1938

. . . Of course you read of our violent blizzard and freezing weather. We have had many harder storms, so far as the sand and visibility was concerned, but never in all the 31 years we have lived in the West, have we seen the thing continued for three days and nights on a stretch, without one minute between violent gusts and lambasting dirt deluging us unceasingly. All over the

South Plains they had heavy snow, and at Pampa it was piled as high as the eaves of the houses. We had some snow too, but the wind was driving so hard it (the snow) could not light on the ground. Just passed us up and went straight by. At Dumas they had the sand and snow combined and were treated to a real mud bath which gobbed all the windows over on the outside.

As if the weather had not brought devastation enough to the High Plains area, there were often clouds of grasshoppers. By the millions, the insects swarmed into the plains areas, turning the sky black. There were times one was reminded of the story in Exodus, of the scourge of locusts inflicted on the Egyptians by God. Some towns were left without a single sprig of greenery — the grasshoppers had devoured everything in sight. Many thought the end of the world was at hand, as they had felt during the terrifying Black Dusters.

May 22, 1938

... You will notice in the *Texan* that the grasshoppers are a greater menace to this country than the drouth. Our people are asking for help from the Govt. to help exterminate these pests. The country people are much exercized and say that if something is not done right now all pastures will be gone etc. Since we have no pastures in this section, we are afraid the hoppers will travel to town and devour our lawns and trees. Right now there are many good looking lawns, and numbers and numbers of lovely trees. In spite of the freeze that took all the early leaves and buds, the trees are beautiful. We are asking the Governor to send men and trucks to help distribute poison to halt this deadly destruction. Everywhere, all over the country, men are organizing and using man power and machinery to combat the plague.

January 23, 1941

Am glad Dr. had the pictures of our trees made when he did for you would not recognize anything in Dalhart or Amarillo. The sleet left nothing but old stumps and snags. Some think they will come out in the spring, and in a few years be prettier than ever, but I remain a doubting Thomas. I do not see how it is possible for those stumps to put out branches and leaves.

Dan Allender was a man who was our tenant-on-shares in 1924–1927 on our farm eight miles east of Dalhart. Allender left farming, moved to town, and became owner of a furniture store, and a radio station. Allender gave a short address over his Dalhart Radio Station, after my Mother died, on March 5, 1954.

The old home place in Dalhart. The trees are Chinese elms planted by my father in about 1918, after the black locusts all fell victim to borers.

This program is dedicated to our friend Mrs. G. W. Dawson, who became our friend first in 1915. I personally knew the entire Dawson family. But somehow I have always had a great admiration for Mrs. Dawson. I had many personal acquaintances with this great person both as a medical patient and in business for I lived on their farm three years. Dr. Dawson and myself always worked in complete harmony. I have seen him give medical care to many people, and often without charge. I know this from personal experience. But always in the background was his faithful helper Mrs. Dawson. She kept the books, gave anaesthetics to hundreds of people while the Doctor performed many a critical surgical operation.

I was present when she was admitted to the Amarillo Hospital. The attendant entered the room and told her he needed some blood tests. I told him she probably knew better what he was doing than he did — that she was a nurse of much experience. She reached for the oxygen mask and settled back on her pillow. And somehow in my heart as I departed from the room, I felt I had had my last visit with someone whom I had loved and respected for many years.

Dr. Dawson delivered my son Joe, September 12, 1923, at about 2:30 A.M. The next morning as she entered the room I shall never forget how her eyes beamed as she said, "You have a son this morning." Her beautiful eyes always expressed as much — or more than — words. She always seemed to know what to say to the sick.

Eyewitnesses said she was judged the most beautiful and useful woman in the great Fourth of July parade in 1923. And as I saw her pass in the car, sitting erect, smiling, with her white hair gleaming in the sunshine, I knew no judge could deny her the diamond ring prize.

She was a lifelong member of the Dalhart Literary Club and the Methodist Church. And was well read on all subjects and would, when asked, give sound advice. I visited in their home many times, and no one could have been a more faithful mother, wife, or helper.

As I departed from the hospital room a few days ago, somehow I muttered a little silent prayer that I could be as good, great, and noble as the sweet little old lady who possessed all the world's grandeur, splendor and life's goodness — the one who has passed from our midst.

My oldest brother, Artis, wrote and sent to her on Mother's Day in 1950, the following poem.

Most cherished Mother,

Now the time has come
When full of years, and memories you pause,
To look upon those years. And we, your sons,
Pause also, and in scanning your long life,
Remember many things with deepest love,
With pride and gratitude and loyalty
And tenderness we don't know how to show,
But yet, withal, with love; that much I know.
Now is the time, not then, when other days
Like softly falling snow, have overlaid
The keenness of your mind, or Death has come
To lift you from your earth-mold, so to bring
You closer to your strongly worshipped God.
Not then, but now, we pause to honor you,
To tell you of our feeling, if we can,
And urgently we try, for if we could,
And you could know, yet could you not know this
That telling you and having you understand
Had given us happiness and a certain sense
Of having partly paid our filial debt.
A little part, but pleasure in the deed
Is all the greater when we come to think
How great the debt, how much we cannot pay.
Yours was a life of sacrifice and work
From that fair day; when, beautiful and young,
You cast your lot and took your place beside
One man; a man who needed you.
Three sons, a home, and yet another life
Equally full, where sons and home were left
A little while each day in valiant work
Beside the man you married, helping him.
Well I remember all the daily toil
As uncomplaining you marched on and on;
If sometimes you looked grim, or sudden storm
Of feeling shook you from your wonted calm,
Then you'd begin to sing: *Amazing Grace,*
Abide with Me, or other old sweet song,
Your mother's songs; and then would roll away

Willie Catherine Dawson, about the time of World War I. She always dressed well and looked beautiful.

The cares and burdens resting on your soul
And you would smile, strong and serene again.
Through all the years, when frailty of men
And all the disillusionments of life
Beat at its gates, yet were you ever strong
To hold within your battlemented heart
Your code, your creed, your faith, and too, your love.
With head held high and calmness in your mien,
How much was hidden, loneliness and pain!
Now, looking back, you see the fight is won,
You've kept the faith, you've fought the battle well;
Grandchildren, great-grandchildren you can see
To prove to you that here you have not failed.
And we your sons can only hope that we,
As well as all those others, can in part
Add to your reckoning of your earthly score,
To make the sum a satisfying whole.
Mother of sons, take this as your salute!
If there is any way that debts are paid
May you obtain your great and just reward,
But, barring that, know that within our hearts
There lies a love that time, distance or death
Cannot destroy.

The Errant Jackass and How to Raise Tumbleweeds

The best side's up. For God's sake, don't plow it under.
Miles to water, miles to wood, and only six inches to hell.
— Texas pioneer sayings

In 1924 when father decided to make a farm out of our section of land about eight miles east of Dalhart, he and Dan Allender, our tenant, decided to use mares to do the plowing. And before long father decided we should use the mares to raise some mules. So he traded for a jackass and had him turned into the pasture with the mares.

He was a very attentive, fine looking young jackass. In fact, Dan Allender said the jackass attended about three mares a night. And he kept all the mares on the run so much that Dan said they were too tired to plow well in the daytime. So, to partly restrain our jack's activity, we put a collar on him and tied about a fifteen foot length of log chain to the collar. This slowed him down a bit and allowed the mares a little more rest. However, after due time we learned that all the jack's work with the mares was for naught. He just didn't produce one single mule.

"That confounded jack's no good," father said. "I'm going to see if I can trade him off."

One day I drove with father on a call west of town, and on the way father saw a farmer plowing with a fine looking pair of mules. "I sure would like to have that span of mules," he remarked.

Some days later father said, "Son, I've been talking with that fellow with that span of mules. I think we can make a trade."

So father put on his great fine black Stetson hat, cut off a large chunk from one of his twists of pure dry, Kentucky leaf tobacco, stuffed it in his mouth, and we drove off to the country.

As we drove along he got to telling me about how he learned the art of horse trading. And he was bragging a little about his ability at this occupation.

"My father was a circuit riding Baptist preacher in Kentucky and poor as a church mouse," he said. "He was always having company for dinner 'though we didn't have enough food for even the family. So I decided at a very early age I had to find a way to earn a decent living. I learned how to take care of livestock and was earning my keep and a bit more as a horse doctor before I was sixteen."

Then he told me he had largely supported himself through medical school by trading horses. He said he would leave for the Indiana hills early each summer with a few dollars, and return in the fall with two or three hundred dollars in cash and a nice herd of horses and mules.

"And I learned some of the tricks about horse trading. For example, I learned how you could use nitric acid to fix a 'U.S.' brand on an old Army mule so you couldn't tell it had ever been there. And how to make a horse with heaves trot up and down the road, heaving not a bit when properly stuffed with oats.

"And I learned that a broken down dejected animal with a sulky, drooping head and tail, would show a real flashy spirit with head held high and tail beautifully arched, after a proper application of ginger root in the rectum."

He was musing thus when we approached the farm where he hoped to trade for that span of mules.

"I think this fellow wants a jack and I'm going to try to trade him ours," he said. "Horse traders have to look out for themselves, you know."

As we approached the man's farm we spotted the farmer. He had that fine looking span of mules hitched to a plow and appeared to be routinely working up and down the field.

We spread the barbed wire fence, crawled through, and walked over the plowed rows to the farmer and the mules. He and father sparred around a while and then father put the big question to him. "Didn't he need that jack?" And, sure enough the man said right off that he sure did and had been looking for one.

Before we left father had made the deal. The jack for the span of mules. It was arranged that the farmer would have the mules delivered at our farm and pick up the jack.

A day or so later father and I drove out to our farm to inspect our prizes. Our tenant, Dan Allender, had been present when the farmer's hired hand delivered the mules and left with the jack. The span of mules were inside our five-bar corral, but each had on a halter to which was attached a strong rope tied to a heavy post.

"Why are they tied up?" asked father.

"Well," said Dan, "when the man brought the mules I thought I ought to level with him about the jackass. So, I said, 'I think I ought to tell you that damned jack won't produce nothin' and he will run everything on the ranch to death.' Then the man said to me: 'Oh, that's okay. There's something *I* know about this span of mules. They can stand flat-footed and jump over a six-bar corral. In fact, we've never been able to build either a corral or a fence high enough to keep them on the place, and we've been trying to get rid of them for about a year.' "

"I *thought* that crook was hiding something from me," said father, as we walked back to the car.

After that the span of mules kept jumping out of our pasture and going back where they had come from and the jack kept running away from his new home and coming back to our mares. Finally we had Dan Allender offer to give the mules back to the farmer we got them from but he wouldn't take them. The farmer did, however, tell Dan he wished we would kill that damned jackass the next time he came on our farm.

One evening, looking up from the weekly *Dalhart Texan,* father called out: "Willie, I'm convinced we can raise cotton on these high plains."

"I think I smell a mouse, George," said mother. "You aren't thinking of trying to raise some cotton yourself are you?"

"That's exactly what I'm thinking about," said Father. "Take section eighteen out here just eight miles east of town. It's too valuable to leave as pastureland. We ought to fence it up, break it out and put about half of it in a cotton crop. Why, if we had three hundred acres of cotton and got a half a bale an acre we could make about enough to pay off the mortgage."

"How much would it cost to fence it up? And how much would it cost to plow it up? And how much will it cost to hire people to chop it and pick it, and where are you going to get the people to do these things?"

"People will be coming here in droves when they hear of this new cotton country," said father. "I always said this land could grow anything, and now with all the ranchland that has been made into farms since the war, we have been getting better crops. More people, more land in cultivation all mean more moisture, you know. We've always known we could raise maize and kaiffircorn and now since the war we've found out we can raise wheat. But cotton! Why, turning these high plains into a cotton empire would bring thousands of people in here; land prices would skyrocket."

"I did read about a few people trying to raise cotton up here last year for the first time," said mother. "The paper said the crops weren't very good."

"That's because of an unexpected cold spring, and an unexpected early freeze in the fall when we expected a frost," said father.

"By now you ought to expect the unexpected in the weather up here," said mother. "I'd a lot rather put the money on the mortgage on the duplex."

Thus, it was that the issue was decided after proper conference. We would go into the business of raising cotton. Not only that, but we would go into raising cotton in a big way.

The May 2, 1924, *Dalhart Texan* carried the following story:

> ### WILL BE BIG COTTON KING
> The original estimate of the cotton acreage in the Dalhart country will fall far short of the actual crop that will be planted, according to those who have made it a point to interview farmers in the different sections. Nearly every farmer will plant some, the acreage running from five to ten or several hundred. Now comes Dr. G. W. Dawson who owns a valuable tract of land eight miles east of Dalhart and says that he is getting ready for 300 acres in cotton at that place.

Shortly thereafter, a neighbor with his turning plow had converted 300 acres of our prairieland, which had theretofore been protected by its beautiful covering of buffalo grass, into a plowed field. It was then planted in cotton.

When I returned to Dalhart late in June that year with diploma in hand from the University of Wisconsin, I drove out to look at the cotton crop. A few miles out I stopped the car and got out on the roadside to stretch my eyes across the prairie, look up at that vast, clear blue sky, and fill my lungs with the dry, rarified atmosphere of the High Plains. What a contrast to the beautiful hills and trees and lakes of Wisconsin! Yet here, in its own way, was an even more beautiful landscape. At least it seemed so to the eyes of one who had spent his childhood on it. Except for an occasional windmill or lonely looking farmhouse, one could look in all directions and see nothing but flat, grass covered land encircled by a horizon which seemed many, many miles away. Somehow the horizon seemed a bit below one's line of vision, giving him the feeling that he was above the whole world about him, and that the earth curved gently downward in all directions from where he stood. Perhaps the high altitude and lack of moisture helped make one feel that pleasant sense of vigor and buoyancy. I somehow felt a master of all the world about me.

As I approached section eighteen I observed thousands of small green bushes protruding from the upturned and drying sod. When I crawled through the fence and walked onto the plowed ground itself, it became apparent that the green bushes I had seen protruding from the ground were not bushes of cotton, but bushes of tumbleweeds. We had had another unexpected cold spring so that such cotton as had come up had been unable to reach sufficient growth to withstand the early hot winds. It soon withered and died. Tumbleweed seed, however, which had theretofore laid dormant under the tight buffalo grass sod cover, once freed from their sod bondage by the plow, had germinated; and once out of the ground, a tumbleweed can stand about any kind of weather. Instead of having a cotton crop we had brought forth a most luxuriant tumbleweed crop. The weeds covered almost all the surface of that 300 acres and we knew that until they were removed that land would be completely useless for farming.

A tumbleweed is really a kind of thistle. It is said to have been brought to this Western plain from Russia along with wheat seed originating there. It is a prickly bush made up entirely of stem and sticker. No leaves. It has branches or spines which grow flat on the ground up to two or three feet in each direction from its center. Other prickly spines extend upward as much as two or three feet to make the whole bush look much like a large stickery ball. The bush stays green until in the fall, then the spines and spikes of which it is composed turn dry, wiry and tough and take on a brownish-gray color. In time the wind will cause the bush to break loose from its roots and then it is free to roam. In the plains country you can nearly always see a few tumbleweeds bouncing along over the surface of the land when the wind blows. They hold their shape and keep blowing around for a remarkably long time. At the tip end of each of the tumbleweed's stickery branches there is a tiny seedpod. As each tumbler spins and rolls before the wind across the prairie, thousands of seeds are scattered from these seedpods. Wherever the prairie retains, or is permitted to restore, its native buffalo grass sod cover, the tumbleweed cannot grow. But where the grass on the prairie is thinned or weakened by overgrazing, cut away by blowing sand or turned beneath the surface by use of a plow, the tumbleweed thrives.

It was late in the summer before we got a house and barn on the place and acquired some mares and plows and a tenant. By then the tumbleweeds had grown so big that we knew we couldn't kill them out with any plow. So we decided just to wait until fall when they would die. Then it should be easy to break them loose from the soil, stack them in piles and burn them. About the middle of September, Old Walt, an itinerant farmhand, showed up in town looking for work. I am sure he had some other name, but I knew him only as Old Walt. Every fall, about time to harvest the maize or other "row" crops, Old Walt would show up. He would come by the sanitarium and let us know he was ready to take on any farm job we might have open. He was an independent, happy-go-lucky old codger, with apparently not a care in the world. He always wore blue overalls and long white underwear that stuck out from his rolled up shirt sleeves. He chewed giant wads of Mail Pouch tobacco and he had a wooden leg that creaked as he walked. In a sense Old Walt was a lot like a tumbleweed in that he sort of drifted with the weather.

Arrangements were made for me and Old Walt to tackle the tumbleweeds that had taken over father's cotton crop. So he and I installed ourselves in our farmhouse one night and the next morning we went out and looked over our tumbleweed problem. The weeds had grown dry enough to burn all right if we could get them loosened from the ground and stacked in piles. Walt said we needed some kind of a heavy drag that we could hitch up to a team of horses and pull along the ground. He thought this way we could pull the weeds loose. Well, we went into town with a team of horses, a wagon and a heavy chain and at the Rock Island roundhouse we were able to get an old piece of railroad rail about fifteen feet long. We rigged the chain around the wagon bed, attached it to one end of the rail and hoisted that end of the rail off the ground. Then we drove back to the farm, pulling the rail behind the wagon. After we got the rail to the farm, Walt hooked a chain on either end of it, harnessed a team of horses to a device called a singletree, attached the chains to the singletree and moved out to attack the tumbleweeds, which Old Walt, right away began calling his "particklar friends."

Old Walt moved right along with this contraption and in a few days he had most all of his "particklar friends" lying there in the field broken loose from the soil. But getting them loose from the soil turned out to be just the beginning of our problem. The big problem was how to get them out of our field.

Old Walt and I attacked the weeds with pitchforks, newspapers and matches and for days and days we struggled.

But every night when we would give up for the day and trudge wearily back to the farmhouse, we would look at the acres and acres of tumbleweeds remaining to be burned and despair of ever getting through.

Once we tried to speed up the operation by using a hayrake. This was essentially about a ten foot row of curved iron spikes about three feet in height and horse drawn. It was designed to gather a nice bundle of hay in the basket formed by the curved iron spikes and then empty itself by causing the spikes to lift upward and rearward.

But the hayrake proved to be more of a hindrance than a help. It made relatively small stacks of tumbleweeds which Walt and I then had to combine into larger stacks for burning. Moreover, when it unloaded itself, the spikes forming its collection basket would lift only about two feet above the ground — not high enough to disgorge the big tumblers it occasionally picked up. We would then have to stop the horses while one of us would go around to the front of the rake and pull the big tumblers out by hand or pitchfork.

So we gave up on the hayrake, but before Old Walt limped back to the barn with the horses and the rake, he said he was going to build a better one. He spent one whole day at this, and when he had finished he had a huge scoop about fourteen feet long and four feet high. The bottom and the backstop were made of two-by-six planks held together by angle irons to which the boards were bolted. Two half circles of two inch pipe were attached at either end with the outer sides of the curves facing to the front. These were intended as rollers which would lift the scoop from the ground when it was rolled forward for the purpose of unloading. A handle for the scoop was made by attaching another iron pipe to the front rail and to the backstop and extending about six feet to the rear.

When Old Walt hitched four horses to this device and dragged it out into the field, he was beaming with enthusiasm. "Jason," he said (that's what he called me) "this here machine can do anything but suck eggs. I'll bet old John Deere hisself would like to have invented it."

Then we went to work, I driving the horses to pull the weed scoop forward and Old Walt swinging on to the handle. We picked up two or three fine loads of tumbleweeds this way, but then, just as Old Walt was pushing up on the handle to make the machine dump its load, one of the horses shied, giving the scoop an extra and unexpected tug. The handle flew out of Old Walt's hand and the scoop rolled completely over, bending the handle double and splitting the backstop board in two.

Old Walt then undid the chain connecting the horses to one side of the scoop, took over the reins and dejectedly dragged his demolished invention toward the barn, his wooden leg creaking as he limped along.

So, back we went to our pitchforks — stacking, burning, stacking, burning. It was a beautiful September afternoon, clear, sunny and warm. I had almost decided to go to town and try to enlist a small army of townfolk in our battle with the tumbleweeds when I suddenly sensed a fresh coolness coming out of the north. I looked up to see a great, black, menacing cloud rising all along the full length of the northern horizon.

Old Walt and I had so far been able to clear only a small patch in the south end of the field and we were working there when we felt that cool breeze. We both stopped working, leaned on our pitchforks and, looking toward the north over about a mile of loose tumbleweeds, watched the storm come down upon us.

"That there is one beautiful norther a coming," said Old Walt.

With the first gentle movement of the north wind, that entire half section of loose tumbleweeds began to stir and inch forward, making the field look much as though it had been covered with giant furry caterpillars which suddenly began to hunch up their bodies and crawl toward us.

The black cloud in the north rose rapidly higher and higher and as it did so, the force of the wind increased and the tumbleweeds began to roll.

Soon the earth grew dark as the black cloud spread out over the entire sky. The wind changed from a gentle coolish breeze to a bit-terly cold gale, and when it hit with full force, the field became a solid mass of rolling, bounding tumblers and windblown sand.

"Most beautiful sight I ever see," said Old Walt as he whirled his pitchfork over his head and let it fly at a passing bush.

In almost no time at all, every loose tumbleweed in that field had blown past me and Old Walt and on down to the barbed wire fence that bounded our farm on the south. There, a great stack of the weeds the full length of the fence was soon formed over which oncoming tumblers began to bounce.

From then on the job was easy. All that Old Walt and I had to do was work up and down that south fence, hoist tumblers into the air with our pitchforks and then watch them fly over our fence and take off like a herd of frightened sheep across the wide, open, uncultivated prairie that lay to the south of our land.

I went into town that night and told father how we had gotten rid of the tumbleweeds. His eyes twinkled and he laughed when I described how those tumblers had taken off across our neighbor's pasture. He said he didn't know who owned that land but we'd be lucky if we didn't hear from him. Then he said we ought to be thinking about what we would do with our land next year. "Now that the weeds are gone, we'll just have time to get that field disked, harrowed and planted in winter wheat," he said.

My Friend: Al Dalton and Bill Bennett: Gentleman

> *If there's a lady present, you never, ever, ask no cowman about the other names of . . . son-of-a-gun stew. The real name is a little different, and the cook used to announce chow by yellin', 'Come get your Son of a ———, it takes a Son of a ——— to eat it!' But when they is ladies around, we calls it County Attorney stew. Why? Ain't you heard that old song?*
>
> — Al Dalton

I don't remember how I got to know old Al Dalton. He was a real close friend of father's and I guess I met him down at father's office. He was an easygoing old codger who spent most of his time when in town playing dominos at Dinwiddie's Pool Hall and Domino Parlor. Father said Al couldn't stand prosperity and that every time he got a few dollars ahead he would come to town and stay just long enough to gamble it all away.

Al was the first man who ever told me you should never ask an old Texan where he came from. He never would tell me where he was from and he would not tell me much about his past, either. I did learn from him that he had been a cowboy all his life, and was one of the last trail drivers. He told me he had once had charge of a trail drive that took a herd of cattle from near Vernon, Texas, all the way to Oregon, one of the longest trail drives on record. That must have been around 1870.

He said he had been married some time in the past and for a time he and his wife were living on a hundred and sixty-acre homestead claim up in the Oklahoma Strip. He didn't tell me why his wife left him but he said that after that he didn't care about the homestead place. We went up there to see it one time. The house was going to pieces and the field he had plowed up was blowing away. It was the loneliest looking place I ever saw and I don't think Al ever went back.

Al used to tell me how to make son-of-a-gun stew. All old cowboys talk about son-of-a-gun stew. There are probably a lot of ways to make a stew that bears that name — or the same stew that bears a *different* name. I may not remember all the parts of the cow that went into it but I do remember that Al said the main ingredient was something called the "marrow gut." "You have to find the marrow gut or you won't have son-of-a-gun stew," Al would say.

"If there's a lady present, you never, ever, ask about the other names of . . . son-of-a-gun stew. The real name is a little different, and the cook used to announce chow by yellin', 'Come get your Son of a ———, it takes a Son of a ——— to eat it!' But when they is ladies around, we calls it County Attorney stew. Why? Ain't you heard that old song?

> *There's the County Attorney I like to've forgot,*
> *He's the meanest dam man we've got in our lot.*
> *Your pockets he'll pick, your clothes he will sell,*
> *And for twenty-five cents he will send you to Hell,*
> *An' it's hard, hard times.*

Jesse James, Andy James's nephew, knew Al. He said that one time Al bought some plain Mexican cows and leased a section of land "about as far out in the country as you could get." Al and his old sidekick, Frank Allen (or "Crip" as they called him because of his bad leg), stayed out there on this place all one winter. Rube Johnson, foreman of the James Brothers North Ranch decided he had better go see how they were getting along. "When Rube got there, Al and Crip weren't speaking to each other," he said. "Al's horse had throwed him and broke his leg. He was trying to make him some leg splints so he could get around. Al had a Ford car and could have come to town to see Doc Dawson, but he couldn't stand on his broken leg to crank the car. Crip couldn't crank it either and, besides, he didn't know how to drive.

"Al told me that one time in the winter of 1911, Rube Johnson and Elmer Gray were staying on the two-section place near Conlen that my father later bought. 'There was a big Indian named Chief staying there and he smelled bad,' Al said. Rube and Elmer wanted to get rid of that old Indian awful bad. That was the first year they were making cottonseed cake in little pellets. They were little brownish pellets about the same size and color as the dung their big old tomcat would leave around. Every day at noon Rube and Elmer would put a stew on the stove to have it ready for supper. Old Rube, he was witty and full of everything so between he and Elmer they decided on a way to get rid of the Indian. When the stew was about ready to serve they mixed a handful of those cottonseed pellets in the Indian's plate of stew. After they had sat down and started eating, Rube says to Elmer, 'What did you leave the lid off this stew for and let that old cat get in?' and when he did that he pulled out one of them little round pellets. Well, that Indian looked down at his stew and saw he had been eating some of those pellets, and when he did that he got up and left and they never did see him again.

"Al told me about Cave Bull and the mustang. He said: 'One time in the early spring of 1890 old Cave Bull, the man the James Brothers bought their north ranch property from, and his son Cave was moving horses to Colorado. Young Cave had just got out of school at Goodnight, and was only about fourteen years old. He was riding a big horse near Dumas and he saw a pretty mustang. He decided to rope the mustang and of course he had the end of the rope hitched onto the horn of his new saddle. Well, he roped that mustang all right, but that was the last time he ever saw his new saddle.' "

Al was a big admirer of my father, and he loved to tell me a yarn about how my father took over Scandalous John McCandless's business of keeping the peace. The story was, that once father had a very sick patient in the sanitarium and was sitting up late one night so he could keep close tab on the patient's condition. Two drunks got out in front of the Cozy Corner Saloon about half a block from the sanitarium and got to shouting and laughing and swearing. Father felt they were disturbing his patient, and he went over and told the men about his sick patient and asked them to quiet down. In a few minutes they were making just as much noise as before, so father called Scandalous McCandless, who was then sheriff, and asked him to get these drunks off the street. Time passed and Scandalous hadn't showed up so father called again. More time passed and the drunks were still raising hell. Finally father had all of this he could stand. He had been cleaning and sharpening instruments, and when he walked down to the Cozy Corner to confront these men he was carrying a handful of surgical instruments in his right hand. He again asked the men to quiet down. They told him he could go to hell — or words to that effect. Father was lefthanded and on the third finger on his left hand there was a huge Masonic ring. Father swung twice and both drunks fell to the street and stayed there. The Masonic ring had ripped through the skin on both men's faces, leaving nasty bleeding wounds. Father then lifted the men, one at a time, to his shoulder, carried them to the sanitarium, sewed their wounds and put them to bed.

Then he called Scandalous again. "Scandalous," he said, "you needn't come to this part of town any more. From now on, I'll keep the peace around here."

One time Al won a beautiful revolver on a punchboard at Dinwiddie's Pool Hall and Domino Parlor. It was a Smith and Wesson .38 calibre on a #45 frame. It had a six-inch barrel, was of blue steel, and had a beautiful checked walnut grip. I found out that Al needed a watch but already had a fine six-shooter. I had a pretty good pocketwatch but seldom had any reason to use it. I asked Al if he would trade the revolver for my watch and he agreed. I was a pretty fair shot with that revolver before I was thirteen.

At the desk on the north side of the platform at the rear of the reception room at father's Trans-Canadian Sanitarium, there usually sat a gaunt, gray-haired, immaculately dressed man. His pale blue eyes seemed to express at once some long endured sadness and generous kindness.

He was father's bill collector and his name was Bill Bennett. Bill Bennett would not talk much of his past and about all we learned of his background was that he was born and raised in Canada. He had come to Dalhart and started working for father a few years before World War I. He was then about fifty years of age.

He lived alone and we assumed he was a bachelor. He was kindly, retiring, considerate, and polite to a fault. And loyal. I doubt that he ever lost a day of work in all the years he served father — and that was from about 1915 until after father died twenty-seven years later.

Bill would substitute as receptionist when mother wasn't in the office. Besides working on slow or delinquent accounts Bill did all sorts of odd jobs for father, whom he adored.

Bill's gentleness and kindness were deceiving. He could show strong mettle when the occasion required.

One fellow who tested Bill Bennett's steel, and regretted it, was Blondie Gibbons.

Blondie was sort of a town rowdy — about twenty years younger than Bill Bennett, and at least a hundred pounds heavier. Blondie, during hours off from his job as cook at the De Soto Hotel, could usually be found draping his huge frame over a pool table at Dinwiddie's Pool Hall and Domino Parlor. Most people silently endured Blondie's coarse bluster and brag for he had a quick temper and a reputation as a mighty mauler in a fistfight.

One time Blondie ran up a little bill for something father had done for him and after the billing statement had gone unnoticed for three or four months, Bill Bennett sent him another — with a reminder the bill was past due. Two or three more bills were ignored, and finally Bill wrote Blondie a hard-line note advising him the bill had gone unpaid too long, and unless there was immediate payment his account would be turned over to attorneys for appropriate action.

A day or so later Bill and Blondie met on the sidewalk in front of the De Soto Hotel.

"Look here, Bill Bennett," said Blondie, "I got your goddam nasty letter and I want you to know nobody pushes Blondie Gibbons around that way and gets away with it. I'm just going to whup the hell outa you, so put up yer dukes."

"Just one moment, Mr. Gibbons," said Bill in a calm, unruffled tone. "If you feel I have offended you and think you should give me a beating, that is your privilege. But just give me a moment to make preparation."

With that, Bill Bennett slowly removed his coat, carefully folded it, and draped it over the edge of a trash barrel that stood nearby. He then with calm deliberation put on a pair of kid gloves and carefully smoothed out the wrinkles. Then he faced Blondie and said, "All right, sir, I am now ready."

Blondie Gibbons aimed a mighty blow at Bill Bennett's head and swung. Bill Bennett ducked and as Blondie's frame lunged past him, Bill planted a firm blow in Blondie's solar plexus. Blondie gasped and grabbed his midsection. At that Bill Bennett clipped Blondie on the chin with a left hook. Blondie staggered forward and toppled over head first — and unconscious — into the trash barrel.

Bill Bennett very deliberately removed his kid gloves, ran his fingers through his thin, white hair to get it back in order, removed his coat from the edge of the trash barrel, put it on and straightened his necktie. He then pulled Blondie Gibbons from the trash barrel, laid him gently on his back on the sidewalk, tested his pulse and, satisfied that Blondie would soon regain consciousness, arose and strode away.

Blondie paid his bill and thereafter looked on Bill Bennett with great admiration.

"You know," he told Joe Scott some time later, "I wasn't going to hurt the old man. I just wanted to rough him up a bit. But, doggone it, I never even touched him and he nearly beat me to death."

After father's death in 1942, Bill Bennett retired to a Masonic home for the aged.

Joe Scott visited Bill at the Masonic home a few years before he died. There Bill broke his long kept silence about his true past. In Canada he had once been a professional prizefighter and had gotten into trouble with the law. His name was not Bill Bennett. He had taken the name Bill Bennett when he came to Texas, hoping to build a new life under a new name unencumbered by the mistakes of his past.

Dalhart's Angel of Mercy:
Mrs. E. R. Stewart

> *Even so, that 1918–1919 flu epidemic took the lives of seventy Dallam County residents. Doubtless that number would have been much greater but for the care afforded by the "Opera House Hospital."*

It is conceivable that a person could have lived in Dalhart between 1914 and 1970, without ever having known or even heard of Mrs. E. R. Stewart.

Not, however, if that person had ever had the ill fortune to reach a state of desperate need for food, clothing, or shelter, or for kind, understanding sympathy and help because of some socially embarrassing waywardness or misdeed.

Those facing such a need somehow migrated almost instinctively to this giant-hearted lady, knowing she would welcome them, hear their stories and render aid — all in absolute, complete, unswerving confidentiality.

She and her husband had come to Dalhart from Kentucky, in 1907, and here had raised a fine family of two boys and three girls. Her husband managed the local branch of the Charles Summers and Sons clothing store. The Stewarts were never wealthy — at least not in a monetary sense — but they lived comfortably on the "right" side of town, enjoyed social acceptance, were church going and were active participants in such goings-on as the Rotary Club, the Masons, and (for her) the Eastern Star and a Ladies' Literary Society.

But for Mrs. Stewart, these activities were not enough to be fulfilling; she could not draw her attention away from those suffering misfortune regardless of the cause, and to them she dedicated herself from about 1914 until her retirement in 1970.

In 1972, I sought out this lady for an interview. She was then eighty-six years of age. She arranged an afternoon's respite from the Coon Memorial Hospital to meet with me in her residence. Piecing together the things she told me with news accounts published in *The Dalhart Texan*, I was able to reconstruct some of the highlights of her remarkable career.

It seems that she had begun looking after people in distress in about 1914, working from her home. Three years later when the United States entered World War I, the work of the Red Cross beckoned, and from then on until she retired in 1970 (as its Dallam County Executive Secretary), she worked under the Red Cross banner. Later, on top of the Red Cross work, she accepted administrative duties and work with other relief agencies. For example: in 1933, the New Deal's Depression-fighting Works Progress Administration enlisted her to head that agency's work in the area. In this role, she brought succor to the destitute by means of a dollar a day "made" work and distribution of food under that agency's surplus commodities program.

But she performed many ministries of mercy that did not fall within the ambit of any such organized charities.

Following the United States's 1917 entry into World War I, Mrs. Stewart, at the call of the American Red Cross, enlisted and directed a group of ladies and girls and boys under military age in making sterilized bandages and sewing or knitting stockings, sweaters, gloves and other items of clothing to be distributed by the Red Cross.

They were thus engaged when the great influenza epidemic of 1918–1919 struck. The town's only hospital (the twelve room Trans-Canadian Sanitarium) was soon overcrowded and the number of dangerously ill persons requiring medical attention became far more than the doctors could handle by house calls. There was desperate need for some method of bringing the sick to some central place.

Mrs. Stewart got the consent of the owners of the Felton Opera House for use of the auditorium as an emergency hospital. Aided by her Red Cross work group, she directed movement of influenza patients from their homes to the Opera House auditorium, and arranged separation of the beds of male and female patients by stacking chairs down the auditorium center. She arranged for volunteers to bring and serve food, and her work group performed nursing chores under the direction of the available doctors.

By these means, many Dalhart area residents received medical care they would not otherwise have had. Even so, that 1918–1919 flu epidemic took the lives of seventy Dallam County residents. Doubtless that number would have been much greater but for the care afforded by the "Opera House Hospital."

Much of the aid to the distressed rendered by Mrs. Stewart was made possible by the generosity of a crusty, self-effacing old gentleman who built and owned many buildings on Dalhart's Main Street. He was part owner in a partnership which raised, near Dalhart, world famous bulls, and was much better known for his high-stake poker games with such financial giants as Jesse Jones of Houston, than for his philanthropies. He was W. H. (Uncle Dick) Coon.

Some time early in Mrs. Stewart's ministry, her work, theretofore performed entirely from her home, reached a point where regularly available personnel became necessary as did space for some type of office available to the public.

Her work and its needs caught Uncle Dick's attention and he promptly made available for Mrs. Stewart's work, rent free, two rooms in his De Soto Hotel.

Later he made available to her, rent free, a house across Main Street from the De Soto. Here, from the late 1920s through the depression and drouth of the 1930s, and on until Mrs. Stewart retired in 1970, her Red Cross and other charitable work was conducted.

"There were a lot of unemployed and hungry people in Dalhart in those times," she said. "And that included people all up and down the ladder — from some who had always had good steady jobs to itinerant Mexican laborers living in temporary shanties over near the Rock Island roundhouse — they all could come to the Red Cross building and get necessary food. Uncle Dick was paying for it. All I had to do was let Uncle Dick's man, Newt Cole, know what I needed and he would buy it.

"We weren't equipped to prepare or serve meals. All we could do was keep stores of staples like dried beans, dried black-eyed peas, apples, oranges and potatoes. Just things people have to have to survive. But we took care of a lot of people this way.

"Along about the middle of 1933, your father started what became known as 'The Dalhart Haven.' It was a place where transients who were then crowding the tops of freight trains headed west would come for a hot meal during stopovers in Dalhart. The way it started was this. There was a kitchen at the rear of your father's sanitarium that wasn't being used because he had closed his sanitarium several years earlier when the Catholic Sisters built the Loretto Hospital. But a lot of the transients would still come to the back door of the old sanitarium begging for food. Your father decided they should have it. He always had two or three men around doing odd jobs and one of them was named Forbes. Your father put Forbes in charge of feeding these transients.

"He arranged with the grocery stores, bakeries and meat markets to give Forbes their bacon rinds and two-day-old bread.

"He bought beans and coffee, and a supply of tin plates, tin cups and tin spoons. Each afternoon Forbes would cook up a supply of coffee, and beans flavored with bacon rind and the transients soon learned they could get a bit of bread, a plate of beans and a cup of hot coffee at the back of the sanitarium.

"After a while the City built a little house on the Fire Station property across the alley from the sanitarium. The Haven operation was then moved to this house.

"All went well until one night Forbes disappeared. Your father called me and I took over running the Haven. I had two men, Lawson and Perkle, who worked at the Red Cross headquarters. Your father kept right on buying the beans and coffee and Lawson and Perkle would go by the grocers, meat markets, and so on, to get the bacon rinds and stale bread. I would go by the Haven in the afternoon and see that the beans, bread and coffee for the evening would be ready. Perkle and Lawson would help serve. Sometimes we would have as many as 200 people lined up for a hot meal. There was a hydrant there and each person in line was required to wash his plate, cup and spoon and bring it in before leaving. To keep the Haven reserved solely for hungry transients, no person was allowed to use it more than once."

Today it is hard to believe that in the 1930s the combination of drouth and depression which hit the people of the High Plains left many in such destitute circumstances that they could not afford even such fundamental necessities as shoes.

In the fall of 1934, as winter approached, Mrs. Stewart's Red Cross office was swamped with requests for shoes — especially shoes for children if they were to go to school. She published in *The Dalhart Texan* calls for the people to clean out their closets of discarded or seldom used shoes and bring them to the Red Cross. What had been the kitchen in the house used by the Red Cross as headquarters was converted into a makeshift cobblerey. Mrs. Stewart's assistants, Perkle and Lawson, were put to work sorting and making necessary repairs on donated shoes. Their cobblers' tools consisted only of needles and thread, two shoe horses on which to mount the shoes for resoling and hammers and nails. What was totally lacking was leather for the resoling work and the resources available could not be stretched so as to afford any significant amount of this leather.

Then one day a Mennonite from that clan's farming settlement north of town came in to see Mrs. Stewart. He said he needed nails so he could resole his children's shoes.

"I told him we could give him the nails, but what was he going to use for the soles?" He said he could fashion the soles from casing of tires on abandoned farm machinery."

"This gave me an idea," said Mrs. Stewart. "I called H. P. Greenough, division head of the Rock Island and asked whether the railroad might have any old belting it could give us. I told him I wanted to see whether we could make soles for shoes with it." Soon the Rock Island began shipping her oil cans filled with rolls of old belting. "With that belting Perkle and Lawson put half-soles on over 1,500 pairs of shoes that fall and winter."

This woman, truly an Angel of Mercy, placed no boundaries on the types of distress to which she would respond. All that was required was that her help was wanted and truly needed. During much of the time of her ministry the pregnancy of an unmarried girl was much less tolerantly observed than is true today. In Mrs. Stewart, however, a girl whose misstep had resulted in pregnancy could find a sympathetic ear — and complete confidentiality.

"You'd be surprised at how many babies I got adopted back before we had child welfare," she said. "Sometimes I would have as many as seven or eight girls who would be in trouble at one time. But no one could ever get from me the names of those girls or of the people who adopted their children."

Except for her relatively short stint as Dallam County Administrator for the New Deal's Works Progress Administration, Mrs. Stewart's ministry to the needy was done at her own expense and without monetary compensation.

In 1964, she was awarded an engraved plaque by the Dallam County Rotary Club reading:

> For 50 years' continuous community service.

In 1965, she was honoree at a Red Cross meeting in Amarillo where she was presented with a silver plate on which was engraved:

>To Mrs. E. R. Stewart
>for over fifty years of outstanding service
>and devotion to the
>American National Red Cross
>and to her community.

And in 1970, the Dalhart Chamber of Commerce awarded her a commemorative plaque reading:

For a lifetime of service to her fellow man.

As she sat in her living room in her Dalhart home in 1972, she said she was eighty-six years old, and it was plain that life was ebbing away from her and that she knew it. It was also plain that she looked back on her active years with a feeling of satisfaction that few others ever achieve.

Dalhart's Golden Cycle and W. H. Lathem

Word had reached the Dalhart residents early Wednesday, April 23, that their well had come in a gusher. The town came ablaze with excitement.

In the spring of 1918, President Wilson issued a call for doctors for the American Expeditionary Forces. Father announced he had always wanted to get in a war, and he had two good assistants that he said could look after the sanitarium (with mother's help). So he enlisted in the Medical Corps and was called up in October. He was commissioned a captain and sent right away to Camp Greenleaf in Georgia. In two or three weeks he was on his way to France on *The Rochambeau*, with a convoy of forty-four vessels. He had barely gotten there when the Armistice was signed on November 11, but had to spend a couple of months bivouacked in a tent in the mud at Brest, in France, before he was shipped back home.

Father got back to Dalhart late in January 1919. Conditions at home were distressing. A great flu epidemic, starting late in 1918, had grown steadily worse. At least seventy Dalhart residents had died. The Felton Opera House, under the direction of Mrs. E. R. Stewart, had been made into an emergency hospital; a quarantine ordinance had required the wearing of masks in all public buildings, prohibited all social gatherings, and forbidden any person with influenza from leaving his place of residence. The great snow that began the previous December had covered the plains from the Sangre de Cristo mountain range in Colorado and New Mexico, to the Canadian River breaks near Amarillo and had remained on the ground, held intact and unthawed by constant below-freezing temperatures, which at times plunged to seventeen below zero. Cattle on the ranges, weakened by the bitter cold weather and inability to nuzzle through the snow to the grass, were beginning to die in large numbers from lack of food and exposure.

And yet, the Dalhart community was filled with excitement and hope. For at long last, the opportunity had come to them to get in on the great Texas oil boom which had commenced with Texas Pacific Coal Company's great discovery at Ranger, a few miles north of Fort Worth. The Ranger field, brought in by a rank wildcat well in October 1917, was producing 10,000 barrels a day by August 1918, with 223 test wells being drilled. It had brought hope to the entire nation which, just previous to the discovery, had been told by the United States Geological Survey that our underground reserves were forty percent exhausted and that we were nearing the peak of domestic production. And this right when the need for oil had risen astronomically due to the requirements of our first motorized war and the advent of the Model T Ford.

Ranger was closely followed by Desdemona, where soon 288 wells were being drilled by ninety-seven different operators and peak production of 55,000 barrels a day was to be reached.

Then came the discovery at Burkburnett, about seventeen miles north of Wichita Falls.

A farmer named S. L. Fowler, discouraged by repeated drouths, blizzards, hailstorms and hot winds, had decided to sell out and move farther west. His wife refused to sign the deed, a requirement of the Texas Homestead Law. Her reason — she was convinced there was oil beneath the farm waiting for the driller's bit. Fowler persuaded a group of Burkburnett citizens to join him in raising $12,000, just enough to get the hole down, to prove to his wife that there was no oil to be found so he could induce her to sign the deed.

On July 16, 1918, with the drill bit at only 1,600 feet below the surface of the earth, the well came in, gushing 3,000 barrels of oil a day, worth $2.25 per barrel.

There was so little faith in the possibility of discovering oil on the Fowler farm that the drilling of the well had excited no leasing activity. As a result, after the well came in, just about anyone willing to take the risk could obtain a lease, drill a well and have a chance at becoming fabulously rich overnight. It was the little man's dream. No tract was too small for a well, quarter-acre tracts making large drilling sites, and drilling extending into the town of Desdemona, where even single town lots were enough. By October, about 200 different operators were drilling about 200 test wells in the field. Many a well came in with an initial production of 3,000 to 5,000 barrels a day, yielding three or four times the cost of the well in the first month's production.

Groups of people in almost every town in the Panhandle organized their own oil companies and set about to get in on the golden play. The Dalhart people were not to be left out.

On November 8, 1918, the *Dalhart Texan* carried the following story:

OIL COMPANY ORGANIZED

A stock company to be known as the Golden Cycle Oil Co., has been organized in Dalhart with a capital stock of $50,000 for the purpose of engaging in the development in the Burkburnett oilfield. A lease on a large acreage has been obtained by the company and it is expected to begin drilling the wells soon. The company will offer stock for sale at $50 per share for the purpose of developing ten acres of their lease and to this end will invest $38,000 in a developing project. It is known that their lease contains some of the best property in the field and is near to proven areas.

The following stockholders are financially interested in the project: T. W. Turner, W. N. Stone, Sam E. Killen, Pem Denton, Roy W. Thompson, Henry Tandy, J. M. Wade, J. V. Powell, W. A. Wolf, E. H. Griffith, W. H. Lathem, Lee Griffith, L. O. Robinson, O. R. Lemman, D. C. Atkinson, S. T. Smith, E. G. and A. J. Schuhart, C. W. Delp, W. L. Hamilton, George Ely, J. L. Smith and M. D. Lowe.

It is reported also that a Texline company has obtained a valuable lease in the same section and will proceed immediately to develop it.

On December 20, 1918, the following advertisement, three columns wide, nine inches deep and surrounded by a half-inch wide black border, appeared in the *Texan*:

W. N. Stone, President; Roy W. Thompson, O. R. Lemman, Mike Kelly, Vice-Presidents; Pem Denton, W. H. Lathem, C. W. Delp, Trustees; W. R. Robinson, Secretary-Treasurer.

THE GOLDEN CYCLE OIL CO.
(Unincorporated)
Capital Stock $50,000
Shares $50 each par value

Holdings, ten acres in the great Burkburnett oil field, Wichita County, Texas

In most every paper you pick up you see where some company, which is not more than thirty to ninety days old, in the Burkburnett field has just declared and paid their stockholders 100 percent dividends. There is no reason we cannot do what other companies are doing and even more, as *our acreage is much larger than the average company's*. The way acreage is advancing in bounds and leaps we firmly believe that our ten acres will be worth the full capital stock before we get our wells started. And if we had not bought this acreage some forty days ago we could not get it and put it into a company with this small a capital and agree to put a well on it as we are now doing.

We are informed that the stock in the Texline Company which was advertised in these columns last week is already all sold and all the stock in our company may be sold before the next issue of this paper, so get your application in at once. Do not hesitate and then after the stock is all sold and we are paying dividends, say, "If."

Send money direct to The Golden Cycle Oil Co., Box 171, Dalhart, Texas.

On December 27, 1918, a Golden Cycle Oil Company advertisement appeared in the *Texan* stating as follows:

Up to date we have not received a bit of bad news from the field. Most every paper tells us something good and something that makes our proposition worth more money as they gradually surround us with big wells, and leases are going up in leaps and bounds out our way.

If you contemplate buying do not wait until it is too late.

Mother had saved the November 8th story and the advertisements of December 20 and 27. Father read them and exclaimed, "Confound it, Willie, here's the first chance we have ever had to make a fortune and they go and wrap it all up behind my back and exclude me just because I'm overseas serving my country! I tell you, they'll have to let me in some way." *

"You know what's best, George," said mother, "but do you think we can afford to gamble right now? As I told you, collections

---

* Aside from being away from his family and his medical practice for four months, the greatest inconvenience caused father appears to have been having to shave himself. In his diary, he noted that, until he had joined the Army, he had not shaved himself in twenty-five years.

have been bad, you being gone, everybody down with the flu and the town closed down with the blizzard. I had to make a note at the bank last week to meet the hospital payroll."

"Don't worry," said father. "You know I can make a good living even on a barren rock trading with sea gulls. We'll have plenty just as soon as I can get back to the office."

Next evening, father came home beaming. "Willie," he said, "I went down and talked to W. N. Stone and W. H. Lathem and told them they had to let me in. They decided to let me have $1,000 worth after they polled the Trustees. I borrowed the money at the Midway Bank. This can put us on Easy Street."

"By the way, I also wired my friend Charlie Mayo and asked him to send me some of that new flu–pneumonia serum the Mayo Clinic has developed. He wired me right back that he was sending me enough to innoculate 1,000 people. I'm going to give it free to everybody who will come and get it."

Altogether, about 690 Dalhart residents became Golden Cycle stockholders. Bankers, ranchers, farmers, railroad men, merchants, doctors, store clerks, housewives — indeed, just about everybody in the town who had a spare dollar or could borrow one — bought a piece of the great play.

W. H. Lathem and C. W. Delp were assigned the task of choosing the particular spot on the ten-acre lease on which the well should be drilled, of contracting for the drilling of the well, and supervising it to completion.

W. H. Lathem recorded in his "Memoirs," the details of what happened thereafter.

On January 28, 1919, he and Delp took the Fort Worth and Denver en route to Wichita Falls. Southeast of Channing, on the south slope of the canyon created by the Canadian River at a point about seventy-five miles southeast of Dalhart, they saw the ground for the first time since the great snow had started on December 16, 1918. It was raining in Wichita Falls and influenza was rampant. The town was crowded with lease brokers, drilling contractors, representatives of oil companies, salesmen and the usual riffraff which in those days gathered in large numbers around each newly discovered oil field.

By February 5, they had made a contract with a firm known as Barkley and Meadows, drilling contractors, to drill a well on the Golden Cycle lease to a depth of 1,700 feet for the turnkey contract price of $17,000.

"I wrote down where to drill same," says Lathem in his memoirs. "But the driller misread the notations, and it's a godsend, because if it had been drilled where I had stipulated, it would have been a dry hole."

By February 21, Barkley and Meadows had begun building their derrick. On February 28, they began moving their rig onto the derrick and by March 4, Lathem and Delp were able to report to the stockholders that the well was "going good at 500 or 600 feet."

By April 1, the well had drilled to the contract depth of 1,700 feet. "We still had a dry hole," Lathem notes in his memoirs. "But it was probably an hour before quitting time, and Mr. Meadows said, 'Let's drill on till quitting time,' and I agreed. In about 30 minutes, the bit struck the oil sand and began to sing, and right there we knew we had oil, but we did not know just how much, but we went out the next morning and drilled into the sand some four feet and it was rich, and Mr. Meadows said, 'I believe we have a good well.' "

At this point, Lathem decided to set casing and clean out the well, then shut down operations until he could see if he could buy more leases. His goal was to raise $20,000 to $50,000. Leases near the well were now commanding about $5,000 an acre whereas the Golden Cycle lease had cost only $300 an acre. Lathem first approached the Golden Cycle Trustees. Before they could reach a decision, the great untimely April 9th, one-day blowing blizzard had swept across the High Plains, resulting in a disastrous loss of range cattle. Already weakened by the prolonged snow, many fell to the ground, stiffened and froze; many simply suffocated when the blowing snow filled their nostrils and froze; many, drifting from the wind, and stopped by a fence or other barricade, were trampled underfoot by those continuing to press on from behind them. Everyone's pocketbook was severely damaged, for the Dalhart area's economy was then based primarily on cattle. Finally, the Trustees wired Lathem they could not raise more funds. They advised him to try to float a loan in whatever amount and on whatever terms he could negotiate. Lathem then turned to Jess Jenkins and Andy James, wealthy Dalhart cattlemen and bankers. They had told Lathem when he left Dalhart in January to let them know if he needed any more money. But when Lathem made this request, nearly one-half of the James's great herd of 17,000 steers had died as a result of the long snow and April blizzard. Jenkins had suffered similar losses. James wired that he was probably broke and was having trouble keeping his Midway Bank open. Jenkins wired that he was already in Kansas City trying to get a loan to save his ranch. Both said they could not send Lathem a dime. By this time, over two weeks had passed since the well had been shut down. Lathem had met disappointment at every turn. Barkley and Meadows then came to Lathem and told him that while they did not have any cash, they had five strings of drilling tools that were clear of debt. They offered to put these tools up for collateral if Lathem could swing a $50,000 loan to be used to buy leases near the well — the Golden Cycle and Barkley and Meadows to own the leases 50–50. On April 21, Meadows and Lathem approached Clint Wood of Wichita Falls. Wood said he would lend them all the money they wanted if they could satisfy his superintendent that they had a well. It was arranged that Wood's superintendent would go on the lease with Lathem and Meadows that very night and examine the well. Lathem notes in his memoirs:

"About dark that evening, we fired up and got up steam and then I went over to 'Burnett and got Mr. Wood's superintendent. He had palsy very bad and shook all the time. We got out to the lease and had coffee and by that time it was around 11 P.M. We slipped the bit in the hole and began to drill. In a few minutes, Mr. Wood's superintendent began to catch the cuttings. He would take a chunk of oil sand and put it in his mouth and begin chewing and shaking and spitting. He would then get a chunk of that sand and look at it. Finally, he said to Meadows: 'Bill, that sand sure has oil in it, but that is the darkest oil sand that I have ever seen.' Mr. Meadows said 'what in the hell do you care about the color of the sand as long as it has oil in it?'

"I took Mr. Wood's superintendent back to his camp about one o'clock the next morning. Then Meadows and I drove in to Wichita Falls, getting there about 2 or 3 A.M., April 22nd. Mr. Meadows said, 'Our money troubles are over because I'm sure Wood will get a good report from his superintendent; he agreed he would give Mr. Wood his report by noon.' Then we went to our hotel and got a few hour's sleep.

"About two or three o'clock that afternoon, that was April 22nd, Mr. Meadows and I went to see Mr. Wood and get the report. When we got up there, Mr. Wood asked us if we would like to see the report. I said I surely would like to see it. He handed it to me and I read the report and it was as follows:

Mr. Wood, I went out with Mr. Lathem and they drilled some three feet in the oil sand, and it is very rich in oil, but I have never seen an oil sand like this. In fact, it is nearly black, and I'm just afraid of this and I personally would not put a dime in this kind of sand.

"Well, this knocked us for a row, and we didn't know what to do next. We went back to our hotel and talked until about ten o'clock that night trying to think of some way to raise money and buy leases before doing more drilling or testing. Finally, we had just gotten to bed when Meadows said, 'Howard, we're at the end of the rope. Let's go out there tonight and drill some more and bale down some and find out whether we have an oil well or just a dud.' Then we got up and dressed and drove out to the well. It was after midnight when we got there. We woke up the fireman and had him fire up the boiler and about 2 A.M. the next morning, April 23rd, we began drilling. After drilling some two more feet, we had the fireman put out the fire under the boiler and began to bale. We baled down probably 500 feet and Mr. Meadows said to the driller, 'That bucket is not going any deeper, let me have hold of that machine.' He took hold of it and let it go down to the bottom and pulled it out and oil came up over the top of the derrick, flowing at an estimated 3,000 barrels a day."

This was about four o'clock in the morning, Wednesday, April 23, 1919. Lathem and Meadows had fervently hoped for such a gusher but had not really expected it. No storage tank had been readied to contain such a flow of oil, no equipment had been readied to install on the control head so as to direct the oil to a storage tank, no pumps had been purchased to move the oil from a storage tank to a pipeline, and no arrangement had been made for a pipeline connection.

The oil drenched Lathem, Meadows, the driller, and the fireman, spread over the Golden Cycle Lease and onto the adjoining land and filled the air with highly flammable and insufferably stinking gas fumes.

News of the well spread quickly. Shortly, Delp appeared on the scene bringing pipe to fit over the control head, and pumps which could be installed to move the oil from a tank into a pipeline. A nearby pipeline operator began laying pipe toward the well. A muleskinner with a span of mules and a Fresno began digging an earthen tank. Finally, by morning of April 24, a pipe had been placed over the control head, an earthen tank created, pumps had been set at the edge of the tank and connected to the pipeline, and the oil was flowing into the slush pit. By noon, this control of the oil had resulted in the gas fumes being reduced about the boiler to a point where it was felt the boiler could be fired up again, so as to create the steam necessary to run the pumps. By mid-afternoon, the oil was being pumped from the earthen tank into the pipeline. Some said the well was producing 5,000 barrels a day. By this time, the posted price for this oil had risen to $3.50 per barrel at point of delivery to the pipeline.

Word had reached the Dalhart residents early Wednesday, April 23, that their well had come in a gusher. The town came ablaze with excitement. The stockholders' dream of sudden black gold riches seemed realized. Three thousand barrels at $3.50 would be $10,500 — more than one-fourth of the total funds raised by the Golden Cycle for the venture. *In twenty days, why — that would amount to $315,000!* At this rate, a $1,000 investment in the Golden Cycle could be yielding over $7,000 in dividends *per month!* Not only that, but maybe as many as four or five more wells could be drilled on the Golden Cycle ten-acre lease. A happy and excited delegation of stockholders left Dalhart for Wichita Falls late that evening on the Fort Worth and Denver in a chartered special coach.

The delegation had driven to the well site early in the morning of the 24th. Gathering as near as the wildly flowing oil would permit, they anxiously watched as Lathem and his crew labored to control the well. When, at last the oil flow was under control, and rumors spread that the well was making 5,000 barrels a day rather than 3,000 barrels as first announced, every man in the delegation shouted and threw his hat in the air. Incredulous, they returned to Wichita Falls recomputing their estimates of their wealth.

Late in the evening of the 24th, Meadows and Lathem, exhausted from working constantly with the well for over fifty hours, decided to go in to Wichita Falls, bathe the oil from their bodies and get some sleep. Before leaving, Meadows gave instructions to his pumper and his fireman: "You see the wind is blowing quite hard from the southwest. As long as this continues, the gas fumes from the oil spill will be blown away from the boiler and it will be safe to keep it fired up. But if the wind dies down, put out that fire at once, because if you don't, the gas will accumulate and drift out to the boiler and the entire thing will go up."

About four o'clock the next morning, the pumper noticed that the wind was dying down. He went to the boiler house and told the fireman to put out the fire. The fireman was shaving. "I'll be through shaving in just a minute," he said. "Then I'll go out and put out the fire."

Lathem's diary notes the following:

"Well, he never finished shaving. The accumulated gas exploded and blew the boiler house and the fireman out in the field, and blew the head off the casing and opened the well full force. The well was on fire." A great geyser of flame shot skyward, burning down the derrick, destroying Barkley and Meadows's drilling rig and lighting the sky for miles. Hurrying back to the scene, the Dalhart delegation, unbelieving and awestricken, watched their wealth literally go up in smoke.

"The well burned for three days," Lathem noted in his memoirs. "Then, all of a sudden, it quit. The hole had sanded up, shutting off the flow of oil. After the well quit burning, we screwed a wellhead on the pipe and put the well on pump, but the explosion had opened the well full force, causing the hole to open into the salt water. The well never made more than 250 barrels a day after that. We afterwards sold the Golden Cycle for $5,000 and it was well sold."

"I still think it was a good bet," said father. "And things aren't so bad after all. This snow is going to give us the best moisture in the ground for next year's crops that we have had in many a year."

Jim Webb's Head —

Or a Stranger's Mysterious Death

I hurried toward the scene as fast as my long-stockinged, kneebreeches-covered legs would carry me.

— John C. Dawson

One sunny afternoon, (I think it was in 1916), a schoolboy, returning to his home along a seldom used road in the outskirts of Dalhart, stopped suddenly when met by a strange, suffocating, repulsively foul odor. He had been walking eastward and there was a breeze coming from the south which had brought the odor to his nostrils. He walked a few steps toward the source of the odor and there, in rich, red ("bluestem") grass, tall enough to shield it from the sight of motorists or others traveling the road, lay the rotting body of a dead man. The boy ran the rest of the way home.

Dalhart was then a small town — perhaps 3500 inhabitants. People in such a town are usually acutely aware of, and concerned with, the doings of one another. Anyway, those in Dalhart certainly were. Every birth, every death, every moral or business transgression which surfaced, was something in which most everyone felt a personal participation. Thus, news of the presence in the town of an unidentified dead body spread as if shouted airborne through some giant loudspeaker.

I had just gotten home from school when one of my fellow seventh graders called and said excitedly, "J. C., there's a dead man by the road out near Felton's house. C'mon." I hurried toward the scene as fast as my long-stockinged, kneebreeches-covered legs would carry me. I hadn't thought it necessary to call father — for he always seemed to be about the first to learn of any town news. He would be there, all six feet, two hundred pounds of him, exuding dignity, interest, charm and competence. He would have his little oblong, black, leather medical kit and his stethoscope. He would be dressed impeccably and with his Kentucky colonel moustache and goatee and his erect, proud demeanor he would, as always, be a striking figure.

When I arrived at the scene, the Sheriff, "Scandalous" John McCandless, Judge Reese, the Justice of the Peace, and thirty or forty other people, including father, were already there. The dead man was lying on his back and father was squatting down looking intently into his face. The man had apparently lain there for days; long enough, anyway, for his skin to putrify and turn black and to assume a revolting, puffy, wet, mushy look. He had brown straight hair, was of medium height and weight, and appeared to have been in his thirties.

For a while we were all so absorbed with curiosity that we forgot to notice the awful odor which shortly moved all onlookers to the upwind side.

Everyone stood quietly, waiting for father to speak. Finally, father arose and said, "This man was choked to death. I can tell because his tongue is sticking out between his teeth."

No one present felt he had ever seen this man before and Scandalous John's search through his clothing provided no identification. However, the name "Jim Webb" was scribbled on a piece of torn wrapping paper in one of his pockets and he was thus to become known to us by that name. Father, Scandalous John and Judge Reese held a little conference after which Judge Reese announced that the body would be buried at once.

Although this man had been a stranger to our community until the stench of his rotting flesh brought him to our attention, he promptly became a well known town personality. I could not remember anything that had ever happened before in Dalhart that so entertained the minds of the people — provided so much free rein for the imagination — so much grist for lively conversation. The why of Jim's presence remained a matter of pure speculation. But myriad theories and rumors were spread. For example, my oldest brother, Artis, who was home for a few weeks from college, said he heard there had been a gang of gamblers in town and that Jim had probably met his end over an unpaid loss. And my brother, G. W., who was home on vacation from military school, said he heard that

Jim may have been among the last of some group of cattle thieves or train robbers and had been put away over a division of loot, or to prevent his being an informer on the others. Who was Jim? Who killed him? Why was he killed? These questions plagued the minds of our people.

On the afternoon following the discovery and burial of Jim's body, Artis, G. W., and I were at home discussing him when the phone rang. Artis answered. In a moment he hung up the receiver and announced, "Father says we should get a tow sack and come to the sanitarium right away. We are going out to the cemetery and dig up Jim Webb!"

The cemetery lay out on the prairie west of town and was reached by an unpaved road. Father, Artis, G. W., and I drove out there in father's old black Maxwell.

When we arrived at the gravesite, four swarthy and sweating gravediggers had already removed most of the dirt from above and around the box in which Jim was buried and Scandalous McCandless and Judge Reese were standing by.

The gravediggers had enlarged the grave sufficiently for one man to stand on the bottom at either end of the box which had been used as a coffin. This enabled the gravediggers to put ropes under the box by means of which it was hoisted from the grave. The gravediggers then placed the box on the ground beside the grave, pried off its lid and turned it on its side. At that, Jim rolled out of the box and onto the ground, stomach down, and emitted a great blast of gas that made me feel he was expressing his total disinterest in, and disapproval of, the whole procedure. Also to be telling us to go to hell and leave him alone.

Father and Scandalous John again searched all of Jim's clothing without finding anything to identify him and finally father cut the labels from Jim's clothing with his pocketknife and handed them to Scandalous John. Then father took a long surgical knife, knelt down, felt with his surgeon's trained hands for the proper place to cut through the membrane separating the bones in Jim's neck and with a swift stroke of the knife, severed Jim's head from his body.

At father's instruction, we put the head in the tow sack, which G. W. somehow got to carry. He seemed always to get the coveted jobs. Holding the sack in his right hand, G. W. climbed aboard the right fender of the Maxwell and stood there, with his left hand holding to the enameled metal framework of the retractable black canvas

Jim Webb's Head — Or A Stranger's Mysterious Death

top. Artis and I then also took standing positions on the car fender, as close as we could to G. W., the sack and Jim.

The sun was setting at the far edge of the high prairie and a slight, coolish breeze was springing up out of the southwest. Nobody said much as we drove back, father at the wheel, we three boys and Jim on the right fender, and the wooden spokes in the old Maxwell's wheels creaking as we went along.

Finally we arrived back at father's sanitarium. Near the alley to the rear was a small brick structure that housed the coal furnace which provided steam heat for the sanitarium building. Father told us he was going to put Jim's head in formaldehyde so it could be kept for people to look at. He said that maybe someone would show up who could tell us who Jim really was.

He had us get an old ten gallon copper boiler from the sanitarium's kitchen, and after we had lodged this just inside the door to the furnace room, it was poured almost full of formaldehyde. The head was then placed in this fluid and after we had put a weight on it to keep it immersed, we went home where mother had supper waiting.

Later, when we removed the weight from the head, it floated face up for several weeks, exhibiting a roundish nose and a mouth fixed in a bit of a grin or smirk. The lips were parted just a little and, as I said before, the tongue was protruding through tightly clenched teeth. Finally, the head rolled over face down, leaving the base of the skull and the top of what remained of the neck floating there slightly above the fluid.

Jim's head stayed in the furnace room about a year. And when I would think about it I would go out to where it was and, with a little stick that we kept beside the boiler, would poke down on the back of Jim's head until it submerged. Shortly it would bob to the surface face up and so remain, long enough for one to study the features. Then, it would seem to grow tired of remaining in this position and, after a slow movement to one side, it would flop back over, face down.

Word somehow spread a long way that Jim was there waiting for someone to look at him and recognize him. People from all around the community and some from across the states came to look at him. I can distinctly recall the pathetic look of failure and resignation that would show on the faces of people, evidently searching for a lost son, relative or friend, as they would turn away and leave after having looked long at Jim. This was especially striking in the faces of the old men and women who came and left.

No one was ever able to identify Jim or explain how he happened to meet his fate in our midst. At long last, the stories and speculation died down, the people ceased to come to look at him and there seemed no further use in keeping his head in the furnace room.

So, with father's consent, we boys took Jim's head home and buried it beside the garage next to the garden. We would dig it up once in awhile and look at it and I remember we used to joke that the turnips that grew above it were the best in the patch.

After my brother, Artis, went back to medical school, G. W., who thought he might also study medicine, dug Jim's head up, filled the old boiler with water, built an outdoor fire and began boiling the head for the skull. In this manner the flesh was removed and the skull cleaned up nicely, after which we kept it out in the sunshine until it was thoroughly bleached.

G. W. then sawed off the top of the skull and arranged some little brass hooks by which the severed portion could be held in place or removed. He took the skull with him to medical school and it provided a good study model. Also, the top of the skull, when unhooked and turned upside down, proved to be useful as an ashtray.

Number 126 and Prohibition's Children

He decided to wage a campaign to close Number 126, and DRIVE SIN FROM OUR CITY.
— John C. Dawson

Get all the doctors you can and get out to the Gunnels farm, Sheriff Alexander and three other people are dying out there.
— Harvey Foust, Deputy Sheriff

Except for the cemetery, there was nothing on the prairie west of the railroad tracks in Dalhart but the baseball park, the pesthouse and the . . . well, the Number 126 house.

Everybody in town knew what kind of a house it was. And most of them called it Number 126, which was its telephone number.

It was about a quarter of a mile west of town, at the end of a well worn automobile trail that wasn't used much in the daytime, but a lot at night.

It was one of the nicest houses in town — structurally, that is. It was a two-story wooden structure, painted a bright canary yellow. It was surrounded by, but clearly visible through, a nice grove of black locust trees which bordered the quarter acre on which it was located. A barbed wire fence surrounded the tract.

It had (so I am told) two great big rooms on the ground floor furnished with nice chairs, sofas and tables, and a player piano. People danced and drank and met other people on that ground floor. The rooms upstairs were utilized for living quarters and other purposes customary in houses of this kind.

In the early days it was a very popular place, especially on Saturday nights, when many a cowboy would come to town after a week on the range, spend some of his wages in the downtown saloons and then spend the rest at Number 126. During Prohibition it was about the only place in town where you could buy beer and this fact resulted in a substantial expansion of its clientele.

Number 126 was also known as "Nettie's Place," for the proprietress, from its founding in 1907 until about 1932, was one Nettie Rittenhouse. Joe Scott owned land near Number 126, and he got to know Nettie. Nettie told Joe how she kept supplied with girls. "Dalhart is just about halfway between Denver and Fort Worth," she said. "When the heat's on in Denver or Fort Worth, this is a good place for the girls to stay till things cool off. Also, it's a good place for the girls to come to for a little vacation when they get tired working in Fort Worth or Denver."

Usually on Saturday nights, Jess Morris, the famous western fiddler, would be there with his band. There would be dancing and singing and drinking until the wee hours of the morning. If Jess Morris and his band weren't there, the player piano could be called into service for the price of a quarter a tune. Sid Johnson says that one time the boys ran out of quarters and one of them jimmied the coin box on the back of the piano by use of a screwdriver. This way he kept the piano going all night long, using Nettie's quarters.

Nettie had good credit at the downtown stores and her girls supplied the beauty parlors and clothing stores with a good deal of business. This was something to be appreciated, especially during the Depression. In a manner of speaking, Number 126 was a respected Dalhart business establishment. Anyway, it ran openly for at least thirty years with no organized opposition.

Nettie prided herself in running a nice, clean, orderly establishment, and she considered she was rendering a valuable service, of a kind, to the community. Cross-eyed Mac, a somewhat retarded handyman about town, usually did the janitorial work. Nettie was well represented in business matters and brushes with the law by Shine Carter and Charlie Dinwiddie, proprietors of Dinwiddie's Pool Hall and Domino Parlor.

In about 1932, Nettie Rittenhouse retired and moved to Denver. Her sister, Lillian Walker, from somewhere in South Texas, took over the proprietorship. Under Lillian Walker's management Number 126 kept right on doing a good business right through the rest of the Depression. During the Depression money became so scarce in Dalhart, that about the only automobiles anybody could buy were Model T Fords. People bought even Model T Fords only when it became absolutely necessary — people other than Lillian Walker, that is. Lillian kept herself supplied with a spanking new pink Cadillac.

Lillian was not as circumspect in the conduct of the business as Nettie had been. In about 1934, she began a practice of loading up her pink Cadillac with several of her most enticing looking girls from Number 126, and driving up and down Main Street in broad daylight.

A lot of Dalhart people thought it was bad enough that Lillian could have a pink Cadillac, right when nobody else in town could afford anything bigger than a Model T Ford. But on top of that, the girls in Lillian's pink Cadillac would be dressed in expensive dresses from Neiman Marcus or similar classy and expensive places and would have been to the beauty parlor for the latest hairdo — luxuries which most of the young girls in town could only dream of. Mother would come home from the office in the evening fuming. "Brazen hussy!" she would cry. "Parading around town advertising sin and bragging about how it pays! How do you think a nice, clean young Dalhart girl who hasn't been able to buy a new dress or go to the beauty parlor in years will feel about this? What's to keep her from wanting also to take up a life of sin and degradation? If George was half the man he ought to be, he'd put a stop to this!"

Some of such protests found the ears of John McCarty, the brilliant, vigorous, young editor of *The Dalhart Texan*. John was outraged. Moreover, he saw in this situation a golden opportunity to attract attention to his paper and increase its circulation. He decided to wage a campaign to close Number 126, and DRIVE SIN FROM OUR CITY.

John sat up several nights drafting and polishing his lead story. Finally, with a headline to read, SO THE PEOPLE MAY KNOW, he delivered his story to George Quigley, his printer, and told him to put out a special edition the very next day.

Half an hour later, Quigley came into John's office carrying a galley proof. "Mr. McCarty," he said, "You can fire me for this if you want to, but I ain't agonna print this story. Maybe Lillian Walker has gone a little too far and ought to be told to quit parading her wares around in her pink Cadillac. But close up Number 126? That's something else. I've been in Dalhart thirty years, and Number 126 has been an important part of this community all that time. It does a lot more good than it does harm. There hasn't been a rape in Dalhart in those thirty years, and how many young Dalhart girls would be in trouble if we hadn't had Number 126? You can't stop sex just like you can't stop gambling. If you close Number 126, you'll drive this business underground, fill our streets with streetwalkers and spread clap and syph all over. No sir, I ain't agonna print this story."

John decided to put the story on the shelf and think it over.

Now, it so happened that a short time before this, a man had come to town and started a little throwaway paper that was getting wide circulation. This was because it did not cost the reader a cent. This paper had been draining off quite a bit of John McCarty's advertising and this was beginning to hurt. John didn't know it then, but Number 126 was about to prove a blessing to his *Dalhart Texan*.

The editor of the throwaway also had seen in Number 126, a *cause célèbre* ripe for the plucking. Thus, on the very morning the *Texan* was to have launched its anti-SIN crusade, the throwaway came out with a huge headline reading as follows: NUMBER 126 MUST GO. This headline was followed by a complete story of the history of Number 126, an account of Lillian Walker's injudicious behavior, and a demand that all good people join forces to close up the place.

The throwaway editor's phone began ringing in a few minutes after his paper hit the streets — not with commendations but with instructions from advertisers to cancel their ads! Within a week the throwaway had gone out of business and shortly thereafter its publisher left town.

Word got back to Lillian Walker, however, that the people didn't like the developments at Number 126, and her pink Cadillac and its painted ladies ceased to appear so much on Dalhart streets.

Number 126 went about its business in a normal way after that, until one night in 1936. On that night, Number 126 caught fire and burned to the ground. Number 126 never again operated in Dalhart — at least not as Number 126. The telephone number ceased to be the private property of anybody after the fire. So some prankster induced the telephone company to assign it to J. T. Mann and H. Coon, the town's liveliest young bachelors. They had to turn away a lot of callers before they were able to get the phone company to rectify the situation.

Ted Houghton used to laugh and say that most of his friends came to town wearing pants that didn't match their coats — the day after Number 126 burned down.

One day in March 1929, George W. Alexander, capable and highly respected Sheriff of Dallam County, dutifully on guard to detect violations of the law, spotted a Mexican named Jesus Esquibel emerging from the home of Lon and Ode Dellinger carrying in a paper sack a pint of whiskey.

This incident led to a chain of events culminating in Dalhart's most spectacular shoot-out, the needless killing of Sheriff Alexander and two of the Dellinger boys, and the wrecking of the life of a deputy.

It had now been nine years since the nation, in a noble effort to legislate the people away from demon rum, had adopted the Eighteenth Amendment to the United States Constitution, declaring that "the manufacture, sale or transportation of intoxicating liquors — for beverage purposes — is hereby *prohibited*."

The nine years since adoption of that amendment had proven frustrating ones for officers of the law, whose sworn duty it was to detect and to prosecute its violators.

The difficulty was that the consumers of such intoxicants kept right on demanding them and when they could no longer obtain their liquor from those who made and sold it legally, they turned to those who did so otherwise. To the consuming public the bootlegger was a necessity. There were "good" bootleggers and there were "bad" bootleggers — so classified primarily on the basis of the quality and consistent availability of their product. But almost everybody had, and patronized, his favorite.

It was commonplace in Dalhart for a person to buy his supplies from his bootlegger in keg lots — then hang the keg in a windmill tower to be aged by swinging in the High Plains wind. Supplies for ready use would then be drawn off into fruit jars. And a prevalent joke was that everyone had a "fruit jar mark" at the top of his nose, put there by the edge of the fruit jar top as the consumer downed the last drop.

So it was that the prohibitionists' well-intended efforts to suppress the social evils attributed to the public use of demon rum turned out to create a frustrating, cynical phenomenon. The otherwise upright, law-abiding members of the public, denied the open saloon but still insisting on having their whiskey, extended open invitation — and rewarding compensation — to those who would supply it. And those who would respond to such invitations could do so only by engaging in procedures forbidden and made criminal by law.

The very same people who thus created and supported this

business opportunity, open only to lawbreakers, joined, by their votes, in the election of officeholders sworn to enforce the law by suppressing the illegal business and thereby denying to such voters the whiskey which they continued to demand.

Most everyone knew — and patronized — some bootleggers who were never caught up in the toils of the law. These bootleggers were equally as guilty of violating the prohibition laws as were the Dellingers — but mayhap they operated more covertly or more cleverly.

At the time Sheriff Alexander saw Jesus Esquibel emerge from the Dellinger's home with a pint of liquor, there were four Dellinger "boys," Lon, age thirty-five, Bert, age thirty-two, Ode, age twenty-three and Oral (or Spud), age twenty. They came from a large family (they also had six sisters). As was true in many families similarly situated, the Dellinger boys (or men) continued as a closely knit group despite their maturity and their disparity in age. And they were fiercely protective of one another.

Prior to Prohibition they appear to have made ends meet mostly as itinerant laborers. They lived openly in the Dalhart area and perhaps were neither sufficiently intelligent nor sufficiently affluent to deliberately follow such lives of crime as cattle theft, burglary, forgery or swindling. But the record is clear that the temptation of making easy money by making and selling whiskey in violation of the Prohibition laws was one they did not resist.

In May 1929, following Sheriff Alexander's apprehension and questioning of Jesus Esquibel after seeing him emerge with whiskey from the Dellinger home, the Dallam County Grand Jury issued indictments against Lon and Ode Dellinger for violations of the liquor laws. The indictments named Esquibel as a witness.

Thereafter, and shortly before the trial of Lon and Ode under these indictments was to be held, their brothers Bert and Spud conceived a plan to save them from being found guilty. They would take possession of Esquibel, spirit him out of the state, and hold him until after Lon and Ode had been tried. Without Esquibel's testimony, there could be no conviction.

This plan was carried out in part. Late one night, wearing masks, Bert and Spud entered Esquibel's shanty near the Rock Island roundhouse, seized him, loaded him into an automobile and carried him to a farm home near Las Vegas, New Mexico. A week or so later, Esquibel escaped and informed Alexander of his capture, the identity of his captors and their whereabouts.

Bert and Spud Dellinger were then indicted for kidnapping.

Spud eluded arrest but Bert was arrested, tried, convicted and sentenced to twenty-five years in the Texas State penitentiary. Later Spud was taken into custody but the kidnapping charge against him was dropped when the District Attorney found that Esquibel had disappeared. Now only Lon and Ode Dellinger remained fugitives. Ode then was picked up and lodged in jail where, on July 19, 1930, he was being held without bond pending trial on the 1929 bootlegging charge.

On that day (July 19, 1930), an informer alerted Sheriff Alexander that Lon and also Spud could be found at the farmhome of one John Gunnels in Hartley County, about five miles south of Dalhart.

Armed with a warrant for Lon's arrest (issued under the 1929 bootlegging indictment) Alexander summoned his deputies, Harvey Foust and Earl Damron, and together they proceeded to the Gunnels farm. As they approached they saw a man resembling Lon enter the outdoor privy at the rear of the house. Alexander and Damron first searched the house and, finding only Lon's wife there, proceeded to the privy. Here they found Lon, took him into custody and began walking with him toward the farmhouse.

A tiny (eight foot-by-eight foot) shack stood at the rear of the farmhouse, between it and the privy. Here all hell was about to break loose. Spud Dellinger emerged from the shack, entered the farmhouse, took a revolver from top of a refrigerator, placed it in the bib of his overalls and, as he proceeded once more into the backyard, said to Lon's wife: "Alexander is here to take Lon and I'm damned if I'll let him do it."

As Alexander, Damron and Lon came within a few feet of the shanty, they looked up to see Spud, with pistol drawn, appear. At this, Lon lunged away from Alexander and Spud fired. Sheriff Alexander fell to the ground with his pistol still in its holster and a bullet through his brain. Damron and Spud fired at each other and Damron found refuge behind a wrecked automobile.

By now Foust had positioned himself near the rear of the farmhouse but his view of the participants in the shooting was blocked by the shanty. Believing the shooting had taken place within the shanty, he raced to it and forced open the nearest door with his revolver drawn. Here he found Lon rummaging through a suitcase on the floor. Lon lunged at Foust trying to wrest his revolver from his hand. The two were struggling when Lon's wife, armed with a shotgun, entered the shanty through a door at Foust's rear. Foust jerked away from Lon, fired first at the woman, then at Lon. Both fell to the floor, the woman dropping her shotgun. At this instant, Spud Dellinger stumbled into the shanty through a door opposite the one entered by Lon's wife. Spud fired at Foust from not over six feet away, but missed. Foust returned the fire and Spud fell to the floor, losing the grasp of his revolver.

One of the bullets fired by Damron had struck Spud in the neck, apparently dazing him, a circumstance which probably accounted for his shot missing Foust, for he was famous as a crack shot with a pistol.

Foust quickly seized Spud's revolver and Lon's wife's shotgun from the floor and hurried out to learn how Alexander and Damron had fared. Alexander lay with a bullet hole entering his brain above his right eye and exiting behind his left ear. Damron was gone. He had assumed both Alexander and Foust dead, and Lon and Spud Dellinger barricaded in the shanty. So he had run to the highway and was hitching a ride to town to summon help.

Foust returned to the smoke-filled shanty and examined Lon, Spud and Lon's wife. He had fired only three shots. One had struck Lon's wife in the hip, a disabling but not a fatal wound. One had gone cleanly through Lon's heart, a wound from which he would not arise. The third had penetrated Spud's lungs near his heart. He was breathing but appeared to be near death. Foust lifted Lon's wife from the floor and laid her on a double bed that stood at one end of the shanty. He then lifted Spud's body from the floor and laid it across the bed at the feet of Lon's wife.

He then went to his automobile and headed back to Dalhart. The first person he met in Dalhart was Weldon Forbes, a part-time night watchman and also a man maintained on my father's payroll to do odd jobs. Foust's face was ashen. He was so shaken he could hardly speak. But he cried out to Forbes: "Get all the doctors you can and get out to the Gunnels farm. Sheriff Alexander and three other people are dying out there."

Rumors of a barricaded gang of killers at the Gunnels farm quickly spread through the town. A citizens' posse was assembled. But when it arrived at the scene, Forbes and three doctors, my father, my brother, Artis, and Dr. Carl Pieratt were all there.

Alexander and Lon Dellinger were dead. Spud Dellinger was fatally wounded and would die late that night in the Loretto Hospital. Lon's wife's wound was superficial and she would survive.

To the Dalhart people Foust emerged a hero, and rightly so. And on the following Saturday, by a huge write-in vote they elected him sheriff to succeed Alexander. He had emerged from the fray untouched by any of the flying bullets. But the affair had left him badly scarred emotionally. It is said that he later sought relief by himself resorting to use of the juice the attempted prohibition of which had given rise to the tragic affair. Moreover, it is believed that Foust's life was shortened by his inability to erase from his memory those agonizing few seconds in the tiny shanty at the Gunnel farm — and the lives which, for such a futile purpose, had been snuffed out.

The Prairie Fires and Bertie Whaley Cecil

The fire burned all the way up into Kansas until it hit the Cimarron River, a distance of over one hundred miles.

Considering the facts that the prairie areas about Dalhart that remain unplowed are covered by buffalo and gramma grasses, that it is a semiarid area, that there are few trees or other obstacles to impede the sweep of the winds, and that the grasses are relatively dormant and dry much of the time, it is not surprising that prairie fires are common.

The constant wind creates a lot of static electricity and this has been known to set the prairies ablaze. The sparks from coal-burning locomotives have been responsible for starting many such fires. A carelessly dropped match or lighted cigarette may do the same. Joe Scott told of a prairie fire near the Punta de Agua that was started by the head of a match breaking off and falling to the ground when a cowboy was lighting a cigarette in a high wind. The grass caught fire and spread so fast the cowboy could not stamp it out.

Nowadays prairie fires do not present the problem they once did, because there are more roads that act as fire guards and each town has a fire department equipped with modern motorized fire fighting equipment designed particularly for containing grass fires.

Mrs. Ted Houghton told me of how the Dalhart Fire Department suppressed a 1950 prairie fire that came near to destroying the headquarters of her Lazy J Ranch near Romero, some twenty-five miles southwest of Dalhart. The fire was evidently started by sunlight focusing on dry grass through a piece of broken bottle. Propel-

The Prairie Fires and Bertie Whaley Cecil

led by a seventy-five mile an hour wind, it leaped a forty foot roadway, spread to the ranch house area, and ignited the giant cottonwood trees that surrounded it. But for the fire department, the headquarters place would likely have been destroyed.

In the old days, when a prairie fire started, the containing of it was a community effort. It was useless and hazardous to try to stop it head-on because the lead fire made its own heat and (as W. W. Steel explained) traveled "lickety-scoot." It would send burning cow chips or tumbleweeds flying ahead a hundred yards or more.

Sometimes, if there was sufficient manpower and time, the plains would be set ablaze *ahead* of the lead fire for the purpose of creating a burned-out area over which the oncoming fire could not leap.

The usually accepted method of combating a prairie fire was to simply try to keep it from spreading laterally, allowing the lead fire to proceed until it met some natural barrier it could not cross, such as the canyon caprock or a wide streambed. Men would sometimes plow fireguards to prevent the lateral spreading. A two-row lister — drawn either by horses or by tractors — would turn the grass under for a width of about six feet. Often the lateral fire line would be attacked directly with wet sacks and brooms. A more effective method was to kill a yearling, and split it open down the middle so as to make a huge wet (bloody) mat. Using their lariats, one cowboy would hitch on to one hind leg, one to the other and then, one cowboy riding inside the fire line, and the other outside it they would drag the yearling's corpse rapidly along the fire line until the heat of the smoldering grass and cow chips would force the inside rider to give up his position. Other fire fighters would follow, beating out any remaining blazes with sacks or brooms.

Rue Wharton, a farmer near Dalhart, told me the railroads used to encourage the landowners to plow fireguards along the rights of way about 300 yards distance from, and parallel with, the rails. When this was done the railroad would keep the grass between the rails and the fireguards burned down.

Ranches like the XIT suffered big losses in grass and cattle as a result of prairie fires, sometimes having to move herds as far away as Montana to find pasture after their own grass was burned. They maintained fireguards around and crisscrossing the pasture. Each would consist of two or three strips of plowed ground, each about ten feet wide and about a hundred feet from the other. The grass between the plowed strips would then be burned. Sometimes the lead fire of a prairie fire would leap even these barriers.

One of the worst prairie fires in the memory of old-timers occurred in 1907. It was started a few miles north of Channing by sparks from a Fort Worth and Denver locomotive. There was a strong wind coming from the southwest. The fire burned all the way up into Kansas until it hit the Cimarron River, a distance of over one hundred miles. Old-timers estimate it burned three million acres of grass.

I was able to get firsthand accounts of this great fire from W. W. Steel of Dumas, Texas, and Mrs. Bertie Cecil of Dalhart.

Mrs. Cecil is the daughter of the George Thomas Whaleys, who in 1904, had come to Texas from Kentucky in a covered wagon and settled on a four-section spread about fifteen miles south of Stratford, Texas, and about twenty-eight miles east of Dalhart. She and her first husband were the parents of Charles Steel, Jr., an official of the Citizens State Bank in Dalhart.

She was seven years of age and living on the ranch when the 1907 fire occurred.

W. W. Steel, brother of Bertie Cecil's deceased husband, Charles, said he had spent his life farming and raising cattle on the four-section spread on which his parents had settled in about 1905. It was some eighteen miles south and west of the Whaley ranch.

Steel was a lad thirteen years of age when the fire occurred. He was in Stratford at the time, and said he could see the fire at night when it was at least thirty miles away. He said, "It looked like it was fire as far as I could see from west to east."

Bertie Whaley and her mother had gone in to Stratford, driving a speedy little pair of mules hitched to a buggy. When they were leaving Stratford to make the fifteen mile drive home (about 4:00 in the afternoon), they saw the smoke rising and Mrs. Whaley judged that, due to the direction of the wind, the lead fire was coming straight toward the ranch house. She headed home, pushing the mules just as fast as she could. As she and Bertie drove along they saw lots of rabbits and birds fleeing in front of the fire. Mrs. Whaley's buggy and the lead fire reached the house at about the same time. In fact, sparks from the fire lit in the buggy and burned holes in some of the packages they were carrying. Bertie spotted her rag doll burning a short way from the house and she ran out and rescued it, but got her hands and legs singed.

Others were already fighting to protect the improvements,

using buckets of water filled from the hydrant in the yard. The home and barn were saved but a chicken house and bunkhouse burned down. Mr. Whaley had started a fruit orchard and the trees were badly singed and died. The cowboys had gone around taking boards off the corrals and cutting fences so as to let livestock get away and not be trapped. The horses and cattle instinctively moved away from the fire and should have escaped it. But a few miles away the cattle drifted into a corner in a pasture where the fence had not been cut. One hundred and twenty-five of them were so badly burned that they either perished on the spot or had to be destroyed. The cowboys failed to take down the lower boards of the pigpen so some of the little pigs couldn't get out and were burned to death.

The "Worst" Blizzards and Sam Wohlford

The Storm was really coming. Finally, I came to a snowbank and climbed up to the top of it and fell all the way down the other side...

—Sam Wohlford
Recipient of Carnegie
Medal for Heroism

In a way, Dalhart area folk seemed to measure time by blizzards. I sensed that they were somehow proud of them and proud of how they had endured them. In any event, people remembered the big blizzards and loved to talk about them.

Like the sudden violent bursts of rain and hail or the searing hot winds, they are a phenomenon of the area. Each one seemed to be worse than the last one. Perhaps the only real difference was in their reporting.

Little seems to be known about those occurring before 1900. After all, the 1880 Census gave Dallam, Sherman, Moore, and Carson Counties zero population.

As late as 1916, it was a rarity to find a telephone at a ranch or farmhouse. Most of those available were operated in a sort of Rube Goldberg fashion by use of the wires on the barbed wire fences. Telephones so connected were, of course, very unreliable during stormy weather.

The earliest full report of a blizzard found in the *Dalhart Texan* told of the one reaching its highest severity on Friday, Saturday and

Sunday the 23rd, 24th and 25th of February, 1912. The weekly issue of the paper appearing Friday, March 1, carried a somewhat complete report under a headline calling it the worst storm in the history of the country. It noted that old-timers were telling of a snow back in 1895 that equaled it, and commented: "That was seventeen years ago and the *Texan* hopes it will be another seventeen years before the Panhandle has another."

The story continued:

> The Panhandle was in the grip of a blizzard, sure enough, Sunday, and bold was the man who left his warm fireside and attempted to weather the elements. The driving wind made the snow cut like fiery sparks, and it was almost impossible to make headway against the wind. Railroad cuts were filled even with the top, and south of every windbreak the snow was piled high, drifts being reported ten feet deep.

The story's coverage on the impact on ranchers and farmers was confined to that of a Mrs. Seyller, the wife of a farmer living a few miles south of Dalhart. Anticipating the blinding snow which fell on Sunday, her husband had strung a rope from the house to the barn with the idea that a person holding to it would not get lost. Sunday morning he had gone out to look after his stock. When he failed to come back when expected, Mrs. Seyller ventured out to look for him. Evidently she lost her grip on the rope, was unable to see her way back to the house, and became completely lost. Mr. Seyller's search for her was fruitless and it was late Monday before a neighbor brought the news to Dalhart. Tuesday some twenty-five Dalhart citizens went to the area horseback to help in the search. Mrs. Seyller's frozen body was found late Tuesday near a neighbor's home — some three miles from her own.

Beale Queen remembered the great snow that covered the ground from December 1918, until April 1919, as the worst. He was about nineteen years old and working at the Matador Ranch at its Alamocitos pasture. "We had twelve thousand head of cattle and six hundred or seven hundred horses in that pasture — the biggest pasture under one fence in Texas, I heard. We ran out of horse feed and groceries, and we found we could not make it into Adrian for supplies by wagon, so the manager had some bobsleds made. We drove one all winter.

"We saved a lot of cattle by culling out the weakest ones and feeding them in the horse corral. When it was all over we found we had lost about five thousand head."

Bob Langhorne of Dalhart, also had a vivid memory of the 1918–19 snow and blizzard. Jess Jenkins, owner of the 101 Ranch with headquarters about twelve miles south of Dalhart in the Rita Blanca Canyon, had talked Bob's father, Joe, into giving up barbering and taking over as manager of the ranch. As a part of the deal his father had bought a hundred head of steers to be thrown in with Jenkins's herd. They had cost him about one hundred dollars a head and he had gone in debt for half the purchase price.

The Rita Blanca Canyon ran through the pasture where Bob's father and Jess Jenkins had most of their cattle. "This storm was so severe and there was so much drifting snow, that all the draws up and down the canyon became filled with snow from six to eighteen feet deep. These cattle were blinded, of course, by this snow, and many of them drifted off into the snow-filled draws and died by freezing or smothering or drowning. We lost all but thirty-seven of our cows. Dad moved back to Dalhart and went back to barbering."

Albert Law, editor of the *Dalhart Texan,* was a lad of thirteen living near Clayton, New Mexico, when the April 9, 1919, blizzard hit. His father had a small herd about three miles east of Clayton. The day after the storm Albert had ridden out to hunt for his father's herd. Some had drifted eight to ten miles. One big four-year-old steer with one eye still frozen shut was found in the bedroom of an abandoned house. It was this storm which caused the James Brothers to suffer the losses that caused them the loss of their ranch. Accounts of this blizzard resided mostly in the memories of people such as Bob Langhorne, Beale Queen, Albert Law and Jesse James. The *Texan* reports were sketchy, possibly because of the influenza epidemic which was raging at the time.

Sam Wohlford, a retired rancher–farmer living at Stratford, gave personal accounts of blizzards on the plains in an interview in 1972. An affable, robust man of eighty-two years, he was obviously proud of the life he had carved out for himself and his family and loved to tell of his experiences.

He had come to the Stratford area in 1907, then a boy of seventeen, hunting relief from asthma, which had plagued him at his family's farmstead in Illinois. On these plains he had not only found relief from his asthma, but had developed a rugged, strong physique. He had built a fortune in farming and ranching. He had traveled throughout practically all parts of the world studying climate and agricultural methods, and had become an authority in these fields. He had become a strong voice in the government of his state and his community. Over the years he had experienced, and learned to adapt himself to, the vicissitudes of climate peculiar to the high plains. The violent sandstorms, the hot, searing winds, the battering hailstorms, the sudden and precipitous changes in temperature, the blistering heat of the summers and the bone-chilling cold of the winters, the prairie fires and the blizzards — all these he had experienced many times. These vicissitudes of climate had caused many a hopeful settler in this new area to move on or return to gentler climes. But Sam Wohlford was proud and happy that he had stayed. He felt the rewards of this land far outweighed the discomforts which it brought, and he loved it above all other places on this earth.

We sat in his den, where I observed that he had a gas fireplace with imitation cow chips instead of logs.

He leaned back at his desk, rolled and lit a cigarette, using a sack of Bull Durham tobacco, and started talking.

He told me first about the 1912 blizzard.

"My brother and I were in partnership in the cattle business on a four-section spread nine miles south of Stratford," he said. "We had gone into the winter with about five hundred steers. There came a pretty good snow in December and it stayed on the ground for about sixty days. Then on February twenty-fifth the cow killer hit. For three days it snowed so hard you felt you couldn't get your breath in it. The cattle were just covered up and died like flies. When the snow stopped it was three feet on a level covering the plains. We had plenty of cottonseed cake and that saved what cows we did save. We decided to cut our losses, so we hired a fellow with eight horses and a little snow plow that made us a path about three feet wide into Stratford. We rented an old livery barn with some corrals and put our cows up there. Then we dissolved our partnership and liquidated. It left me with seventeen old cows, five saddle ponies, a crippled mule, a fifteen hundred dollar feed bill and five dollars in cash. I got married on that five dollars."

Then he told me about his experiences in the 1948 blizzard.

At about 4 o'clock on a Tuesday afternoon, February 11, 1948, he had seen a great black cloud rising rapidly in the north, felt a chill north wind springing up and a sprinkling of snowflakes beginning to fall. Sensing these conditions could bring early darkness, he had gone out to his corral earlier than he usually did to see that the corral gates and barn doors were securely closed and fastened, and that plenty of feed and water had been made available to his saddle horses. Until then, the day had been calm, sunny, clear and beautiful.

As he walked out to the corral, he noted that the cattle in the pasture were beginning to drift toward the north, as is their custom at the onset of a norther. He would keep an eye on the action of these cattle for if they turned about and began drifting southward before the wind, it would tell him the norther would be a severe one.

He was still working at the corral and making these observations when he saw a stranger walking toward him along the trail used in travelling from his farmhouse to the farm-to-market roadway about a mile to the south. The man introduced himself. "I am Bob Reynolds," he said. "I am working over at the Prongers's ranch. Moved up here from South Texas about a month ago. My wife is having a baby and Mr. Pronger got the people at the Cactus Ordnance Plant to let her come down there where she could stay in their little hospital and have the plant doctor look after her. My wife's mother, my three kids and I are on our way down to the Cactus Plant to see my wife and the new baby. I got a little four-year-old girl and two boys. One boy's about two and a half years old and the other about fifteen months. We're in an old pickup truck Mr. Pronger loaned us and we're stuck in a sanddrift and out of gas."

"Mister," said Sam Wohlford, "you might not know it, being new out here, but this norther looks like a bad one to me — and it can be dangerous to be out in. Did you notice them cows turning round and drifting south? That's a bad sign. I'll be glad to get my jeep and pull you out of that sanddrift and give you a tank of gas, but I don't think you ought to try to drive to the Cactus, even if it is only about fifteen miles. Especially not with a woman and three little kids. I'll pull you out and bring you all up here to the house and you can all just settle down here and stay with us until this storm blows over. I'll tell the missus to fix you some supper."

After supper, to Sam Wohlford's great consternation, Reynolds announced that he and his mother-in-law had made up their minds they just had to get on down to the Cactus and see that baby. Then, despite all of Sam's pleadings and warnings, Reynolds, his mother-in-law and the three children loaded themselves into the pickup truck and drove away.

It was now about seven o'clock at night and the wind had risen to a gale, forcing a fine, powdery snow before it, a condition which Sam knew would cause the snow to build into huge, sometimes impassable drifts, and to fill the borrow pits along the roadways, making it difficult for a motorist to keep from running off the road. Already the temperature had plunged downward to below freezing.

Sam stood shaking his head as he watched the pickup disappear. *It'll be a miracle if they get there,* Sam thought as he returned to his house.

Throughout the night and all the next day the storm continued without a pause, the force of the wind rising constantly, the snow becoming thicker and the thermometer moving relentlessly lower until by mid-afternoon it was below zero. Sam had not ventured outside, and from the way his sturdy frame house strained and creaked before the force of the wind, he judged it was blowing about sixty-five miles an hour. Looking out through his windows he noted the snow coming down so thickly that it reduced visibility to but a few feet. He was barely able to detect the drifts of snow which now rose eight to ten feet in height on the south sides of his house and barn.

Sam had just said to his wife that this was one of the worst blizzards he had ever experienced when there came a knock at his door. (It was now about 5 P.M.) Sam went to the door and opened it. There, sagging heavily against the doorsill, was Bob Reynolds. Sam put his arm around Reynolds and helped him into the house and laid him on a sofa near the doorway. "I left the door open so he could just kind of thaw out for a little while," said Sam. "I knew if he had a quick change from that cold out there into the warm air of the house that he would just pass out. I had him down a slug of straight whiskey and pretty soon he began to talk."

"We ran into a snowdrift by that little grove of trees about five miles down the road," said Reynolds. "The car just sunk down in that snow and wouldn't move. There wasn't nothin' for us to do but just bundle up and spend the night right there. We didn't have no heater in the truck, and one window glass was out. We did have some quilts, though, and we wrapped up in them. By daylight this morning the snow had nearly covered the truck, the blankets was frozen and we were terribly cold. I knew your tenant Wilson lived a mile or two north of where we were so I decided to try to find my way to his house and get help. When I got out of the truck and tried to stand up, I just collapsed. I couldn't walk at all. But finally I did get up and made my way to Wilson's house. He was in bed with a bad back and Mrs. Wilson was sick, too. They didn't have no phone. I thought if I could find my way back to the farm road, I could find my way back to your house so I lit out and I've been on my way here all day. Please, Mr. Wohlford, try to go and get my mother-in-law and those kids. I'm afraid if somebody doesn't get them out of there pretty quick, they'll all freeze to death."

Hastily, Sam changed into his warmest gear — heavy woolen long john underwear, woolen socks, woolen shirt, woolen high-necked slipover sweater, a pair of denim blue jeans and laced boots equipped with rubber cleats. He gathered together two tarpaulins and two large eiderdown quilts. With his lariat, he tied these securely in a bundle. He put on his sheepskin-lined greatcoat and his fur-lined cap with flaps that would come down over his ears. He put on a pair of fur-lined leather gloves. He then carried the bundle of tarpaulins and quilts to the barn, gassed up his tractor, attached to it a little mobile platform ordinarily used for carrying cottonseed cake to cattle, and tied the bundle of tarpaulins and quilts securely on the platform. He returned to his house, got his strongest flashlight, and then said to Reynolds,

"I think you can make it now. You got to come with me and help me find your pickup."

A few months later at a gathering in Stratford, Texas, after Sam had received the medal awarded by the Carnegie Hero Fund Commission of Pittsburgh, Sam told what then transpired.

"It was just about dark when we got down to that grove of trees and we began looking for the pickup, but all we could see was just a bunch of snowbanks about fourteen feet deep. Finally, we spotted the top of the car sticking out of one of the drifts, just a little bit of the top sticking out. The rest was all covered up. We began to dig but we didn't have nothing to dig with but our hands. Finally we dug down until we could see inside the pickup. Nobody in there seemed to be moving. I thought they was all dead. Then we got the door of the pickup open and I got inside and pulled those frozen blankets off Reynolds's mother-in-law and the three kids. The mother-in-law and four-year-old girl and the two and a-half-year-old boy were unconscious. The fifteen-month-old baby was trussed to his grandmother's arm with his head on her breast. He was sobbing. And that was the only sign of life there was in that car.

"My tenant Wilson's house was just about a mile north from where we were, and I decided to try and take Reynolds, his mother-in-law, and the children there. I told Reynolds to go to the platform on the back of the tractor and untie that bundle of tarpaulins and eiderdown quilts so we could wrap his mother-in-law and children in them. I pulled Reynolds's mother-in-law out of the pickup, and how I got her up on my shoulder and got her over to that tractor, I'll never know. She was a big woman and weighed about a hundred and seventy-five or a hundred and eighty pounds. But I got her over there somehow. When I got to the tractor I laid Reynolds's mother-in-law on the platform, covered her with the blankets and tarpaulins, and then went back and got the kids and carried them out to the platform. Reynolds's face and hands was frozen and he was in bad shape so I had him get on the platform, too. I wrapped them all up together in the tarp and quilts with a little hole left there where their heads were so they could breathe. I tied that bundle of blankets and people down tight to that little platform.

"Then I started the tractor and headed out toward where I thought Wilson's house was. This made me face directly into that screaming wind, and the snow was coming so thick I couldn't see nothin'. I tried to find the wagon trail to his house but it was covered up. The only way I could tell where I was going was to head just a little to the left of where the wind was coming from. I figgered that ought to get me to the Wilson place. Well, when we got about a quarter of a mile from Wilson's house the damn tractor stopped. I cranked and cranked — but the dang thing just wouldn't start. I think the snow had hit the coil. Finally, when I got so tired I just couldn't crank anymore, I went around, took a-hold of Reynolds's arm and shook him. I said to him, 'If you got any strength at all, get out of those covers and come around here and help me get this dang thing started, because if we don't we're all going to stay out here and freeze to death.' Well, he crawled out of the blankets and got around in front of the tractor. He just took a-hold of the crank and kind of fell over against it. Well, hell — the dang thing started! That wouldn't happen again in a hundred years.

"It was about ten or eleven o'clock when we got to Wilson's house. I woke them up and then I carried Reynolds's mother-in-law and the three kids in there and laid them on a bed. I said to Wilson's wife, 'Now you work with these people. If you got any whiskey or anything else hot, pour it down 'em.' I said to Reynolds, 'You stay there in that house. It's about twelve miles from here down to the Cactus; I'm going to try to go down there and get a doctor.'

"I guess it was about midnight when I went out and started the tractor and headed back to the road. Well, I was almost to the road when that blamed tractor died again! I got out and started cranking that dang thing and I was cranking away, when I heard a roar that was louder than the roar of that wind. I stopped and listened a minute and then I knew it was a train. In a minute I could see its headlight coming toward me through the snow. I ran toward the railroad right-of-way and tried to wave the train down, but I guess the engineer never did see me because the train just went right on by. Later I learned it was the Fort Worth and Denver rescue train that had set out late Wednesday evening from Amarillo to go to Boise City. It was on its way back to Amarillo.

"I knew there was a man named Robbins who had a house about a quarter of a mile south of where I was on that railroad and I headed out for his house. When I went to cross the railroad right-of-way I came to a little shack where the railway people kept a phone. I thought maybe I could call the Cactus or Amarillo or somewhere. I broke down the door and cranked and cranked on that phone but I didn't get no answer so I struck on out for Robbins's house. I kept going along, kept looking and looking for his house, but I just couldn't see it. I didn't have anything to guide me. I just went toward it by instinct. The storm was really coming. Finally, I came to a snowbank and climbed up to the top of it and fell all the way down the other side and rolled right up against a building. It was a snowdrift that had built up on the south side of Robbins's house. I didn't try to go in right away — just sat there out of the wind for thirty or forty minutes to get my breath and thaw out; I knew if I didn't do that, why, when I hit the warm air in the house I would pass out. I went ahead and finally got the attention of the Robbinses. Now, as if there wasn't enough trouble already, I'm blamed if that fellow's wife wasn't having a baby! He said he had meant to take his wife into Dalhart, but the baby kind of caught them by surprise and of course they couldn't go nowhere in that storm.

"Well, while Robbins was giving me a good slug of bourbon, he told me that his brother-in-law, Bob Ferris, lived about three miles to the south and had a pickup truck with snow tires on it. He said that if I could get to the brother-in-law's house, maybe he could take me to the Cactus to get a doctor. So I started out *again*. By now it was about two o'clock in the morning. I was going to try to *walk* that three miles south to Ferris's house, and was the snow blowing! Christ A'mighty! You couldn't see *nothin'!* And I stumbled around awhile and I came up to a telephone pole and I knew that the telephone line ran on down right by Ferris's house. I also knew those poles was set about three hundred steps apart. I figured that if I could keep going from one telephone pole to the other I would finally get there. Well, I started out from that first pole trying to look straight ahead, but that snow was blowing just straight parallel with the ground, and it was so thick I couldn't see two feet. But then I noticed that when I looked up at an angle through the snowflakes I seemed to see for some distance. I guess there was a little moonlight or starlight high up in the sky. This way, pretty soon I was able to glimpse the top of the next pole. But I kept running into snowdrifts and my legs would sink down to my waist every step forward, and then when I would try to pull my hind leg out, my front leg would just sink deeper. Pretty soon I got so weak I began to fall down every few steps, and when I would go down I would think I couldn't possibly pull myself up again, just couldn't muster enough strength to stand up. Well, somehow I did get back up every time, and I just kept going and finally I found Ferris's house. I leaned up on the door and began knocking. When he opened the door I just fell on in.

"Ferris and his wife got dressed and we got in his pickup truck and we drove back to Robbins's house and left Ferris's wife there so she could help Robbins's wife while the baby was being born. Then Ferris and I got in the pickup and lit out for the Cactus. It was now about four o'clock in the morning and all we could do was creep along — even with that pickup truck and its snow tires. We would hit them snowpiles and the old pickup would just barely creep, and then finally edge its way on through. We finally got to the Cactus about seven o'clock Thursday morning.

"The Cactus people got out their rescue team of a truck, a jeep and an ambulance. They added two stretchers and dispatched a driver and two other men together with the plant's doctor, and we all headed out for Wilson's house.

"We got to Wilson's house about ten thirty, Thursday morning, and when we got there we found Reynolds's mother-in-law was dead, and his four-year-old daughter and two- and a-half-year-old son were dead. But Bob Reynolds and his fifteen-month-old baby were alive. We loaded the corpses, Bob Reynolds, and the baby in the ambulance, and started back to the Cactus.

"On the way we stopped for a few minutes at the Robbins's house and the doctor went in. Mrs. Robbins and the newborn baby were doing fine."

When he had finished telling me the story, Sam stepped over to his bookcase, got out the Carnegie Medal and showed it to me.

It was a silver disc about three inches in diameter.

On the front side appeared an embossed profile of Andrew Carnegie, above which (around the edge) were the words, *Carnegie Hero*

Fund, and below it, also around the edge, the words, *Established April 15, 1904.*

On the reverse side was an outline of the United States, Canada and Newfoundland, with the seals of each country. Around the outer edges there was relief work picturing the laurel (typifying glory), the ivy (typifying friendship), the oak (typifying strength), and the thistle (typifying persistence).

In the center of the reverse side was a cartouche or inscription plate which read:

Awarded to Sam C. Wohlford who rescued Kenneth H. Reynolds and others from exposure near Stratford, Texas, February 11, 1948.

Around the edge on the reverse side was the following quotation from John XV, verse 13:

Greater love hath no man than this, that a man lay down his life for his friends.

The Skunk In the Opera House

and Return of a Native

> *Some day, I thought, I should come back and write a book about these people and their land. I wondered: would it be a story of a strong people building a new land, or a story of a new land building strong people?*
>
> — John C. Dawson

Miss Sally Childers (Aunt Sally) was my teacher in the seventh grade. She was real strict but she was fair and seemed to understand boys. I liked her a lot. But you couldn't walk outside of Miss Sally's classroom without feeling you were being watched by the new school principal, whom I will call Old Man Scrooge. Just the way he looked told you he was going to be hard to get along with. He had a leathery, pockmarked face always fixed in a scowl. Somebody must have told him that Dalhart boys were incorrigible little hellions intent on making life miserable for school principals. He made it known right away that things were going to be different. He put in a lot of new rules: like no more scribbling jokes on the blackboard, no more sliding down the fire escape at recess and no more running in and out of the school building. Not only no more running — no *going* in or out except when told to do so by his ringing his big cowbell. When we went to leave a class we had to line up in single file in the hallway, stand absolutely quiet and at attention, and wait for Old Man Scrooge to ring his bell, telling us to go.

He would stand scowling in front of his office until everybody was in his place in line and everything had quieted down. Then he would ring his bell and we were expected to march out keeping in step and with our mouths shut. The same procedure was followed when we were to leave the schoolyard and go back to our classes. Old Man Scrooge would stand out on the front steps of the school building and ring the bell to tell us all to get in line ready to march back to class. Until then we didn't dare go in. When the lines were formed to his satisfaction he would ring the bell again to tell us to march on in.

He just seemed determined to take all the fun out of school and I felt all the time that somehow, sooner or later, he was going to pounce on me.

Well, it wasn't long before he did. When it turned cold late in October, mother bought me a beautiful white knit sweater with a big comfortable rolled up collar. Recess time came and I lined up just the way I was supposed to but after Old Man Scrooge rang his bell telling us to march out, I somehow got out of step. We were right in front of his office and he saw me. He ran up behind me, grabbed me by the neck of my beautiful new sweater, lifted me off the floor and shook me until my eyes were popping. When he put me down he growled: "Maybe that'll teach you to keep step!"

That sweater never did regain its shape and you can imagine how I felt about Old Man Scrooge.

Pretty soon he pounced on me again.

It happened one day after a recess when he rang his bell to tell us to line up and get ready to march to class. Three boys from my class (one was Gene Carr) were having a ball with a piece of fire hose about fifteen feet long. One boy was tugging at either end of the hose and the third had the hose coiled around his midsection. The boys were still tugging away at this hose after everyone else had taken his place in line and come to attention.

The three boys dropped the fire hose and lined up behind me for a moment. Then, however, Old Man Scrooge leaped from the steps, seized the fire hose and came running toward us. At this, the three culprits, one at a time, pulled out of line, scurried forward and edged back in somewhere near the front. In my innocence, I remained behind. So, when Old Man Scrooge got to the line, the culprits were gone but I was still there. Old Man Scrooge then proceeded to give me a thorough thrashing with that fire hose.

After that I made up my mind that some way I would get even with that old tyrant if it was the last thing I ever did.

At the time I was trapping skunks down in the Rita Blaca Canyon. I had six or eight traps set in little caves along the base of the caprock. After school, every day, I would go home and change into hunting clothes, then walk down into the canyon and run my traps. Whenever I found a skunk in a trap I would shoot it with my .22 rifle. Then, after making an incision with my knife along the rear of the belly and down the inside of each of the rear legs, I would skin the skunk. I would then carry the pelt home and stretch it, furry side down, over a board which I had sawed into the proper shape to hold it. The hide would then be scraped and left to dry, after which I would sell it to the Schuhart Grain Company which made a business of buying these and other pelts.

I laid plans for Old Man Scrooge. Specifically, I got an empty pint whiskey bottle and took it along while trapping. When I had killed a skunk I would open the sac containing the liquid that skunks squirt at their enemies and would squeeze that liquid out into my bottle. In this way, by the end of the school year, I had almost a full pint of essence of skunk. I didn't know exactly how I was going to use that essence, but it was reserved especially for Old Man Scrooge.

When it was announced that commencement exercises would be held on an evening at the Felton Opera House, my plans began to jell. It was on the second floor of a two-story building in the center of the town on Main Street. There was a stairway about six feet wide leading up to it from Main Street and another stairway about twelve feet wide leading up to it from a side street.

I reasoned that Old Man Scrooge's automobile would have to be parked somewhere around that opera house while the commencement exercises were going on, and I made up my mind that my essence of skunk and his automobile should meet.

Some days in advance of the day for the commencement, I got out my bottle of skunk essence and washed it carefully to remove fingerprints. Then, handling it with cotton gloves, I went to town and hid that bottle in the alley near the opera house. Also, I took a pair of black tennis shoes, some black trousers and a black shirt and hid these in the storeroom in father's sanitarium building.

On the night of the commencement, I waited until it got dark and I felt most everybody in town would be inside the opera house attending the commencement exercises. Then I strolled down to the sanitarium, changed into my black tennis shoes, black pants and black shirt and, going into the alley, went down to the opera house to look for Old Man Scrooge's auto.

I found it parked exactly at the foot of that twelve foot wide stairway that led up from the side street. Then I went around in the alley, got my bottle of skunk essence and, quite deliberately, emptied it over the front and back seats and the canvas top of that car.

I then disposed of my bottle in the alleyway and returned to the sanitarium storeroom. There I changed back into my ordinary clothes and strolled down Main Street to Guy McGee's Drugstore, the principal place for ice cream sodas, *et cetera*, in the vicinity of the opera house. I ordered a strawberry ice cream soda, and was sitting at a table in the rear enjoying this when suddenly the Main Street door to the drugstore opened to admit a great mass of jabbering people. I heard them saying over and over — "How do you reckon that skunk got loose in the opera house," or words to that effect.

Well, I hadn't realized that when I perfumed Old Man Scrooge's car that the stairway before which it was standing was the principal source of air being brought into the opera house for ventilation.

My skunk essence had thus swept into the opera house, its occupants had fled for fresh air and the commencement had come to an end.

After that skunk episode, mother and father decided that I ought to go to some other school, so they got me enrolled in Northwestern Military and Naval Academy at Lake Geneva, Wisconsin. I was only thirteen years old and the main idea, I think, was to get me near my brother, Artis, who was a premed student at the University of Chicago.

That was the year father bought a two section place about twelve miles north of town. There was a little house and a windmill already there but father put up a big red barn and corral and a lot of new barbed wire fencing.

He bought eighty-seven Black Angus yearling calves and took me with him when he decided to have all of them branded and marked and the bull calves made into steers. He had registered a brand that was fashioned out of a *D* and an *R* (for doctor). It looked like this: (ᗡR). His calves were to be marked also by clipping about an inch off the right ear. The corral was really in two parts; one was an enclosure in which all the calves were held until we were ready for them, the other, a much larger enclosure, was reserved for roping, bulldogging and branding the calves one at a time.

As best I can remember, it took me and three cowboys to handle each calf. We would open the gate of the enclosure that held the calves and let one out into the larger enclosure. A cowboy would then rope the calf by a rear leg. I would grab it by the head and wrestle it to the ground, left side down. The cowboy with the rope would move closer, place his feet against one rear leg, his hands on the other, and, with him pushing with his feet and pulling with his hands and me holding the calf's head to the ground it would be pretty well immobilized. I would hang on to the calf's head and try to stay out of reach of its flailing front feet.

Outside the corral was the fire used to heat the branding iron. When we had the calf down, the cowboy handling the branding iron would open the gate to the corral, come in and place the red hot iron on the calf's right hip. Smoke and smell of burning hair and singed flesh would arise. Another cowboy would clip the calf's right ear. If it was a bull calf, the operation required in order to make it a steer was performed. We would then release the calf and let it out of the corral and into the pasture. There were a few whiteface yearlings that got the same treatment as did the black polled Angus. They were tame in comparison, and would lie down submissively when bulldogged. But those polled Angus calves would buck and kick in all directions. They could even kick forward with their front feet.

For a while I had a job hauling cement by wheelbarrow from a cement mixer to a *porte cochere* being added to the De Soto Hotel. Then mother, Aramita Killen, and several other folks made up an auto caravan for a trip to the mountains near Taos, New Mexico. We carried tents and cots for sleeping, and utensils for cooking, including a giant iron kettle in which the women would boil Mexican beans and such. It took us two days to drive from Dalhart to Taos, with an overnight stopover at Mount Dora, New Mexico.

After that I packed up a pup tent, blankets, a coffeepot, skillet, condiments and so on and rode the Fort Worth and Denver to the Magenta station near the Canadian River. There was a good bass fishing lake some club had built in a valley near Magenta, and near it was a beautiful grove of cottonwood trees. Here I pitched camp and spent a wonderful week, sleeping on the ground, fishing, walking over the prairies flushing coveys of Mexican quail and practicing shooting with my .38 Smith and Wesson revolver I had gotten from Al Dalton on a trade.

Pretty soon after I got home from this camping trip I packed up for my trip to Chicago and Lake Geneva, Wisconsin.

When father drove me down to the Rock Island Depot and bought my ticket, he saw a little sign on the ticket window that told him he could buy a twenty-five thousand dollar life insurance policy on me for twenty-five cents. Father bought the policy, then turned to me with a mischievous little grin and said: "Just too good a bargain to pass up, Son!"

Between the day father put me on the train for military school and the day I came back with a diploma from the University of Wisconsin, eight years elapsed.

It was now June of 1924. In a lot of ways Dalhart and Dalhart folk hadn't seemed to change much. The town had grown a little. The *Dalhart Texan* said the town now had a population of about 4,000. But life every day seemed to be still directed mostly by what kind of weather they were having and the people still seemed to enjoy surviving blinding sandstorms, searing hot winds, killing blizzards and snowstorms and destructive hailstorms. These weather phenomena seemed merely to punctuate life, help keep it from being too dull and humdrum. They were still experimenting with ways to do something with the land other than what it seemed to have been intended for, namely for grazing cows. And they were still trying to induce people from somewhere else to come there and convert the beautiful open prairies into farms.

The way cattle strengthened on the bluestem, gramma and buffalo grasses had told them way back in the beginning that the soil was nutritious. There was a deep sandy loam topsoil and the land was flat and easy to plow. Despite the fact that only about eighteen inches of rain could be expected — and that mostly in gully washers — the people had learned ways to raise maize and kaffir; and later winter wheat and still later, corn.

Now, I learned, farmers all over the north Panhandle and even up in the Oklahoma Strip were planting cotton. This was only the second year this had ever been done in this area. Somebody had started the rumor that folks could grow cotton just as well here as they did down by Lubbock or McKinney. That would give them a cash crop to add to the winter wheat and the fall crops of maize and kaffir and corn. So they were all for giving it a good hard try.

The 1923 cotton crop had been mostly a failure because (they said) first, there was an unseasonably late spring that delayed the germination of the seeds and, secondly, there was an unseasonably early freeze that closed the cotton bolls just when they needed a frost to bring them open. People were so enthused with the prospects for this new crop, however, that they built a gin at Dalhart capable of ginning one hundred bales a day. A list of the stockholders in the *Dalhart Texan* included the name of my father. After the 1923 cotton crop proved disappointing, the *Texan* editorialized that the failure of cotton in 1923 should not be regarded as indicating its future. It said 1923 was an "off" year weather-wise — declared that cotton was there to stay, that Dalhart and Channing would be cotton centers in a few more years and that loads of people would be flocking in. Land prices, they editorialized, would skyrocket.

One of the biggest arguments for trying to raise cotton up in our area was that we wouldn't have boll weevils. "No boll weevils north of the Canadian," farmers would say. Maybe the real reason there were no boll weevils could have been that the weevils were smart enough not to go where there was no cotton. The truth of the matter was that spring in our 4,000 foot altitude came too late, and the winters came too soon. Most importantly, the nights were too cool. Cotton requires long warm nights to do well.

The 1924 cotton crop was a bigger disappointment than the 1923 one had been, and the cotton boom died about as quickly as it had started. There wasn't much in the newspaper about it, but the gin was sold and moved off and everybody just went back to raising wheat, maize, sorghum and some corn.

You didn't have to be a farmer or a rancher to be a landowner in a town like Dalhart. Everybody believed in the land and most everybody owned some of it. Father was reputed to be a big land owner. The trouble with him was that he was such an easy touch for land salesmen that while he had title to tracts all around, he never got any paid for. He just kept on acquiring more land and more mortgages. Before the war he had about gotten his two-section "thoroughbred" place north of town paid for, but he sold it to the James Brothers in 1918, when he was called for the medical corps.

When I got home in 1924, he had really loaded up on land but was not farming or otherwise developing any of it except section eighteeen, eight miles east of town. That's the place he was going to make into a great cotton farm that turned out to be a tumbleweed disaster.

All the other land was raw prairie. A two section tract about twenty miles west near the New Mexico line was so sandy we wouldn't dare drive our car out over it. "Great broomcorn land," said father. One section was north of town near the land Andy James was trying to drill for oil on. And two sections were twenty miles east of town where Moore, Sherman, Dallam and Hartly Counties join.

Father just loved all that land and every now and then he would ask me to go with him and look at it. He would put on his great black Stetson hat, get a big mouth full of that dry Kentucky leaf tobacco he kept in twists, and off we would go.

When we would come to one of the pieces of land, he would get out of the car and gaze across it looking proud and satisfied and then he'd pick up some of the dirt, roll it around in his hand, look at it, smell it and then say, "Finest land on earth, son. All it needs is moisture."

He didn't seem a bit fazed when the cotton crop on section eighteen turned out to be a tumbleweed crop. Nor did he seem the least bit worried about the fact that none of the rest of the land had any kind of improvements on it and had no way of producing any income to help pay off the big debts against it.

I never tired of the tales he would tell me on these trips, about how his mother's massaging his legs helped him overcome crippling infantile paralysis as a boy; how he had taught himself veterinary medicine before he was sixteen; how he had put himself through medical school trading horses in summertime in the Indiana hills, stealing bodies for dissection at the university, doing the dissection for the rich boys, and so on.

Andy James was stubbornly fighting for a comeback from the disasterous losses suffered by the James Brothers Ranch in the 1918–1919 blizzard. The ranch's creditor, Interstate Bank of Kansas City had required the sale of the 50,000 acre "north" ranch but was allowing Andy to test his convictions that oil could be found on the remaining ranchlands and that a great revival of prosperity could come through the advent of cotton farming.

Andy had planted cotton on five separate one hundred-acre tracts over the ranch "to test all kinds of soil" and had put together an oil venture he was sure would find "the mother pool."

The proceeds of the sale of the north ranch went on the bank indebtedness except for a barn full of huge Winton "Jackrabbit" touring cars. These went to Andy and his brother, Walter, a giant assembly of machinery for which they had little use. The cars were not entirely valueless, however, to the restless, innovative Andy. He proceeded to use them — as long as they lasted — pulling listers to dig fire guards to protect the land from prairie fires and as auxiliary power helping his one-man desperate effort to complete his oil well test after the contractor had gotten his drill bit stuck at 1,500 feet and had given up.

I drove out to see Andy and his well that summer. He was all alone in the middle of the derrick floor. It was an old standard drilling rig and Andy was trying to pull and reset casing using a rope run through the top of the derrick and tied to one of those Winton Jackrabbits stationed about a hundred yards away.

Old Fred Wynn had been out with his doodlebug (a little bottle on a string) the actions of which, he thought, could detect oil. Andy told me, "Old Fred Wynn went all around here swinging his little bottle and finally told me I had just missed the oil a thousand feet. I told him, 'Hell, this hole varies that much!' "

Andy got the well down about 1,800 feet before abandoning it as a dry hole. The failure of the well and the failure of the cotton venture ended Andy's efforts to salvage some of the ranchlands. Even so, he and his brother, Walter did not give up. With local backing from Dalhart's Citizen's State Bank, they went back in the cattle business and finally left nice cattle ranches to their heirs.

Back before father bought the building at the north end of Main Street and converted it into a sanitarium, the building had been occupied by a land company. When he bought it in 1912, it had big signs painted on the north side advertising a hundred thousand acres of Capitol Syndicate (XIT) ranchlands for sale. "Ten per cent down and 40 years pay," it said. I found a snapshot of the building taken in 1909, and the sign was on it then. So at least as early as 1909, there was a big movement to sell off the big ranchlands. The idea was to split these lands up into little farm tracts that would bring actual farmers into the area to settle. Personally I never understood why the people wanted so much to move cowboys out and move farmers in. I liked the cowboys.

Well, when I came home in 1924, the big push to sell off the ranchlands and bring a large population of farmers was on again and in a big way. High prices for grain to feed Europe following the war, plus unusually good rains (over thirty inches in 1923, while the average since 1904 had been about eighteen) was making the cheap lands of the Panhandle look like a bargain, and folks with the big tracts were trying to cash in. The newspapers were full of stories about what a boom in land sales was going on, how many new farmers had come in, how much business was being benefited and so on.

One story declared that 520,000 acres in Dallam and Hartley Counties, the last of the old Capitol Syndicate (XIT) lands, would be broken into small tracts and sold at twenty dollars to forty dollars an acre, ten years to pay and six per cent interest. Another said 60,000 acres in Dallam and Hartley Counties, recovered by the state from the XIT after a resurvey, would be offered by the State Land Commissioner one fortieth down and forty years to pay at five per cent interest.

Another story told of 80,000 acres out of the James Brothers Ranch being offered for sale in small tracts by the Kansas City Bank that had taken over after the 1919 storm.

The paper remarked gleefully, "It won't be long until the largest ranch in this part of the country will give way to the plow and maize and kaffir, wheat and corn and cotton will take the place of the far renowned bluestem, gramma and buffalo grasses."

Such talk was absolute heresy to old-time ranchhands who felt The Old Man Up Yonder had intended for this country to be held together forever by those grasses, and to be used exclusively for grazing cattle.

Jess Jenkins had decided the area was getting too crowded and was moving his operations to a new ranch near Corona, New Mexico.

Despite all this effort and talk about filling the land up with farmers, there were still worlds of land that had never seen a plow on which you could chase a coyote for miles in your car and never see a fence. The area was still — and maybe would always be — mostly a cow country.

Charlie Woods, who had bought Andy James's interest in the Midway Bank after the 1919 blizzard, took me out several times to inspect herds of cattle which secured much of the bank's loans. In the bank itself, giant horns from Longhorn cattle of an early date made the framework for the chairs and sofas in the lobby. The new Citizen's State Bank — with men like Orville Finch, Charles Steel, Eck Brown, Lon McCrory and W. H. Lathem — was doing a lively business of lending on the security of cattle. The lobby of the De Soto Hotel was still a great place for cattlemen to gather, enjoy the company of one another and do business. The bulls raised on the ranch of Uncle Dick Coon and Bill Culbertson had become in demand worldwide — a tribute to the strength-giving qualities of the high plains grasses.

Bobby Dyche, the artisan, had made a great set of miniature wood carvings of the hats of prominent townspeople — all cattlemen to some degree. Each cowman developed his own distinctive way of creasing his Stetson and slanting or curving its brim. Any Dalhartan could look at the display of these little wooden carvings shown in the show window in front of the Charles Summers and Sons store and recognize whose hat was depicted.

The Skunk in the Opera House and Return of a Native 173

There were hats of Orville Finch, W. H. Lathem, John (Scandalous) McCandless, Dad (Cyclone) Logan, Smokey Bonner, Arch Sneed, Ealy Moore, Tobe Pitts, Bob Beverly, Henry Tandy, Hugh Exum, Billy Jarrett, Bob Duke, Frank Farwell, Andy James, Walter James, Henry Boyce, Uncle Dick Coon, Bill Culbertson, Malcolm Stewart, Joe Reynolds, Berkley Dawson, Malcolm Shelton, Ted Houghton, Vic Stewart, Al Dalton, Jess Jenkins, Webb Wharton and others.

I read in the *Texan* that Dad Logan was candidate for mayor and John (Scandalous) McCandless for sheriff and tax collector. The paper said that Scandalous McCandless had held that job since 1912.

Joe Langhorne, Joe Bass and Shorty No Legs were still entertaining people in the De Soto Hotel Barbershop.

Joe Bass gave me a good feeling about how my father was regarded thereabout. He was giving me a haircut when father came down the street on his way for his daily face massage and shave. "Just look at him!" Joe exclaimed. "How proud he carries himself! How fine he looks in his fine clothes!"

Shine Carter and Charlie Dinwiddie were still running Dinwiddie's Pool Hall and Domino Parlor. Bill Wanser and Shorty Wolf were running the drugstores. Also, for those who might wish to know, Number 126 was still doing a flourishing business.

Prohibition had closed all the saloons, but everybody in town knew a bootlegger who would supply his needs. The stuff they sold had to be cured awhile — was sometimes hung in a keg on the windmill tower to swing in the wind. The druggists could fill whiskey prescriptions issued for *medicinal* purposes by doctors, however. The doctors got three dollars a prescription and some of the doctors (I am told) got so tired of being pestered for prescriptions that they just signed whole books of them and sold them to Bill Wanser or Shorty Wolf for three dollars per prescription. This let Shorty and Bill take care of the problem of deciding who was entitled to have whiskey *prescribed*.

T. L. Jacques would be seen striding toward town from his fine home down the street from ours. He had, in the early days, been a leading clothing merchant with stores in several towns in the northern Panhandle and in the Oklahoma Strip. His business had met disaster somewhere along the way. He had already used up too many of his allotted years and too much of his energy to undertake rebuilding his fortunes. He was now clerking for some other store owner. His demeanor showed his deep sadness, yet in his erect stride, impeccable dress and courtly manner, he exuded pride, courtesy, honesty and fine breeding.

Miss Sally Childers, who had despaired of making a learner of me in the seventh grade, was now our postmistress. Every day after each passenger train had come through, almost everyone congregated at the post office. Aunt Sally could be seen there back of the post boxes sorting the mail and otherwise managing the place.

Mrs. E. R. Stewart, Dalhart's "angel of mercy" was looking after the needs of the unfortunate from a house across the street from the De Soto Hotel, furnished her without charge by the owner, Uncle Dick Coon.

Long strings of railroad cars, carrying cantaloupes and other perishables from California to the Midwest and the East, were coming through town frequently. The cars were refrigerated by large blocks of ice put into compartments at each end of each car. The Rock Island Railroad and owners of the local icehouse maintained a long wooden platform about level with the tops of the cars. The long trains of cars would be shuttled to a stop on a spur track along this platform. Using ice hooks, men would slide hundred-pound-blocks of ice along the platform, then open the hatches leading in to the ice compartments of the cars, and drop the ice in.

The Rock Island's *Golden State Limited,* crack luxury passenger train running between Chicago and Los Angeles, made its first run in 1924. W. H. Greenough, Division Superintendent for the Rock Island, at least since the 1912 snow, was still Division Superintendent. He was a courtly, well-mannered, dignified man and a close friend of my father's. His beautiful private car, still equipped with a very efficient Japanese porter, was still being parked on a spur track down back of the Ely–Hesse Produce Store near father's Trans-Canadian Sanitarium.

Mother, Mrs. Greenough, Mrs. Swearingen, Mrs. Stewart and Mrs. Gushwa were still meeting regularly at sessions of their literary club. Mother was still singing in the Methodist Church choir with Lydia Fountain still at the piano. Father was still refusing to attend *any* church, due to a stubbornly held resolve born of some early-day difference between him and some clergyman. Yet he had a well-worn *Holy Bible.*

People were enjoying a new story about Val Powell and the turkey. It seems that he was invited to Thanksgiving dinner at the Killen's. Mr. Killen (a civil engineer) was called away on a business emergency, and only Val and Mrs. Killen were left to handle the turkey. Both Val and Mrs. Killen were noted for their enormous appetites and love of good food. Afterward Val observed: "You know, a turkey is an awfully inconvenient bird. Too big for one person to eat but not big enough for two."

At the Sanitarium, mother was still keeping the books, giving the anesthetics, running the kitchen, doing the buying of supplies, and handling the taking and developing of X-ray pictures. Bill Bennett was still the bill collector and all around handyman. He and mother still occupied desks on the platform built at the rear of the reception room. The stuffed owl and stuffed dog were still occupying their own small platforms on the wall beneath the platform where Mother and Bill Bennett sat — the owl with outstretched wings and Old Prince reclining with one front paw over the other, just as he did when he used to lie in front of Old Betsy.

These were the early-day people, the people who came to this harsh, undeveloped land lured by the very fact that it was harsh and undeveloped. Independent, perhaps a bit primitive, self-reliant, good humored and, it seemed to me, possessed of a distinctive and even unique sense of the histrionic. A people living always in close relationship to the land and what it could produce.

Some day, I thought, I should come back and write a book about these people and their land. I wondered: *would it be a story of a strong people building a new land, or a story of a new land building strong people?*

After the Storm
Once again the air has that cleansed, invigorating, freshness found only on the High Plains when, after a violent hail or rain, the storm clouds are torn and forced into retreat before the evening breeze.

Painting by John C. Dawson

Part Two

Survivors of the Dust Bowl Era

The storm was upon them before Hazel and her husband noticed the child's absence. Reasoning that she would have fled homeward, but seized with fear that the child would become lost, Hazel's husband grabbed his flashlight and hurried out to search for her.

By now the swirling, powdery silt had become so thick that he could not see. Hazel described it as "not just black — not just thick — it was black thick." He tried his flashlight but it would not penetrate the blackness. On the sidewalk he dropped to hands and knees. With his head at this level he could see a few feet underneath the impenetrable black cloud. Staying on his hands and knees so as to see the sidewalk, he crawled the five blocks to the child's home.

— Hazel Shaw

INTRODUCTION

The way most Dalhart area old-timers remembered the Depression and Drouth of the thirties was succinctly expressed by farmer-rancher W. W. Steel of Dumas, Texas:

"The Depression? Well, the Depression wouldn't-a-been so bad if it hadn't-a-come in such hard times!"

Hard times indeed! Citizens everywhere in the United States were victims of the Depression. Also the drouth eventually spread throughout most of the Great Plains. But in the area that became known as the Dust Bowl, the drouth's effect, added to the Depression, brought singular and unique hardship and deprivation.

The so-called Dust Bowl area comprised southwestern Kansas, the Oklahoma Panhandle, southeastern Colorado, northeastern New Mexico and the north Texas Panhandle area in which Dalhart is located.

Dalhart was my residence until I left there in 1929, to take up law practice in Houston. Until then, the area was still a beautiful grassland supporting a great abundance of wildlife and domestic livestock, and one populated by a people proud and vigorous in their high, dry atmosphere. Returning for a visit in the 1930s I was greatly disturbed to see what the drouth and wind had done to that once beautiful land and its people. The land had become virtually a bleak, hideous desert, abandoned by most forms of wildlife and even domestic animals whose life depended on grasses. Plowed fields were blown out to plow depth; barbed wire fences had been turned into mounds of tumbleweeds and sand. Pastures had been denuded of grass. Farmers had despaired of being able to raise crops either for sale or for sustenance of livestock. The economy, almost entirely dependent on farming and cattle raising, was shattered. The people seemed benumbed by their misfortune and to be simply holding on with dwindling hope.

From my relatives and friends I was given an intimate glimpse of the hardships the area residents endured and of the courage and

Introduction

fortitude they displayed in holding on, and seeking ways to restore their land to productivity.

All this intrigued me and made me yearn to some day go back and try to learn the causes and meaning of this disastrous period of our history. I wanted to try to put something on paper that might help future residents prevent a recurrence. However, it was not until my retirement from active practice in 1970, that I was able to undertake this research. Some thirty years had passed since the end of the Depression and Drouth of the thirties. The physical evidences of the devastations of that period were then generally obscured by new vegetation, but memories of the period were still vivid in the minds of the residents.

I made many trips to the Dalhart area and drove widely over the rest of the Dust Bowl, interviewing ranchers, farmers and other residents. Most people interviewed permitted me to record our conversations on my tape recorder. In Washington, D.C., I searched the archives of the Department of Agriculture and the Library of Congress for pertinent information and photographs.

I concluded that if there was any contribution I could make which would be of value either to the old-timers who had lived through this disastrous period, or to the young people who have, or may, come along at a later period, it might be to simply record the story of the times as related to me by the people, especially those in the Dalhart area. In this way, perhaps I could at least convey to others the feelings and the experiences which these people had endured, and the actions they took in their efforts to undo the damage the elements, aided by man, had wrought.

What is here recorded seems important and worth preserving. Perhaps it will bring back proud memories for those who were there. For those who were not there, it may bring a valuable lesson as to the importance of properly treating the area's most valuable resource — the land.

The Black Dusters

On the side of the road nearest the storm, every little spike on the barbed wire fence was glowing; it was a brush discharge of electricity — that phenomenon called Saint Elmo's fire.

— Artis Dawson

It was the constant winds, picking up and moving sand from an earth parched by heat and drouth, that inflicted the greatest damage throughout the Dust Bowl in the 1930s. But it was the suffocating blinding dust storms, commonly referred to as *black dusters,* which began in 1934 and continued at least through 1937, that seemed to signal nature's most unendurable destructiveness.

While these storms were felt to some extent as far south as Odessa, Texas, as far west as the Denver, Colorado area, as far east as Dodge City, Kansas, and even, on occasion, Washington, D.C., and the Atlantic Ocean, they appear to have had their origin in the Dust Bowl area. Without doubt, they appeared in that area with greatest frequency and wrought in that area their greatest hardship to land, man and beast.

John McCarty, editor of the *Dalhart Texan* during the Dust Bowl days, once wrote that he had learned of somewhat comparable dust storms occurring elsewhere in the world. These, he said, were the *black dust black storms* on the Russian steppes and deserts, the *palousers* of northern Idaho in which the fine dust sifted through every crevice and, when mixed with rain, covered glass with red mud, and the *simooms* of the Asian and African deserts, described as a kind of suffocation caused by excessive dryness and dust-laden wind. Also

The Black Dusters 181

whirlwinds or *dust devils,* he said, sometimes rise more than 2000 feet in Death Valley where they are called *sand augers.* Then he opined that the Dalhart area's 1934–1935 model Black Dusters seemed to be a sort of cross between simooms, palousers and sand augers.

The Black Dusters were a strange phenomenon attributable to a set of unusual conditions both of climate and of environment.

The soil in the Dalhart area is a sandy loam easily stirred by livestock or by the plow. Also there is perhaps no area other than the seacoast where the wind is so strong and constant. Blowing sand that stings the face and hands, pits windshields, peels paint from automobiles and sometimes limits visibility to a few yards, is commonplace. It is a nuisance but one easily tolerated, especially considering how clean, clear, calm and invigorating it seems when the wind subsides. But after two years of the great drouth of the 1930s, the Black Duster, a new and much more frightening visitation of nature, made its appearance. It was composed of a much finer element of the soil than sand, an element so fine that it would separate from the heavier windblown sand particles and lift high into the atmosphere, float there in great clouds, and then descend softly to earth when forced down by wind currents.

A soil conservation engineer at Dodge City explained that the earth particles composing the Black Dusters were silt (as distinct from sand). It was black in the Dodge City and other Kansas areas, red in much of Oklahoma, whitish or gray in eastern Colorado and northeastern New Mexico. He demonstrated the lifting action of the wind by holding a sheet of writing paper to his mouth and blowing over it. "Like the lifting action of the windstream above the wings of an airplane," he said.

These great clouds of silt came to the earth as huge, soft billowing masses, blotting out the sunlight, bringing pitch-darkness to the earth and leaving deposits of silt on everything over which the cloud passed. The silt was so fine that it would penetrate areas that blown sand could not reach. It was sticky, and it smelled. It penetrated even the best constructed homes and filled the air within them. Some said it could even penetrate glass. It was choking and blinding. The darkness created was often such that drivers of automobiles would be forced to stop still even in daylight hours, and wait out the storm. Even with their headlights on they could not see to drive.

The Black Duster would blank out an area for hours; then usually there would follow a strong wind, carrying sand. Anyone caught out in one of these dusters would instinctively place a handkerchief (a wet one if possible) over nose and mouth to make a mask through which to breathe. Those who could not reach shelter would lie down on the ground and wait for the storm to pass. From late in 1933, through most of 1935, there were many of these Black Dusters. Some came as late as 1939.

These giant clouds of fine silt evidently rose to enormous heights. For example, on April 17, 1935, the *Dalhart Texan* reported that Laura Engels, famous female pilot, was forced down at Alamosa, Colorado, by a black duster. She said she struck the storm somewhere over the Texas Panhandle and though she climbed to over 23,000 feet, she could not free herself of it.

The people in Dalhart said they learned to tell where each "black" duster came from. They believed the black ones came from Kansas, the gray (ghostlike) ones from Colorado and New Mexico, the red ones from Oklahoma. But accounts in newspapers and periodicals showed that while some of the windblown silt may have come from these areas, there was more than origination there — the storms struck these areas just as they did in the Texas Panhandle. Once, three such fronts converged over Dalhart: black, red and gray.

Hoping to learn how widespread these storms were and where, in fact, they had originated, I flew to Dodge City and rented a car. From there I drove westward along the Arkansas River to Lamar, Colorado, then southward to Springfield, Colorado, south and east through Boise City, Oklahoma, and on to Dalhart. Then north through Stratford, Texas, and Guymon, Oklahoma, eastward through the Oklahoma Red Lands to Woodward and Vici, Oklahoma, then on back to Dodge.

People in each place had vivid memories of the dusters. But all felt those that struck their areas had originated somewhere else.

Most people said the dusters came on winds blowing out of the north. However, one (a red one) came into Dodge City apparently on a wind from the south, indicating, I thought, that there may have been a great cyclonic movement of dust-laden air sweeping southward along the east side of the Rocky Mountains, then curling eastward and northward after passing through the Texas Panhandle and picking up dust when passing over the Oklahoma redlands.

The breadth and the speed of movement of such dusters is indicated by the reports on the great "granddaddy duster" of April 14, 1935.

A. A. Justice, U.S. Government Meteorologist at Dodge City, noted in his daily journal that the storm struck there at precisely 2:49 P.M., bringing instant darkness. The *Panhandle Magazine* of November 2, 1980, declared there was total darkness at Liberal, Kansas, (seventy miles southwest of Dodge City), at 4:00 P.M. The caption of a U.S.D.A. photo taken at a ranch in Baca County, Colorado, says the storm struck there at 3:52 P.M. with instant total darkness. A report from Lamar, Colorado, (about 160 miles west of Dodge City), says it hit there about 4:15 P.M. also with instant total darkness. A Boise City, Oklahoma, report says it struck that town (about seventy miles south of Lamar) at 6:00 P.M., with the black dust causing much darkness until after 10:00 P.M., that drivers were unable to see their way even with headlights at full strength. The *Dalhart Texan* reported the storm engulfed Dalhart at 6:20 P.M. with similar impenetrable darkness continuing until 10:30 P.M.

These reports seem to verify that the storm struck an area over 200 miles in width and that it traveled at about sixty miles an hour. Stephen Eastin, editor of the *Range Ledger* in Cheyenne Wells, Colorado, confirms that dusters struck (and produced impenetrable darkness during school hours) as far north as Eckley, in Yuma County, Colorado.

Words do not seem adequate to describe these Black Dusters.

Perhaps the fiercest dust storm of the 1930s *was* the one on April 14, 1935, which is now remembered as Black Sunday. Flocks of crazed birds tumbled in the sky. The horizon was black, and soon the dust was so thick and everything so black, that mother's holding their children could not see them. "I thought the end of the world was coming," was said over and again.

Mr. Justice, with his meteorologist knowledge, provided us with the following description of the duster generally regarded as the "granddaddy" of all. In his official report for April 1935, he said:

"The storm that will longest be remembered came on the afternoon of Sunday the 14th, striking at 2:49 P.M. Instant darkness followed, lasting for forty minutes. Then for a period of about three hours there was darkness, with occasional breaks of very short duration. By midnight the dust became light . . .

"As a meteorological phenomenon this storm was very interesting. Many people saw the dust cloud coming, even though visibility was limited to a few miles by the dust then prevailing. The cloud extended east and west as far as could be seen in a straight line. As it came on it presented a rolling, tumbling appearance, something like a great wall of muddy water. The base of the cloud was inky black, the top portion of a lighter color, due to the amount of lighting falling on the two portions. The height of the cloud was estimated to be about 1000 feet. According to the most trustworthy observers, the upper portion of the cloud appeared to be rolling forward and downward, the extreme lower front was lined with columns of rapidly rising dust, as though these were forced out by the falling heavier air layers above and behind. Apparently this was a well-developed polar front; all the air movements in it seemed to conform to the idealized structure of a cold front. According to some who took the trouble to check up on the movements of the front of the storm, it was traveling at about sixty miles per hour in this area.

"An interesting thing observed was the great number of birds flying straight in front of the onrushing cloud. Hundreds of geese and ducks and smaller birds too numerous to count were racing for their lives . . ."

My brother Artis was once caught out near Dalhart in one of these storms. His description:

"A very majestic sight was this roiling black cloud towering a thousand feet or more above and before you. By then there was a stillness you could *feel*, and only a gentle, restless stirring of the air. Seconds later, darkness and wind. Not a very hard wind.

"Sitting in the car with the windows closed waiting for it to get light enough to see to drive, one of the boys said: 'Do you see what I see?' I looked. On the side of the road nearest the storm, every little spike on the barbed wire fence was glowing; it was a brush discharge of electricity — that phenomenon called Saint Elmo's Fire."

Beale Queen was wagon-master at the famed JA Ranch (originally the John Adair–Charles Goodnight Ranch) during much of the period of the black dusters. The ranch lay largely in the Palo Duro Canyon southwest of Clarendon, Texas.

Beale talked of sandstorms and black dusters:

"Well, in a sandstorm, that sand is clean. It will sting you and it will get into whatever you're trying to eat, but it doesn't choke you down. A sandstorm is entirely different from those dust storms. The dust storms we had would leave a kind of greasy looking dust on everything it could get to — a different color from other dust that we had.

"You'd see a black duster coming. It was just like a high wave rolling over and over toward you. When it got to you, it looked like it had hit the ground about a hundred yards on the other side of you. From then on it was so dark that you couldn't strike a match and see the light. You could see the light but you just couldn't see anything. It was the blackest dark you ever saw.

"Usually within an hour it would go over, leaving a foggy look in the air. Maybe you couldn't see over fifty or a hundred yards. And in the Palo Duro Canyon it would stay that way for weeks at a time.

"Sometimes, for at least a day in advance of the dust storms, the horses in our remuda would be nervous and just as jumpy as they could be and it was hard to control them, hard to catch them out of the rope corral, and they were not sensible and wouldn't calm down. They could feel that storm coming, and they'd stand looking north or northwest. That's where most of those dust storms came from.

"As the storm came on, the horse's tails would flare out and I guess they were full of electricity, and their tails would stick to whatever part of their body the tail touched."

Bob Langhorne, prominent Dalhart banker:

"In the years when the drouth was so bad I was in the old First National Bank and we would have the clouds almost as regularly as we had had them in years past when we didn't have a drouth and they would roll in from the northwest — which is our direction to get a rain from — and they'd be beautiful looking clouds. You would just know that it was going to rain.

"We had these large plate glass windows on the north side of our building. We'd watch those clouds as they'd roll in and in the front of them it would begin to sprinkle. Within five minutes or less after a light rain, a terrific wind would hit. Those clouds would immediately blow on off and the dust and dirt would accumulate and your windows would be darkened until you could hardly see out of them and our rain was gone. We've seen that happen so many times it just became frightening.

"The dust storms were a phenomenon within themselves. They would roll in from the north, northwest, and the entire area for several hundred miles to the north, northwest of us was also experiencing them.

"The front end of the dust storm would be this rolling, billowing cloud that would just roll in and envelope the area and then behind it would be these severe winds and practically all of them came out of the northwest. Now we would have hard sandstorms out of the southwest, but these dust storms, almost without exception came out of the northwest.

"You couldn't keep it out of the house. I don't care what kind of a house you lived in or how well built it was. When these things would roll in, those old dusters, that fine dust would just seep in and you could turn the lights on in a room and it was still dim — real dim — because of there being so much dust in the room. People would hang wet sheets, wet blankets and things over the windows trying to keep some of that out of their home."

Every person I interviewed who had experienced the Black Dusters told me they were impossible to adequately describe; yet every one eagerly told me of his or her experiences and undertook to tell me how the dusters looked and felt. None of the residents were harder hit than the housewives struggling to keep the fine, sticky, smelly silt from covering every inch of their homes. Some concept of what these dusters meant to them may be conveyed by my mother's letter of May 23, 1937:

Dear Son:
    Our weather continued hotter than blazes, with a terrific wind until Friday afternoon. Late it became quite calm and smothering hot. Your father and I were sitting in the porch swing when we noticed what seemed to be a nice cloud coming up in the northwest. It looked black, but I said at once, 'I'll bet a horse it is dirt.' Your father thought not. Then suddenly all the north horizon was yellow with dust. Harriett [my brother's wife whose home was next door] was downtown and called me by phone asking me to close her windows. (She had cleaned house all day.) I knew the monster of the sky was traveling fast so I ran out and toward Harriett's but before I could get to her walk it was so dark that I could not see where to turn in. I called back for your father to turn on our porch light so I could find the walk. Finally made it into their porch and thru the door, but the house was already in such a fog one could hardly breathe or see the lights. Everything was covered with dust before I could close the windows, tho I ran from one to another as fast as I could heel it.
    You can't imagine how those storms look when traveling. No one can who has never seen one. Artis [my brother] and Porter Montgomery had gone to the country to 'dig' for Indian artifacts or petrified fossiles said to have been uncovered by wind erosion. They saw the storm coming and started for home. Just then they had a flat tire, and they and another man worked as fast as they could changing the tire, but before they had quite finished the

storm was upon them in all its fury and almighty power. They had to sit there, what seemed to be an eternity, before they could start driving, then they all had to watch the road and creep along at a snail's pace. Meanwhile, Dr. and I sat in a dense fog, nearly crazy with uneasiness for fear that Artis had gone into a ditch, and no one knew which way he was. And the children were at the show, and Harriett had phoned them to stay there until she could see to drive down for them. Nobody could see to drive, and you may be sure there were no cars going for an hour or more. Finally all rounded in by some hook or crook, but the wind and dirt kept up its villainous work until after midnight. You should have seen our houses the next day.

Artis said they could see all over the whole country from where they were, and that for a scope of twenty miles or more they could see the dust coming. First like a dark cloud low on the earth which did not seem to move for several minutes. Then the billows of colors, rolling and tossing, so fast that before you could snap your fingers twice it was here. I said, 'Well, since it had to happen, I am sorry it did not happen while J. C. was here.' It is a sight never to be forgotten. But just to stir up a little bit of cheer, will tell you that we had a good rain Monday night on Section 18 and clear on out thru Sections 23 and 25. So much for that. It is better than for five years.

With love,
Mother

Photo of April 14, 1935 dust storm, Dunlap Ranch, Baca County, Colorado. The legend states: "Ten seconds after this picture was taken one could not see his hand in front of his face."

Courtesy U.S.D.A. Soil Conservation Service

"You'd see a black duster coming. It was just like a high wave rolling over and toward you. When it got to you, it looked like it had hit the ground about a hundred yards on the other side of you. From then on it was so dark that you couldn't strike a match and see the light. It was the blackest dark you ever saw."

— Beale Queen

Photo of April 14, 1935 dust storm taken in Baca County, Colorado.
Courtesy Library of Congress

"This dust got up into the upper cloud and air movements and then when you had a front come in, the dust, which is very fine and powdery, would come in on that front and drop down in on you instead of blowing through you like a sandstorm."
— John McCarty

The U.S.D.A. legend says this photo was made in Texas, probably in 1935. From all accounts, it is the way the April 14, 1935 duster, and many others, looked as they approached.

Courtesy U.S.D.A. photo

"A very majestic sight was this rolling black cloud towering a thousand feet or more above and before you. By then there was a stillness you could feel and only a gentle, restless stirring of the air. Seconds later, darkness and wind. Not a very hard wind."

— My brother, Dr. Artis Dawson

Homesteader's Struggles:

C. C. Lucas Family

In a matter of minutes the great black cloud had covered the horizon from east to west and was blotting out the sun . . . we all just sat silently with our wet handerchiefs over nose and mouth. . . . All the while it was so dark we could not even see each other in our cars.

— Virginia Lucas

About thirty miles north of Dalhart is the Oklahoma Panhandle, the area known as No-Man's-Land (because not a part of any state or territory) until 1880, when Congress enacted a law joining the Oklahoma Panhandle to Oklahoma Territory.

When the Panhandle became part of the Territory, the Federal Homestead Law became applicable and much of the former No-Man's-Land became open to settlement under that law. This meant that a man could acquire title to 160 acres (later 320) by meeting certain rules designed to prove intent of permanent occupancy.

Persons putting their hopes on these small parcels of land suffered the Drouth and Depression of the 1930s more severely than did their neighbors in the Texas Panhandle where the Federal Homestead law was never applicable and the pattern of land acquisition suggested larger tracts (such as the four section spreads of the Whaleys, the Steels and the Wohlfords). For example, an April 11, 1935, news story out of Washington, D.C., declared that all but three of the forty families in sixty-nine townships in Cimarron County had been driven out.

I wanted to get a firsthand account of life on such a homestead. Albert Law, Editor of the *Dalhart Texan* referred me to the C. C.

Lucas family (in 1972) then living in Dalhart. From C. C. Lucas, his wife, Zumie, and daughter, Virginia, (there on a visit from her job with the Bureau of Land Management in Arizona) I obtained the following:

In 1906, John J. Lucas, then a tenant cotton farmer in south Texas, migrated to the Oklahoma Panhandle and filed for homestead rights on a 160-acre tract in Cimarron County, about fifteen miles southeast of what is now Boise City. There he raised a family of six boys and three girls.

Others, similarly motivated, soon joined the Lucases and by about 1914, the area around Lucas's farm had become a community of homesteaders. It called itself the Union Chapel Community.

The community was compriseed of a cluster of 160-acre homestead tracts on most of which there resided a family living in a dugout. A dugout was a shelter created by digging a hole in the ground about fourteen feet wide, twenty-two feet long and five feet deep. Using concrete or boards, walls were constructed to about three feet above the surface of the earth. Sometimes the floor was covered with concrete though more commonly the earth itself formed the floor. A slanted roof of boards covered with tar paper or corrugated sheet iron would be built. In the portion of the walls above the surface of the earth, there would be windows, each capable of being opened or closed by means of a wooden flange or shutter suspended by hinges. A door on the south side (to face away from the northers) provided the means of access to and from the residence. From the ground outside, a small set of stairs led down to the level of the floor. The interior walls might be papered — often with newspaper.

The flat, treeless, landscape about the Lucas residence was dotted with these dugouts.

Sometimes a homesteader, instead of building a dugout, would construct a home of adobe (sun-dried brick made of earth mixed with dried grass or hay, or heavy clay).

In 1917, C. C., John Lucas's youngest son, and Zumie Enlow, the comely teacher of the one-room Lone Star School were married. Zumie was a daughter of another homesteading family from south Texas.

C. C. and Zumie began their married life in a fourteen-by-twenty-two foot adobe house constructed by an early homesteader on a 160-acre tract about two- and one-half miles southeast of C. C.'s parents' home. It was a "relinquishment," the original homesteader having relinquished his rights to it. C. C.'s purchase of this tract

Homesteaders' Struggles: C. C. Lucas Family 193

and an adjoining 160-acre relinquishment was financed by a loan from the Oklahoma Public School Fund with a repayment obligation of about $100 a year.

In 1918, a son was born to C. C. and Zumie. Zumie then gave up her position as teacher of the Lone Star School. In August of the following year, a daughter was born to them. She was named Virginia.

The occasion of Virginia's birth was something of a community celebration. For days before the event, the friendly people of the community had congregated in and about the residence of C. C. and Zumie.

The women took over all the housework, cooking, serving meals and cleaning up, and they brought with them food in abundance. Pork, beef or lamb canned the previous winter; fresh sweet corn, lettuce, okra and tomatoes from their gardens and wild lamb's quarter and careless weed, picked on the open prairies. This with stores of dried beans and peas, cakes, cookies and coffee. And flowers — zinnias, cosmos, lantanas, periwinkles and sweet peas. Also fluffy dresses for the baby, handsewn from flour or sugar sacks.

She was named Virginia, because some of C. C. and Zumie's ancestors had come from Virginia, and because a beloved childhood friend of Zumie's had that name.

Among those who gathered there were C. C.'s older brother Carlie, his wife, Dee, and their eight-year-old daughter, Hazel. Carlie had been operating a dairy herd on rented land in the old Cherokee Strip near Shawnee, the area settled in the Oklahoma land rush in 1892. Although moisture conditions there permitted a farmer to make a living on a tract as small as eighty acres, values had risen beyond Carlie's means. So, in 1914, Carlie had sold his dairy herd, loaded his wife and five children in a covered wagon and in two weeks was at his parents' home in the Oklahoma Panhandle searching for a farm he could buy. He found and bought (for $1500, borrowed from the State School Fund) a 320-acre relinquishment, five miles from his parents' home and forty miles west of Texhoma.

Virginia's parents had been in their home on their 320-acre farm for two crop seasons when she was born, and the land had been good to them. With his six workhorses Lucas had each year raised and harvested about fifty acres of milo maize, thirty acres of sorghum, thirty acres of broomcorn and ten acres of wheat (which was just being introduced in the area as a cash crop). The moisture had been marginal in the 1917–1918 crop year, but spring rains in

1918 had resulted in satisfactory yields. The heavy snows late in 1918, and in early 1919, had provided exceptionally good moisture for the row crops, and in August, when Virginia was born, C. C. was planning to put in fifty acres of winter wheat to take advantage of the moisture still in the ground.

He had marketed all the broomcorn and most of the wheat and maize, reserving only enough to feed the chickens. The corn was dried and stored in one end of his harness shed. He would reserve this for his four pigs. The sorghum was reserved as roughage for the workhorses, the brood cows and milk cows. Zumie's garden had kept the family in fresh vegetables and she had canned a goodly supply of okra, tomatoes, squash, and green beans. Supplies of dried beans and black-eyed peas were also at hand. Each fall C. C. had butchered a fat hog, had cleaned, salted down and dried the carcass and hung it in the smokehouse at his parents' nearby farm.

He was milking two good milk cows, providing adequate milk for the family and some cream to take to the store along with fryers and eggs to trade for salt, pepper, coffee, sugar, flour and perhaps a bolt or two of calico for Zumie's dresses.

Most importantly he had survived the severe snows and blizzards of 1918–1919 without loss of livestock. This was because all the livestock had good shelter in his feedlot. This contrasted with the results of the storms on range cattle such as those at the nearby James Brothers Ranch where the staggering losses in cattle spelled the end of that spectacular ranch operation.

So in the fall of 1919, after Virginia was born, C. C. and Zumie looked with considerable satisfaction and optimism on their fortunes.

By 1926, when Virginia reached the age of seven, four more children had been born to C. C. and Zumie. Virginia had become an able assistant to her mother in keeping house and helping care for the younger brood, carrying water to the house from the windmill and, each Saturday, helping bathe the younger children in a washtub in the kitchen. But it was not all drudgery. C. C. had acquired "Old Rabbit," an aged but gentle gray mare which Virginia was permitted to ride. In the springtime she would take horseback rides over the pasture or to visit neighbors and in the fall she would go on Old Rabbit to the Lone Star School. There, at recesses or after school, other children would join Virginia astride the willing beast. The open prairie beckoned to Virginia and she would ride Old Rabbit out over it, drinking in the invigorating dry, clean air and occa sionally dismounting to search for wild flowers which abounded there.

From time to time she would see a coyote or an antelope and she learned to spot and identify the many birds. Some were migratory like the red-winged blackbirds, woodpeckers, mockingbirds, bluebirds, doves, ducks and geese; some were indigenous to the area such as chaparrals, meadowlarks, prairie chickens, sandhill cranes and sparrowhawks. Occasionally she would ride over to the neighboring Haversticks to listen to their player piano, or to her Uncle Carlie's to listen to his battery-operated Atwater-Kent radio.

In time, C. C. acquired a second saddle horse for the children. Called "Prince," he was a fine, spirited, young bay gelding. Prince was reserved for Virginia and her older brother. The gentle Old Rabbit was left for the younger members of the family.

So, Virginia was a child of the prairie, and she loved it. Even in the winds (the ever-present winds!) Virginia found a source of invigoration and pleasure. In spring when the winds from the southwest were strongest, they would often lift the glass-like particles of sand from plowed fields and hurl them with stinging force against Virginia's face and legs. Sometimes they even obscured the sun and drove those exposed to the blowing sand to shelter.

Then, especially in the late afternoons when the wind would abate to a point where it would cease to lift and carry the sand particles, Virginia would slip a bridle on Prince, let her hair down, mount the animal bareback and race across the prairie as the western multicolored sky would come ablaze with daylight giving way to darkness.

Braced against the wind, clasping her legs tightly around the horse, she would welcome the feel and smell of the clean air filling her lungs and sending her hair streaming backward in an abandoned freedom. She would go this way as far as she could, then return, hair flowing forward and even obscuring her view, but still tingling with excitement.

Each fall during the next years following Virginia's birth, after the row crops were harvested and the winter wheat planted, C. C. and Zumie would assess their finances and debate their prospects for building a better home for the family. Every year another child was born to them and the little two-room adobe house became increasingly much too small for their brood. And, after a few years, with normal wear and tear, the adobe house had become a fragile shelter.

But each year the debate about when to build a better house would end in resolution to wait for better times.

Finally, in the spring of 1928, as C. C. surveyed his crops, he believed the good year, so long awaited, was at hand. Increasingly, since the end of the World War, world demands for wheat had risen. And with this development, the fortunes of the plains farmers had benefitted significantly. So, in 1927, C. C. had broken out an additional thirty acres and thereby increased his wheat acreage to eighty acres. Good rains, June through September 1927, had given the land a good moisture base. And equally good rains in May and June of 1928 had brought the wheat to splendid maturity.

C. C. could see that the wheat crop might even approach that of 1914, when many of the area farmers had harvested up to sixty bushels to the acre. Maybe over 4,000 bushels! — and at about two dollars a bushel, C. C.'s 1928 wheat crop looked like his bonanza.

C. C. had acquired a Ford pickup that could take the wheat rapidly to the market at Texhoma, forty miles away. He traded his ten workhorses for an International 1530 tractor and bought, on time, a threshing machine.

Eagerly, C. C. and his family awaited the time when the wheat would be ready for the harvest. And, one day late in June, C. C. determined that the time had come. Tomorrow he would hitch his tractor to his thresher and work would begin.

But, late that afternoon a menacing black cloud appeared in the north, followed by a sudden chilling breeze. And as C. C. gazed at the clouds and felt the breeze, he was gripped with fear that he might be visited by the wheat farmer's greatest enemy, *hail*.

Suddenly the sky darkened and pelting rain began to fall, quickly followed by hailstones. C. C. ordered the children to stand alongside the wooden wall which partitioned the adobe house. For he knew that a severe hail could demolish the ageing and flimsily supported roof. As the family huddled by the partition wall, the bright flashes of lightning, the loud claps of thunder, and the ear-splitting deluge of hailstones on the roof made C. C.'s fear for his family's safety obliterate, for a few moments, his realization that this event of nature would likely spell the end of his dreams of sudden wealth and a new home.

The storm lasted only a few minutes, but that was enough. When it had ended there was still enough daylight for C. C. to see that the wheat he had been about to harvest and also the sprouting maize, corn and sorghum had all been completely flattened to the ground.

Nothing could be salvaged from the wheat crop. With luck, a late but stunted crop of maize, corn and sorghum was possible, and could provide some feed for the hogs and chickens and some roughage that might sustain the cattle and horses through the winter. But there would be no crops whatever to take to market in that year. Even this devastation, however, was not without compensation to Virginia and the other children. The ground lay inches deep in hailstones. And hailstones are, after all, made of ice. Ice, for this family, was a rarity — usually found only on the water tank during winter. Immediately the children went forth with pails and gathered ice. Then the ice cream freezer was hauled out and soon they were enjoying homemade ice cream — all they could eat of it.

Of course, the storm meant that the building of the new home would have to be postponed again. But C. C. resolved that he could no longer leave his family sheltered only by the old adobe. With the help of neighbors, and at a cost of about $500, he constructed a new residence. A five-room, concrete-floored and walled basement, covered with a roof of sturdy sheeting and tar paper. On this basement he and Zumie would, some day, build the home they had planned for so many years.

Following the hailstorm in 1928, unusually good rains came and continued through 1930. In fact, in nine of the twelve years following the end of the first World War, the area enjoyed much better than average moisture. World demands for grains seemed insatiable. In 1921, wheat was bringing two dollars a bushel at Texhoma, and good prices prevailed the other years. Virgin prairielands in the Oklahoma and Texas Panhandles could be bought for as little as thirty-five dollars an acre, and word quickly spread that here a man could buy land, plant it to wheat and in one year get back his purchase price. The result was that vast areas of hitherto untouched grassland in the Oklahoma and Texas Panhandles, and in southwestern Kansas and eastern Colorado, were plowed up and planted to wheat.

Much of this new planting was by people who did not live on the land. They would plow and plant in the fall; then the following spring — if there was a good crop and prices remained up — they would return to harvest and market the wheat. If the crop was a failure or the prices fell, many would not return. They would simply abandon the plowed up land and leave its destiny to the elements.

The inevitable result of such procedures was overabundance of grains, driving prices down, and abandonment of newly plowed farmlands. Added to this condition came the Great Depression.

In spring of 1931, C. C. Lucas's eighty acres of wheat yielded a satisfactory fifteen bushels an acre, and his fall harvest of row crops (and calves) was exceptionally good. But these crops were to fall victim to the overproduction which had preceded them, and to the Depression which began in the east in 1929, but reached the prairie farmlands two years later.

By June, when Lucas's 1931 wheat harvest began, the price for wheat had dropped to eighty-five cents a bushel. And by the time he reached the Texhoma market with it, the price had plunged to twenty-four cents a bushel. His 1200 bushels sold for $288. The same amount would have brought him $4,600 in 1921! Ten yearling calves brought him $250 and his thirty tons of maize sold in the fall at four dollars a ton — half what it would have brought ten years earlier.

But he had enough corn, pummies (ground maize and cornstalks) and bundled sorghum to carry his pigs, cattle, and horses through the winter and until another year could bring fresh grasses in the pasture and new crops of grain for sale or feed. Maybe *next* year would be better . . . and C. C. and Zumie could look again at the prospect of a new house.

Virginia was thirteen years old now, and in the fall of 1931, she had gone in to Boise City to live with her father's niece, Hazel Shaw, so she could go to the Boise City High School.

C. C. Lucas doggedly turned his attention to putting in new crops. By June 1932, when Virginia came home for the summer, C. C. had a fair stand of wheat and his row crops of milo maize, sorghum and corn were coming along well, standing about six inches above their seedbeds.

He was constantly searching the skies for signs of rain, but not the kind that came. One day late in June, the heavens opened and there came a downpour of nearly nine inches. Lucas's row crops of milo maize, sorghum and corn (planted in this country between the ridges of the plowed fields) were covered with soil and the nearly matured wheat was flattened to the ground and rendered unharvestable. Lucas knew the flattened sandy soils of his fields, if left untended, would soon begin to blow and erode. He moved at once with replowing, both to keep down the blowing and to be able to replant the row crops for possible late harvest.

But many who had broken out new lands around Lucas with no

purpose other than to gamble on a good wheat harvest elected to abandon their fields to the elements. And the elements appeared to be determined to punish these farmers for their neglect and desecration of the soil. Except for the June deluge, rainfall, in all the year 1932, was at least seven inches below normal. Soon the prevailing winds from the southwest began picking up sand from the abandoned lands and carrying it away. Lucas's sprouting row crops were cut down by the blowing sand. And the sand, deposited on the pasturelands, then picked up by the next blow, was soon cutting away even the grasses upon which Lucas had depended for pasture.

Before summer was half gone, the exposure of the mother cows to the windblown sand particles had so chafed and irritated their udders that they were refusing to let their calves suckle milk from them. C. C. bought axle grease and he and Zumie would massage the mother cows' udders with this grease to try to soften them and relieve the chafing. Even so, they would have to rope the cow and hold her down in order to make her let her calf have milk. Lucas's milk cows which, in the past, had yielded two- and one-half to three gallons of milk per day were soon yielding less than half that much. Zumie Lucas's garden became entirely covered with windblown sand and there were no fresh vegetables for the table.

Lucas's supplies of pummies, sorghum, corn and maize saved from his 1931 crop were exhausted by mid-1932 and it soon became clear that there would be no replenishment for that year — for there would be no crops. None. And without them, Lucas would have no means of feeding his livestock — not even his pigs and chickens. Denied crop yields for two successive years, Lucas was without funds with which to purchase feed for the livestock, and even if he had had the money there was no feed to be had, for the crops of every farmer in the area had met the same fate as had his.

Lucas moved to cut back on the livestock, selling ten of his mother cows and three of his milk cows on the market at Texhoma. This left him with four brood cows and one milk cow. Perhaps these and his pigs and chickens could survive.

The two saddle horses, Old Rabbit and Prince, presented Lucas with an agonizing dilemma. They were growing gaunt for lack of feed. None of his neighbors would or could, take them. Besides, their removal would be heartbreaking to Virginia and the other children. He determined to keep them as long as he could possibly do so.

Spring of 1933 brought no relief from the drouth. Indeed, in the months January through July, less than two and a half inches of rain fell on the lands of Lucas and his neighbors.

A job on the new railroad being built from Elkhart, Kansas, to Boise City, provided Lucas with means to maintain his family, commencing late in 1932. His milk cow perished early in 1933, but with fifteen dollars saved from his salary on the railroad he purchased another. Now the family was subsisting largely on salt pork, dried beans, milk, biscuits and molasses.

Late in 1933, under a federal program designed to reduce starving herds, Lucas sold all his remaining brood cows at eight dollars to fourteen dollars a head. Under the program the cows were to be taken to a slaughterhouse in Amarillo for conversion into meat — distributable under the New Deal's surplus food program. The calves, however, were to be separated from their mothers, removed to a remote spot on the farm, and destroyed.

Virginia and her brothers and sisters did not watch the destruction of the calves. Instead, they huddled together in a bedroom in the basement-house. Here Virginia tried to comfort the younger children who broke into sustained sobbing at the sound of each shot signaling the death of a calf.

Now the only livestock left on the farm were the milk cow and the two saddle horses. Miraculously, the milk cow survived until late in 1934. But the saddle horses were to go earlier. In the fall of 1933, there was not only no remaining grass, there was not even a green tumbleweed left for the horses to eat. No one would buy the horses or even accept their care on any terms. Turned out upon the highway they would die of starvation or be run down by traffic, and in that case they would meet their end without even the presence of those who loved them. Each day Virginia and the other children would go into the pasture and the saddle horses would come to them. And they would pet them and pray for them and then resignedly return to the home.

Eventually the horses began eating the boards that formed the corral. Old Rabbit was the first to die. A few weeks later Prince died.

The desolation and despair which beset Virginia and her brothers and sisters was punctuated by the whining sound that would be made by vibrations in the wind of the wire on the windmill used for deactivating the wheel when strong winds threatened it. It sang a stricken, sad and lonely tune after the horses were gone.

The desperate condition to which the Great Drouth and

Depression had brought Lucas and his family typified the conditions generally existing throughout the area.

Housewives in Cimarron County formed several home demonstration groups, and pooled their resources to import salt pork, black-eyed peas, dried beans and even some fresh vegetables. These would be distributed among the members. Zumie Lucas joined one of these groups. C. C.'s job on the railroad continued through 1935.

By these means the Lucas family was able to subsist through the years 1933–1935 and to stay on their farm.

But the drouth which had commenced in 1932, continued. The rainfall for the years 1933 through 1936 averaged only ten and a half inches a year — eight inches below the average. As time went on, more and more of Lucas's neighbors packed their belongings on their jalopies and fled from that devastated land, leaving their farmlands to be further eroded by the winds and adding to the clouds of sand which settled upon their neighbors or continued on elsewhere.

The pastures, already barren of grass in 1933, continued that way, or grew into fields of tumbleweeds which would entrap the blowing sand and create huge hummocks — or would blow and lodge against the barbed wire fences which themselves would soon be covered with sand.

There was no escaping the sand, even in the best-built home. In farmhouses like the Lucas's, the sand would sift under doors and through the cracks about the windows. Often, in order to leave or enter the home, it was necessary to shovel sand from the floor or from the stairs leading down from the outside ground to the front door.

As long as Lucas's job on the railroad continued, he was able to sustain his family on his salary and to buy gasoline and oil for his tractor. With this tractor he continued doggedly to plow his farmland to do such planting as he could afford. Thus, if it ever rained he might make a crop — and even if the rain never came the plowing would help prevent the soil from blowing away.

Day after tedious day, Virginia would sit by a window and look hopefully at the sky for signs of rain. Many times beautiful rain clouds would form and she would become so convinced the rain would come that she imagined she could smell it and feel its welcoming cooling effect. Then the wind would resume and blow the clouds away. Sometimes it would even begin sprinkling, but the droplets themselves would be filled with fine sand, leaving dirty splotches on the window as the clouds left.

Often Virginia would walk out over the barren pasture and recall how beautiful it once had been, and she would look for the wild flowers she used to gather, and the lamb's quarter and careless weed she used to pick for the table. But there would be none.

And she would look and listen for the birds that had been there back when she used to ride over the pasture on Old Rabbit or on Prince. But she would find none.

The year 1934 brought death to Lucas's milk cow bought in 1933 with money earned from his job on the railroad. Nineteen thirty-four also brought the scourge of the Black Duster, blanking out the sunlight in mid-afternoon and covering the barren pastures and fields, every living thing exposed to it, and every inch within the home with fine, black, powdery, sticky, smelly silt.

It was as if nature had decided to bring a dark, soft funeral wreath with which to cover the things and the lives its fierce winds and its denial of moisture had rendered so barren.

The Black Dusters came with increasing ferocity and increasing frequency in late 1934, and early 1935.

Little Ruth Nell Shaw, the daughter born to C. C.'s niece, in Boise City in April 1934, fell victim to the Black Dusters. Virginia Lucas gave me the story:

"When the Black Dusters seemed to be coming every few days back in the fall of 1934 and spring of 1935, Ruth Nell would just cough and cough. It kept getting worse and late in 1934, Hazel asked me to come and stay with them and help look after Ruth Nell.

"They had one of the best-built houses in Boise City and they had put sort of shutters around the doors and caulked all the cracks around the windows to try to keep the dust out. Still it just filtered right on in. We even kept damp sheets hung over the windows, but couldn't keep it out.

"Little Ruth Nell's pillow and sheets and bedclothes and her face and arms and hands would get covered with the oily, sticky, black silt. She kept growing worse, and early in April 1935, she developed whooping cough. Then they took her down to Enid to get away from the dust. Two days after they got to Enid, little Ruth Nell developed pneumonia and died.

"The same day Ruth Nell died, my father's mother, Loumiza Lucas, who was eighty, also died. We always thought the dust had contributed to her death.

"Hazel and her husband owned the Boise City Funeral Home and it was right in the same house they lived in.

"It was decided to have both grandma's funeral and Ruth Nell's funeral at the same time — on Sunday, April 14, 1935. Little Ruth Nell was to be taken to Vici, Oklahoma, the next day for burial, but grandma was to be taken to Texhoma that same day for hers.

"The burial service for grandma was to take place at the Texhoma graveyard at 6:30 which would be about an hour before sunset.

"We thought it would take about three hours for the funeral procession to go the forty miles to Texhoma, because we would be driving over a somewhat bumpy dirt road, and, of course, the driver of the hearse would be going real slow so as to keep from jostling grandma too much.

"So we planned to leave about 2:30 to give us plenty of time. But the two funerals lasted longer than we had planned and by the time grandma was in the hearse and the cars all lined up to go, it was after three in the afternoon.

"Altogether, counting the children and all, we must have had about fifty people in the procession. The hearse and every auto had a chain attached to the rear and dragging on the ground. Ever since the persistent sandstorms began late in 1932, everybody kept such a chain dragging from his car. This was because the static electricity would become so bad when the sand was blowing that you had to have the chain to ground the electricity or it would foul up the ignition system and kill the engine.

"We finally got started about 3:15 and then just crept along. Of course, we would have gone slowly just because it was a funeral procession, but we went especially slow to try to make the ride over the bumpy dirt road as smooth as possible for grandma. Besides, the chains dragging behind each auto stirred up little clouds of dust, and you wanted to stay far enough behind the car in front of you and go slowly enough for the dust it kicked up to settle or blow away before you got to it. Another thing, at several places the sand had drifted across the road and two or three times we had to stop the procession while the men got out and pushed the cars to get through.

"We were about ten miles out of Boise and it was about 5:00 o'clock when we saw a big black cloud rising out of the north. The way it was roiling and spreading, we all knew right away it was a Black Duster.

"Everybody pulled to a stop and the men and women got out

and had a little conference about what we should do. We all knew the storm would be upon us in a few minutes and would probably make it pitch dark and if a high wind would follow the black cloud as was customary, then between the darkness and the wind, we would have a hard time getting to Texhoma in time for the burial. Not only that, but if we did go on and even got to Texhoma, and any of the children got out of the cars and started running around, there was danger they could get lost. The older heads counseled stopping the procession until the storm passed, then go back to Boise. Some of the women, however, felt we should not stop the funeral procession for anything. It would bring bad luck they said. But the older heads prevailed. So, as quickly as possible, the hearse and all the autos were lined up about three feet apart on the north side of the road and facing south.

"Some of the men had brought drinking water in canvas bags tied to their radiator caps, and with it handkerchiefs were dampened and made ready for use as masks. In a matter of minutes the great black cloud had covered the horizon from east to west and was blotting out the sun. It rolled over us from the rear and we all just sat silently with our wet handkerchiefs over nose and mouth. We were that way for over an hour and all the while it was so dark we could not even see each other in our cars.

"Finally, it was decided we should try to get on back to Boise. But it was still too dark for the drivers to see the road. In order for the cars to be driven without danger of running off the road and into the borrow pits alongside, four white-shirted men were lined up side by side to hold hands and walk ahead of the hearse with the cars to follow, each as close as possible behind the other.

"This way we crept back to the funeral home in Boise City, arriving at about 10:00 o'clock that night."

For the first hour or so after the funeral procession had left that afternoon, Hazel Shaw was busily packing for the trip next day to Vici, Oklahoma, where her baby, Ruth Nell, was to be buried. Hazel's niece, Carol, then four years of age, had begged to stay with her to be near Ruth Nell.

At about 5:00 in the afternoon the child happened into the yard, looked to the north and saw the great black cloud forming and bellowing forward. Instinctively she started running to *her* home, five blocks away.

The storm was upon them before Hazel and her husband noticed the child's absence. Reasoning that she would have fled homeward, but seized with fear that the child would become lost, Hazel's husband grabbed his flashlight and hurried out to search for her.

By now the swirling, powdery silt had become so thick that he could not see. Hazel described it as "not just black — not just thick — it was *black thick*. He tried his flashlight but it would not penetrate the blackness. On the sidewalk he dropped to hands and knees. With his head at this level he could see a few feet underneath the impenetrable black cloud. Staying on his hands and knees so as to see the sidewalk, he crawled the five blocks to the child's home. She had beaten the storm and was safely there."

The following day was clear and sunshiny, as if made to order to erase the memory of the previous afternoon and evening. Virginia and the others who had turned back to Boise the previous evening, again left for Texhoma to bury grandmother Lucas and Hazel Shaw and her husband left for Vici, Oklahoma, carrying the coffin of their baby, Ruth Nell.

Late in 1936, C. C.'s job on the railroad ended. Since 1931 his farm operations had produced no income whatsoever. His salary from his railroad job and a few dollars picked up now and then from hauling with his pickup or plowing for others with his tractor had been his only source of income. By these means he had sustained his family, but barely so. Nothing was left to apply on the Oklahoma School Fund's purchase-money mortgage on his farmland.

The Fund agreed to postpone mortgage payments if he would just stay on the land and keep plowing to hold down the wind erosion. Lucas then found a job driving a school bus in the Coldwater Community several miles to the south of his farm. This called for moving the family nearer to C. C.'s work. A settler who had abandoned his Coldwater farm offered it on a tenancy basis to Lucas. Lucas moved his family there and for two years tried, with his tractor, to fill the holes and flatten the sand hummocks produced on this farmland by the long drouth and constant winds and to prepare the land for planting in hope of making a crop. Eventually this last effort at farming was given up and his job driving a school bus ended. Lucas then sold his tractor and moved in to Dalhart where he could find occasional hauling jobs for his pickup.

So ended Lucas's dream of farming independence.

When I talked with Virginia Lucas and her parents thirty-six years later, they did not appear to show any scars from the hardships they had endured. The pleasant things that happened in those years seemed uppermost in their memories.

But Virginia spoke philosophically of the drouth and Depression years, and she reached in her purse and drew out a copy of a piece she had found in some magazine. It was titled "An Eleventh Commandment." It read as follows:

Thou shalt inherit the Holy Earth as a faithful steward, conserving its resources and productivity from generation to generation. Thou shalt safeguard thy fields from soil erosion, thy living waters from drying up, thy forests from desolation, and protect thy hills from overgrazing by thy herds, that thy descendants may have abundance forever. If any shall fail in this stewardship of the land, thy fruitful fields shall become sterile, stony ground and wasting gullies, and thy descendants shall decrease and live in poverty or perish from off the face of the earth.

Homesteaders' Struggles: C. C. Lucas Family 207

Abandoned farm in Cimarron County, Oklahoma, in the 1930s
Courtesy U.S.D.A. Soil Conservation Service

208   HIGH PLAINS YESTERDAYS

Abandoned farm in Baca County, Colorado, in the 1930s
Courtesy U.S.D.A. Soil Conservation Service

A "Normal" High Plains Sandstorm
Sandstorm on a farm in Baca County, Colorado. This is blowing sand, a normal occurrence on the High Plains. It was the lighter, finer, blowing silt which developed the Black Dusters of the 1930s. As Beale Queen said: "in a sandstorm, that sand is clean. It will sting you and it will get into whatever you're trying to eat, but it doesn't choke you down. A sandstorm is entirely different from those dust storms."

Courtesy U.S.D.A. Soil Conservation Service

Deserted homestead of the 1930s. Dallam County, Texas
Courtesy U.S.D.A. Photo

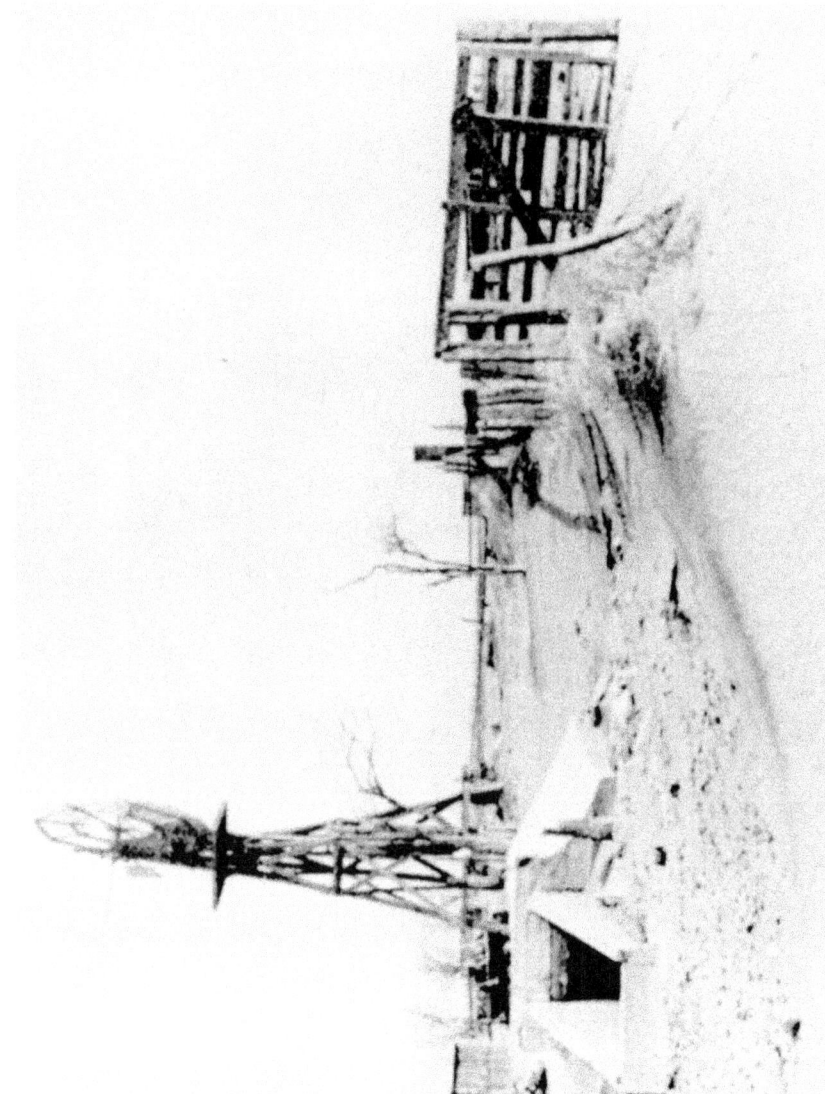

Drifting soil in a farmyard, Hartley County, Texas, in the 1930s

Clovis, New Mexico area. A formerly cultivated field that lost as much as ten feet of soil in the 1930s.

Courtesy U.S.D.A. Soil Conservation Service

The Barbed Wire Crows' Nests
Said Andy James: "I went out there to look at the old James Ranch place the other day and I can tell you that what I saw made me sick. There is not a blade of grass in miles of that place. The roads are all covered with sand. All the fences have sand held by tumbleweeds piled up on them to where you can walk over them. And right out in front of where the old ranch house used to stand, the tumbleweeds and sand had built a sand dune about as big as this Courthouse. In front of that, there used to be a pretty row of cottonwood trees that my mother planted. Now, they are all dead. In fact, there are only two of them that are still standing and all they have for branches are stubby, broken spikes. The only sign of life I saw out there was crows' nests. I ran off one old crow who was sitting in one of the trees and I looked at those nests. Those nests were made of bobwire and tumbleweed. I guess that is all the crows could find out there to build the nests with."

John McCarty, Albert Law and the Weather Reports

At last we have had two light rains, and the air is, for once, clear of dust. You know, it got so for the last month or six weeks that we did not have one half day any time without a dust storm, and some of them so bad that they entirely excluded the sun for hours, turning the day into Egyptian darkness. The blackest dark you ever looked into. . . . It seems strange and unnatural to have rain, wet ground to walk on, moist air to breathe, and real moist clouds hanging around, instead of billows of dust.

— Willie Catherine Dawson
Letter, May 15, 1935

The survival of Dalhart during the Dust Bowl days was so closely related to day-by-day weather conditions that the weather reports in *The Dalhart Texan* were uniquely colorful. The reports not only glimpse the heart of the community and its concerns, but give a genuine picture of the struggle between man and nature as it was actually lived daily.

Albert Law was editor of *The Dalhart Texan*, from 1936, until his retirement on the first of January 1982.

He had come to the paper as a reporter in 1929, the same year that Wilbur C. Hawk, Gene Howe, and John McCarty acquired the *Texan* from Herbert Walker, and McCarty came to it as editor. McCarty was moved to editorship of the *Amarillo Globe News*, in 1936, and Law succeeded him as editor of the *Texan*.

As the Great Depression began late in 1929, and was shortly followed by the Great Drouth, the writings of both McCarty and

The Dalhart Texan's *Albert Law, at his desk in 1972, many years after his colorful reporting of the Dust Bowl days.*

Law in *The Dalhart Texan* are firsthand accounts of much that went on in the Drouth and Depression years of the 1930s.

Both men did much in this period to encourage the residents to find humor amid their hardships, and to keep faith with the land. But each had his own individual style and approach.

In addition to McCarty's editorship, his work included direction of certain relief efforts. As editor, he proposed programs for rehabilitation through road building and other construction projects. In his "Cactus, Sage, and Loco" column, and elsewhere, he drafted beautiful descriptions of sandstorms and Black Dusters. He wrote scathing denunciations of the proposals of New Deal "armchair farmers" to move the drouth-stricken residents to milder and more humid climes. He urged the people *not to give up*, with such salty pieces as his "Grab a Root and Growl," and "Spartans!" pieces, likening the hardy folk sticking it out to Spartans of old. McCarty organized Old Loco's LAST MAN CLUB, in which each member pledged that, barring acts of God, unforeseen personal tragedy or family illness, he would be *The Last Man to Leave*. He forgot, however, to include an order by one's boss requiring a change of location as an acceptable excuse for not being the last to leave. So in March 1936, when Hawk died and *Amarillo Globe News* needed a new editor, he was called to that position.

One piece of McCarty's writing particularly deserves preservation, in my opinion. It is the piece written in 1935, in humble praise of the majesty and force of the Black Duster. He called it, "Tribute to Our Dust Storms," and it read, in part, as follows:

> Let us praise nature and the powerful god that rules nature. Let us in centurion tones boast of our terrific and mighty dust storms and of a people, a city and a country that can meet the test of courage they afford and still smile. Let us humbly and in shame admit our part in the rapacity our land has suffered at our hands, but vow, with the raging winds of the prairies, that we will with God's help carpet our lands once again with grass and vegetation, and with our heads unbowed, our spirit undaunted, view the magestic splendor and beauty of one of the great spectacles of nature gone rampant — a Panhandle dust storm — and smile even though we may be choking and our throats and nostrils so laden with dust that we cannot give voice to our feelings. Let us realize that the force and the god capable of such gigantic and destructive demonstrations of nature can be just as calm and tender as the hushed quiet before the storm or the bright day which follows.

In a 1972 interview, John McCarty told me of another notable, sand, dust, and rainstorm. "I'd just been to Guymon and had visited with the people up there. We encouraged them in the 1930s," McCarty said.

We did everything to keep the moral and the spirit of the people up, and we encouraged them in the formation of their Pioneer Days, a celebration on May the second. They started that back in 1934.

They had trade trips and things and of course we went with them. The people of Dalhart made one batch of trips with them, the Guymon folk came into Dalhart. We all went out and met out on the edge of town. Boy! There had been a sandstorm blowing first, and right in behind that was a dust front. It was in from New Mexico, and it was red. So we put a big flatbed truck in the middle of the street and got the Guymon boosters on that. *They* had a quartet — *we* had our Dalhart quartet — and both groups joined hands. The dust was just coming in over us in billows, and it was trying to rain. Once in awhile the rain would come down through there. It would make a great puddle of red mud, almost an inch and a half thick. But we all stayed right there and listened to the quartets. Of course the crowd was joining in. They were always singing *Old Faithful*. It was quite popular at that time and you know. 'Old Faithful, we rode the range together' . . . What a time and what a storm! To me, it was one of the most dramatic experiences illustrating the spirit of the people. And by God they didn't go inside either. They just stayed out there in all that weather singing.

The wonderful spirit of these people and what they put up with! They could stick it out and laugh about it. It was an interesting thing. It was amazing.

From McCarty's Old Loco Column:

May 1, 1935: T. L. Jacques, who was just in and joined the Last Man Club says he has seen it worse here. He said about 1907 the sand would get waist deep in the streets here in one night. He said one night the sand blew in against a small house his brother Gus was living in and covered up the house, so that they had to dig Gus out the next morning. Mr. Jacques believes the wind was a lot worse then than now also. He said it was nothing uncommon for the wind to pick up cinders, pebbles and coarse gravel and severly beat up the poplars that exposed their faces to the wind.

All I've got to say is that if Mr. Jacques will just keep that Last Man Pledge and hang on we'll show him some sandstorms that are sandstorms before many more seasons. Anyhow, I saw a cow leaning against a big telegraph pole yesterday nibbling away the short grass showing up through the sand, I'll bet Mr. Jacques never saw a cow so thin she had to lean up against a telephone pole to keep from blowing away and yet still have enough guts, hope, faith and courage to nibble around in the sand for short grass. If I could get her pedigree, number and name, I'd enroll that cow in my Last Man Club. She had the old Dalhart spirit.

Then later, of course, McCarty went to the *Amarillo Globe News*.

But Albert Law stayed on, and continued with his own distinctive reportorial style. His reports dramatized the land-saving effects of following the teachings of the U.S. Soil Conservation Service, and of H. H. Finnel, director of its local Demonstration Project, that farmers use contouring and terracing, and avoid destruction of stubble or other soil-holding vegetation. His accounts served as powerfully persuasive editorials.

Law was best, perhaps, at finding and expressing color and interest in what most influenced and interested the people — the weather. In doing this, he could make one feel — and almost like —

the sting of the wind-blown sand, the dreadful heat of midsummer, or the bone chilling cold of a norther. He could make the reader derive hope of relief from the drouth because of a heavy mist, or the smell of possible rain. Some examples follow.

July 12, 1933. On the heels of a barrage of dust from the southwest, .13 of an inch of rain fell in Dalhart late Tuesday. Temperature reached 103°.

July 27, 1933. (A Fox Hardware Advertisement) Aside from the fast, hard, 8 inch rain of June 1932, we have had but little in the way of moisture for two years. It seems we are due.

November 2, 1933. Clouds that came up rapidly toward noon Wednesday blanketed the entire north Panhandle of Texas, Oklahoma, Kansas and New Mexico with rain that ranged from one-quarter of an inch to two inches yesterday afternoon and last night. Wheat farmers this morning were jubilant.

December 2, 1933. Records at the U.S. Government Field Station four miles southwest of Dalhart, where weather data has been kept since 1906, showed that rainfall in the Dalhart area, as registered there, is 7.86 inches behind the average. The first eleven months of this year totaled 10.14 inches of precipitation against an average of 18 inches.

February 26, 1934. Old Man Winter set a new season low Sunday night with 6° above zero, according to the U.S. Field Station. The Rock Island Lines reported a skift of snow from Dalhart to Liberal.

March 30, 1934. Shrieking Windstorm Causes Great Damage in Dalhart. The biggest single damage was at the ice dock, owned by the West Texas Utilities Co. and the Rock Island Lines. Eleven hundred feet of the huge structure was torn and twisted leaving only 120 feet standing.

The northbound Denver train due here at about 10:20 last night was approximately thirty minutes late as a result of sand drifts on the tracks between here and Channing.

April 18, 1934. Tuesday's rain total in Dalhart still stood at .40 of an inch this morning. The total for the week is .65 of an inch or since January 1, precipitation has been 1.08 inches, about 50 per cent of normal, the station said.

However, many farmers report an unexpected amount of moisture in the soil and say they could plant except they fear high winds would cut off the young vegetation after it is up.

May 1, 1934. Whipping in from the east, rain clouds doused scattered Panhandle communities with showers and gave a few places heavy rains last night. Precipitation came as near to Dalhart as Dumas, Four Ways and Tascosa.

May 2, 1934. Preceded by a terrific dust storm, rains swept into Dalhart late Tuesday giving .21 of an inch of moisture, according to the U.S. Field Station. It raised the year's total to about 1.45, about 40 per cent of normal.

May 21, 1934. Last Friday, with 98°, established this month as the third hottest May in the history of the U.S. Field Station here. May, 1918, had a 99° and the same month in 1927 had a 100°. May, 1925, had 96°.

May 22, 1934. The big old hospitable face of the north Panhandle country, drawn, dry and cracked from months and months of drouth, relaxed into a broad smile today after a rain which ranged from $1/4$ to 2 inches splattered over it slowly and methodically for the past twelve hours. Farmers who have hung on by the skin of their teeth picked up their belts a notch and prepared to plant row crops.

August 13, 1934. The terrific heat has practically ruined hopes for a crop throughout the Middle West and the only remaining hope is that sufficient winter moisture can be received for the planting of wheat. The corn crop in Kansas is only 9 per cent of normal with the lowest harvest ever made being freely predicted.

August 17, 1934. For the 34th day this summer heat Thursday reached 100° or above. The mark Thursday was 100° according to the U.S. Field Station southwest of the city. Normally this section has four days each summer of 100° or more, the Station said.

August 27, 1934. Rain was slowly falling this morning and bringing cheer to farmers throughout the northern part of the Panhandle.

September 1, 1934. Walls of water from heavy rains northwest of Dalhart were threatening to wash out a bridge across the Punta de Agua where it is crossed by the highway. Water was said to be the highest that it has been since this country has been settled. Carrizo Creek is filled and out of the banks with floodwaters. Visitors to Rita Blanca Lake say that it is filling rapidly and should be full by night. The rain here Friday night brought the total for this year up to 5.93 inches. The average rainfall for this section for one year is 18.5 inches.

November 16, 1934. Fingers of fog dressing the world in gray, this morning further buoyed spirits of northwest Panhandle residents. Since September 1 precipitation in this territory has been normal, records at the Field Station show. Since January 1 total precipitation has been 9.51 inches, the Station revealed.

November 27, 1934. Howling in on a chill north wind, snow

last night left only a trace of its furrow wind journey southward. Streets this morning had only a skift of snow and the U.S. Field Station, 4 miles southwest of Dalhart, reported only a trace of moisture. The temperature dropped to 24 degrees, within one degree of the coldest of the winter, recorded the morning of November 22. At 7:30 this morning the mercury had come up to 30°, the Station said.

February 10, 1935. On the heels of a brisk east wind, moisture in the form of mist began falling in Dalhart about midnight last night amounting toward noon today to .15 of an inch. The fall was .03 of an inch between early this morning and 10:15 A.M. when the mist began turning to snow. This follows .13 of an inch of rain here early Thursday morning, giving the total for this year to date of .28 of an inch.

February 19, 1935. Saturday turned out to be a freak day in that the wind blew from at least two directions — west and north — and that dust and rain played hide and seek with each other in this immediate vicinity.

February 22, 1935. Rolling out of the northwest, appearing at times like a giant range of mountains, then as swirling vapor, a dust storm descended on Dalhart between 6:30 and 7:00 last night. Objects a half block distant were obliterated or only loomed at intervals between the stifling dust clouds. Dust seemed to float in the air. It settled over sidewalks and pavements as a fine snow leaving traces of footprints and automobile wheels this morning.

February 25, 1935. Scourging a howling dust storm ahead of him, old King Winter again claimed possession of the Texas Panhandle Sunday night sending the mercury scurrying to 8° above zero.

April 15, 1935. Black robed, regal, swift and menacing, the great-granddaddy of all Panhandle dust storms engulfed this area at 6:20 o'clock Sunday evening. Traffic was paralyzed. The darkness was like midnight though there had been a brilliant sun a moment before. Former dust storms had rolled up slowly. This one moved with awe inspiring speed.

After it struck, people in the same car could not see each other. Powerful electric lights were invisible across the street. People became lost in the city. One nine-year-old lad laid out three- and one-half hours within less than a block of several houses. One man was within 75 feet of his barn when the storm struck. It took him more than an hour to find his way to it.

Thanks are due the Dalhart Fire Department and the West Texas Utilities Company for the fine bath the streets in the downtown section got this morning. The fire boys donated their services and the West Texas Utilities donated the water. A noticeable improvement in the atmosphere was evident after the streets and sidewalks were washed.

May 17, 1935. The great moisture offensive started two weeks ago by courageous little snowflakes pointing into Dalhart in the teeth of a four year drouth and unprecedented dust storms moved to new victories this week.

This morning Dalhart and this area had had 1.49 inches of rain since Tuesday night. This was in addition to .28 two weeks ago, ushered in by the little white messengers of a justified faith in the great Texas plains. Rain is still falling through most of this sector. Up to yesterday morning .66 of an inch of rain had fallen.

Farmers and ranchers looked forward confidently to a great year. Unusually heavy grain sorghum plantings are likely, to help overcome wheat losses due to drouth. Ranchers feel that grass lands will stage a phenomenal comeback from the searing winds of the past two or three years.

May 21, 1935. Dust billowed over the Panhandle yesterday; resumed the attack this morning, shattering the belief that the first sizeable rain would constitute wind erosion control in this area.

The dust followed on the heels of an inch and $^3/_4$ rain; ranging up to four inches in many parts of the Dalhart territory. As early as Sunday sand rode across denuded pastures and farmlands, the moisture within a fraction of an inch of the surface being powerless to stop the stinging devastating attack of the hurtling particles.

The rain last week proved the effectiveness of contouring and terracing. On land neither contoured or terraced about half an inch of the inch and a half rain ran into lakes, highway ditches, or other waste places. On terraced land it was all saved, and on land both terraced and contoured it was held virtually where it fell. With terraces alone the distribution was not so even.

June 17, 1935. Rolling up out of the northwest, clouds at noon drenched Dalhart in a miniature cloudburst. Estimates are [that] at least an inch of rain fell. The U.S. Field Station, 4 miles southwest, got only a sprinkle. How far the downpour extended in other directions could not be determined before the *Texan* went to press.

More moisture refreshed the Texas Panhandle early this morning. The Field Station near Dalhart registered .11 of an inch, bringing to 1.09 inches total rain since last Friday night."

Hail, some of it the size of large marbles, pelted lustily in

Dalhart for a few minutes late Sunday afternoon. Damage, if any, was light; moisture was only a trace.

June 21, 1935. Mother Nature flipped her skirts in high disdain again Thursday in repudiation of the talk that wind erosion is past. She flounced through the northwest Panhandle Thursday afternoon, accompanied by billowing clouds of dust that whipped up out of the northwest.

Many have taken the attitude that with rains apparently starting again, the drouth definitely broken, that wind erosion control methods are a nuisance, a needless expense and totally unnecessary. This is revealed by random street talk among various classes of persons.

Thursday made the second or third time within a short period that had just drunk deeply of rains ranging from $1/2$ to several inches of moisture. As soon as the actual mud is gone from the top of the ground the soil is ready to blow again, proponents of the control point out. Only a vegetative covering, blanketing the soil, is adequate protection, say agricultural experts.

June 22, 1935. Following the hottest day of the year — 102° at the U.S. Field Station near here, Dalhart was lashed last night with a howling wind out of the northeast. Sand was picked up from fields, soaked only a few days ago, and hurled far and wide. Harbingers of the coming gale appeared about noon yesterday when a sand bank appeared high in northern skies. Sand drifted lazily into Dalhart all afternoon on a mild north wind that later became a gale.

For this writer, the highest point in Albert Law's colorful reporting was reached in his reports in 1935, about the efforts of one Tex Thornton to bring rain to the Dalhart area by use of TNT.

The April 29, 1935, edition of *The Dalhart Texan,* reported that a group of Dalhart businessmen had "guaranteed $300 to Tex Thornton, noted oil well shooter, and explosive expert of Amarillo, and told him to start moving his equipment in to bomb the skies in an effort to produce rain."

I received this newspaper clipping, and the following note from my father, dated the first of May.

. . . Wind and dust as usual. Tex Thornton now exploding T.N.T. four miles west of town. Exploded much this evening, and is now shooting every twenty minutes. The balloons did not arrive but will be here tomorrow. So far, I haven't had to get rain coat or umbrella. 'Tis now ten P.M.

Here the 1st of May and the country looks like dead of winter except a little foliage on trees and not much of that, 'tis really getting to the breaking point, people's nerves are slipping, many sick and many on the ragged edge, just holding up on their nerve, in that condition just a little trouble with lungs and they can not resist.

Reporter Law's view of the events were as follows:

May 2, 1935. Starting at 2:30 yesterday afternoon, Thornton and his bombs stunned a howling souwester into temporary submission. Awed, the dust storm, which a few moments prior had been whipping with unholy abandon the seared prairie where the experiment is being held, watched with bated breath the rapid series of early explosions. Then realizing, as clouds approached, the danger to its grip over this drought ridden sector, it rallied its sand legions and by 6:00 o'clock had forced Thornton and his helper, Tom Eldridge under cover.

Thornton caught the wind napping again at 8:00 o'clock and started more blasting, but the clouds had been beaten so far down by the stinging dust of the afternoon that they could not be wooed back. Gigantic calcium flares were used last night, casting a weird eerie light giving Thornton the appearance of a director of a huge inferno.

Bombing was discontinued this morning as the barometer indicated wind and high clouds for today. Gas balloons to carry TNT bombs to cloud ceiling will be delivered this afternoon to Thornton who has pitched camp on the wind whipped prairie, ready to blast aid to any moisture laden clouds that venture over this harrassed land of dust and drought.

A sprinkle of rain fell in Dalhart during the height of the sandstorm yesterday afternoon, when Thornton was putting TNT to get the Vitamin K relief. [See the end of this chapter for explanation of Vitamin K.] Rain peppered down in the Chamberlain and Conlen communities east of Dalhart late Wednesday, and more fell here last night according to persons who were up.

May 3, 1935. Tex Thornton, Amarillo explosive expert engaged by Dalhart businessmen and farmers and ranchers of this area to bomb the skies to induce rain, announced at 11:30 this morning he would resume the attempt at 4:00 on the Billy Jarrett place four miles northwest of Dalhart on the South Sudan Road. Everyone is invited to watch the experiment though warned to stay at a safe distance.

Thornton is bringing special suits and masks so that the most vicious sallies of wind and dust cannot deter him in his efforts to aid moisture laden clouds to drop their cargoes on the parched plains. Small gas balloons will carry the TNT bombs to cloud ceiling. Strange will control the balloons so they cannot float loose and endanger anyone. He also will have some other special type aerial bombs.

Low clouds rolled into Dalhart this morning, van-guard of those that were laying down a barrage of snow at Tucumcari; that at noon had forced the battle lines of the tyrant dust back at Nara Visa, forty-five miles west of here.

Barometric conditions are favorable for the bombing, the weatherman said. Snow was also reported from Tucumcari west of Vaughn and east to Wilderado. Snow is also reported as far west as Albuquerque.

Saturday, *May 4, 1935*. WET SNOW COVERS PANHANDLE; MOISTURE HERE IS .10 OF AN INCH. Dust is Defeated by Leaden Skies.

May 4, 1935. Optimism of nitroglycerin power has come down with each individual snowflake since the little white messengers of a justified faith and hope in the great Texas plains started their victorious offensive against the twin tyrants of dust and drouth at 3:00 P.M. Friday. THE TYRANT KINGS WHO HAVE RULED THE NORTH PLAINS WITH THE STINGING LASH OF SAND LADEN WINDS AND THE THROTTLING POWER OF CHOKING DUST CLOUDS FOR FOUR YEARS THIS MORNING WERE COMPLETELY ROUTED, SCURRYING BEFORE THE MACHINE GUN LIKE PELTING OF THE MYRIAD SNOWFLAKES. Leaden skies, grim, determined, rolled reserve ammunition to the front lines as the tyrants fled releasing their grip on the roiling soils of broad and fertile Panhandle farm and ranch lands.

Tex Thornton, Amarillo emperor of high powered explosives, watched the moisture invasion this morning with growing satisfaction. Last Saturday he was engaged to bomb the skies here for moisture and last Wednesday opened his bombardment to rout the tyrant kings. At noon today he said he planned no bombing so long as the present snowfall continued. It's getting along all right, he said.

Moisture at the U.S. Field Station four miles southwest of Dalhart, was .10 of an inch at noon, having been .03 of an inch at 8:00 this morning. Snow still sang merrily through the air at 12:30 P.M., with the moisture total mounting steadily. This is the most moisture since the first week in March, the Field Station said.

The Denver lines at noon reported two inches of snow on the

ground from Texline, thirty-six miles northwest of here, to Pueblo. Much had fallen and melted. Snow was falling in Denver. From Texline southeast to Dalhart snow was mostly melting as it fell. The Rock Island estimated three inches had fallen at noon here. The Denver said the snow had extended as far south as Amarillo.

The Rock Island at noon reported four inches of snow having fallen at Nara Visa, forty-five miles west of here, Logan and San Jon. Ten inches at Tucumcari, two to three inches at Dalhart, Vega, Wilderado, Groom, and Amarillo. Roughly the boundaries of the snow belt seem to be from Vaughn, New Mexico, east to Sayte, Oklahoma, from Vaughn east to Guymon, Oklahoma, from Guymon to Sayre, and all points west; and from far below Amarillo to Denver, Colorado, and north the snow pushing into Wyoming, it was said.

The temperature at the Field Station here dropped to thirty-one last night but experts said they believe fruit and other vegetation was not damaged because of the moisture.

May 6, 1935, Monday. Snow, Sleet and Rain Bring Moisture to Area; Explosives Expert is Happy

Snow which started at 3:00 P.M. Friday later turning to sleet and then rain brought the Dalhart area .25 of an inch of moisture, according to records at the U.S. Field Station four miles southwest of here Sunday afternoon. Tex Thornton, Amarillo explosive expert who had been engaged by Dalhart businessmen, farmers and ranchers a week ago Saturday, to bomb the skies for moisture, left for home Saturday night. Men prominent, in the move to bring him here started by Frank Machokta, farmer, near Dalhart, were well pleased with results. "We'll bring him back again if the drouth returns," they declared. Others discounted the benefits.

Thornton and his assistant Tom Eldridge, also of Amarillo started their Saturday bombing about 2:00 P.M. after the morning snow flurries had ceased. In fifteen minutes after the first discharge roared into the moisture laden skies floating past, sleet was falling. In fifteen minutes rain had started which by 4:00 was so heavy at the site of the bombing that a ranch house 300 yards distant, could not be seen. At noon Saturday, moisture was only .10 of an inch.

Thornton Saturday was using two aerial TNT torpedoes, specially made by him and one ground charge every ten minutes. Bombing continued about three hours. Three of the special torpedoes, which ranged up to a thousand feet are equivalent to a quart of nitroglycerin. Some of the ground charges comprise as many as ten sticks of TNT, dynamite or nitroglycerin solidified, these ten stick charges equal to about two quarts of nitroglycerin, Thornton explained.

An idea of the power in these charges can be seen in the comparison of nitrogylcerin and sixty percent dynamite, ordinarily the highest type sold commercially, Thornton said. A quart of nitroglycerin weighs $3.^3/_4$ pounds. The same weight in sixty percent dynamite is at least thirty percent less powerful.

Thornton was modest as congratulations and thanks poured in on him late Friday and all day Saturday. "I did the best I could," he said "I'm mighty glad that the people of Dalhart and the Panhandle got moisture and if I had anything to do with it I'm doubly glad."

So, it would seem, a good time was had by all.

Charles E. Johnson, who was the manager of the J.C. Penney Company in Childress, and R. S. Brashears, at that time publisher of the *Childress Index*, sent a telegram to Dalhart, in care of Editor John L. McCarty.

> WISH YOU FELLOWS WOULD QUIT STIRRING UP THE DUST UP THERE. IT IS GETTING IN OUR EYES. BELIEVE BATTERY OF WATER SPRINKLERS WOULD BE MORE EFFECTIVE THAN TNT.

People found laughter in the most trying times.

Gene Howe, ("Old Tack,") editor of the *Amarillo Globe News*, in a hilarious article, claimed the blinding dust storms must contain vitamin K, because people felt so much better when the storms were over.

A Long Dead Outlaw Brings A Sense Of Relief From Drouth and Depression

I wish they'd hurry up. I want to be in Hell in time for supper.
— Tom (Black Jack) Ketchum

Old-timers of the Dalhart area say that, during the Drouth and Depression of the 1930s, there was little other than playing softball and hunting arrowheads, to relieve people of the boring hopeless tedium visited upon them by the deadening effect of curtailed business activity, the constant and unrewarding hope for rain and the ever present dust-laden wind.

In 1933, however, there was a strange, gruesome occurrence that brought, in a perverse way, a welcome respite.

The occurrence referred to was the exhumation and reburial of one Tom Ketchum, otherwise known as "Black Jack" Ketchum, a man who had been hanged in 1901 for attempted train robbery.

In a way, Black Jack Ketchum ranks as one of Dalhart's best known characters — although Clayton, New Mexico, forty-four miles northwest of Dalhart has the much better claim on him since it was there that he was tried, sentenced, hanged and buried.

Black Jack's hanging occurred in the first year of Dalhart's existence but the stories of it, and of the exploits attributed to him, were a part of the traditional lore of the town. Here, though surely not a soul felt a desire to emulate him, many seemed to look back at him with a sort of irreverent sense of admiration, perhaps seeing him as an out of this world character who epitomized rebellion against all things orthodox and proper, and a devil-may-care attitude of, *To hell with it all.*

A Long Dead Outlaw Brings a Sense of Relief

It is a strange fact that somehow, perhaps especially in sparsely settled communities such as those of the Dalhart and Clayton areas, persons achieving reputations as ruthless gun-toting outlaws in the early days of the West were often remembered long after most of the upright and law-abiding citizens were forgotten. Jesse James, Butch Cassidy and his Wild Bunch and Billy the Kid were good examples.

One might think that in 1933, thirty-two years after Black Jack Ketchum's demise, the memories of him would have faded into oblivion. Such memories may have faded a bit or become blurred by the many versions of his exploits that came from the pens of his chroniclers but a few facts were clearly remembered by all: He was a cowboy turned outlaw who had tried to hold up a passenger train all by himself. In this attempt he had been shot and captured; for it he had been indicted, convicted and sentenced to death by hanging; on mounting the scaffold and taking his place on the trap door, he had jauntily admonished the sheriff to *Let 'er go!* — and when his body reached the end of the rope, his head had been completely severed from his body. Some said he was rather handsome, and he was only in his early thirties.

His act of attempting a train robbery all by himself was an injudicious act of derring-do, an act which alone would have brought him a certain kind of fame. For the records of past train robberies establish that such an act requires the services of several desperados, one to hold the getaway horses at an appointed spot, one to hold the engineer and fireman at gunpoint, and one or more to uncouple the express car from the balance of the train and — after the engine and express car had been moved a proper distance — to break open the express car, take care of the expressman, dynamite the safe and sack up the loot.

Even more rare — and hard to believe, by those knowledgeable about hanging procedures — was the fact that this man's head was somehow wrenched from his body as a result. His chroniclers had suggested numerous reasons for that. They suggested it was due to Black Jack's weight or that the fall had exceeded the accepted length, or that sandbags used the night before to test the rope had remained tied to it (adding intolerable weight), or that Sheriff Garcia had greased the noose to be sure it would do its job.

None of these theories seemed to satisfy persons knowledgeable about human anatomy and hanging procedures. That it was a very rare occurrence was well known and the fact that it happened here and was not satisfactorily explained, did much to keep the legend of Black Jack alive.*

Other accounts of Black Jack's life — and death — had abounded in earlier days. These included several books and numerous magazine and newspaper articles. Anyone visiting Clayton's Eklund Hotel Bar could see on the wall a framed photograph of Black Jack exhibiting his great shock of black hair, his bushy black moustache and his carefree air. Also in the Eklund Bar were photographs of Black Jack on the gallows at his hanging and of his headless body lying on the ground beside a great pool of blood.

Perhaps it was because of these reminders that, over the years, a constant stream of curious travelers had come to seek out the grave in which Black Jack's body had been deposited. That grave was in a seldom used repository for the dead on a remote cactus covered hillside about a mile northeast of the Clayton city limits.

In 1933, at the insistence of a group of old-timers, it was decided that the body of the man remembered by many as "New Mexico's most famous outlaw" deserved a better resting place. There was now a well established and well managed cemetery for Clayton and the decision was that Black Jack's body should be moved there. It was this decision which resulted in a series of events which, as I have said, brought to the area's citizenry a pleasant respite from the ravages of the Drouth and Depression.

In the September 9, 1933, edition of *The Dalhart Texan* Albert Law reported that the exhumation was to occur at 2:00 P.M. the following day, which was a Sunday, that elaborate ceremonies were planned; a Mr. H. H. Everitt would speak of Black Jack's career at the reinterrment rites and that a moving picture company would send a photographer. Present would be several who had witnessed the hanging — A. W. Thompson, then of Denver, Jack Potter,

---

* In 1977, a professor of Forensic Medicine at Glasgow University declared that: "At a properly conducted judicial hanging, such a thing is quite impossible." A well-researched book on hanging titled *Hang by the Neck*, published by Charles C. Thomas of Springfield, Illinois, in 1967, cites only three such decapitations, Black Jack's being one of them. The book seems to suggest, but does not conclude, that the manner of tying the knot may hold the answer. The curator at the little museum in Cimarron, New Mexico, is positive this is the answer. He exhibits two loops with knots above them. One, he says, is a correctly tied hangman's loop and knot. The loop on this one will not slip. The other, though it looks like the nonslip hangman's knot and loop, allows the loop to pull closed when the rope is pulled. If the latter type was used on Black Jack, it could well explain his decapitation.

prominent Clayton cattleman, Vincent Garcia, cousin of Salomi Garcia, the sheriff who had been in charge of the hanging, Tom Gray, R. W. Isaacs, and Carl Eklund all of Clayton — and many others whose names were not learned.

Law's article then recounted much that had been told about Black Jack that operated to make him a legendary devil-may-care figure. He (Tom) was the brother of Sam Ketchum, who had been killed in a pitched battle with a posse in Turkey Canyon in New Mexico, following an 1899 train robbery in which Tom Ketchum took no part. It was believed that in 1891, he and his brother Sam were the men who robbed a grocery store owned by Levi and Morris Herzstein at Liberty, New Mexico, and later killed Morris Herzstein when he tried to trail them. However, no indictments had ever followed the incident.

James D. Horan's book, *Desperate Men*, based on Pinkerton files, puts the Ketchums with Butch Cassidy's Wild Bunch when on the dodge in Alma, New Mexico, in July 1899. The train robbery which resulted in Sam Ketchum's death, followed. Tom (Black Jack) did not participate, and the solo effort in August that year that ended his career, is the only one in which the book says he participated. Horan wrote,

> . . . Curry and Logan then decided to leave the Hole in the Wall and enlist under Butch Cassidy, who was becoming the most talked about outlaw in the West. On August 18, 1897, with nearly a hundred riders, the Logans and Curry left for Cassidy's headquarters at Powder Springs, a few miles north of Brown's Hole.
>
> With the Logan and Curry gang and the Ketchum brothers and their riders moving in to join Cassidy, the Wild Bunch was now, without a doubt, the largest and strongest outlaw band in Western history.
>
> On April 25, 1898, President William McKinley declared that a state of war existed with Spain. — Cassidy, in a burst of patriotism, proposed to the riders that they select a group and call it the Wild Bunch Riders. . . . Steamboat Springs, Colorado, was selected as the meeting place.
>
> Here was Harvey Logan, Elza Lay, Camilla Hanks, Blackjack Ketchum and his brother Sam, who had come in from Texas way, Ben Kilpatrick, Harry Longbaugh, the Sundance Kid and all the rest of the less important thieves and rustlers who had heard about the great plan. Everyone wanted to ride to Denver and enlist.

In the summer of 1899, Blackjack Ketchum and his brother Sam were allied with the Wild Bunch now on the dodge at Alma, New Mexico. Sam led the gang's next strike. Cassidy may have planned it but Ketchum was the leader that night. — The other riders were Elza Lay, Harvey Logan and Deaf Charley Hanks. The holdup took place at 11 p.m., July 11, 1899. . . . at Folson, New Mexico. . . . Sam [then fatally wounded] admitted he was Sam Ketchum, brother of Tom Ketchum, the original Blackjack.

The Wild Bunch riders were still a magnet for violence and death. Blackjack Ketchum became a wolf, as they said, to hold up the Southern Pacific singlehanded. It was a bungling job, done more in rage over Sam's death than a desire for money.

Blackjack was sentenced to death, some say pressured by the railroads to the gallows, and still big and handsome, with his mustache carefully trimmed, stepped on the trap.

Let 'er go, he said calmly and disappeared in the hole. The hangman was an amateur who had bungled the job. The sandbags were too heavy and the outlaw was decapitated.

Possibly due to the poor means of communication at the time, there seems no solid record of any killings on the part of Tom Ketchum. But there was something about him that inspired the imagination and romanticism of those privileged to meet, see and hear him after his capture and incarceration. Thus, Albert Law, dealing in 1933 with the impressions of Black Jack recounted by earlier reporters declared:

"Though his record is dark and his name still sinister, Thomas E. (Black Jack) Ketchum, one of New Mexico's most famous badmen, was a paragon of courage, with nerves of steel and a heart of flint. He was no cowering gangster, bolstered with bombs and machine guns, and cut his swath to freedom through the ranks of those equipped as well as he, so far as guns and bullets went. The early history of this man of granite is shaded with doubt. The Ketchum boys were marked men, but no man could beat them to the draw; no posse could run them to earth among the boulders and canyons of their Northeastern New Mexico haunts."

Telling of the solo train robbery which spelled Black Jack's doom, Law said:

"The *Night Flyer* often carried money in those days because there was no bank in Clayton and when the saloons wanted money they wired Trinidad banks to express it down. The Black Jack gang wandered into Arizona where they quarreled, and all deserted their chief, even Tom's brother, Sam.

A Long Dead Outlaw Brings a Sense of Relief 233

"Black Jack, now a lone wolf, returned to his old haunts, assertedly with two more notches on his gun, for two fresh graves in Arizona. He decided to hold up the *Flyer* alone. He cached his dynamite and tied his horses at Twin Mountains. In the blackness of night, August 16, 1899, he swung on to the front of the baggage car, as the fast mail shrilled out of Folsom. At the Twin Mountain curve the engineer felt the muzzle of a rifle in his ribs and heard a sharp command to stop. Black Jack's eyes flashed with mad lust that night. He brooked no delay.

"Passengers hurtled from their seats as the *Flyer* screamed to a halt. Frank Harrington, conductor, now a Houston insurance man, realized that for the third time, his train was being robbed. With the rear brakeman he made it to the baggage car where he stumbled over the mail clerk, writhing in agony on the floor, shot in the face by the bandit.

"Black Jack was on the ground, cursing and raging, threatening to kill both the engineer and fireman if they didn't hurry and uncouple the baggage car from the rest of the train. Suddenly the brakeman moved his position, giving Harrington his chance. He leaned out the baggage car door, raised his gun, fired. So deadly was Black Jack that even though he did not see the gun until the moonbeams glinted on its polished barrel, he swung his six-gun on Harrington, the slug nicking his arm.

"The bandit crawled away in the darkness. Sheriff Saturnino Pinard's posse from Clayton found the outlaw 300 yards from the track next morning, astride his rifle, dazed, his right arm riddled with buckshot, his body drained of blood. He had been too weak to mount his horse and had waved the posse down with his huge black hat.

"At Trinidad he refused an anesthetic and watched the doctor cut his arm off. When it was over he smiled, said 'Doc, I hope I can do as much for you sometime.' "

There was more:

"If you'll bring a fiddle, we'll dance," he is said to have told the *Padre* who tried to bring him solace as the last nails were being driven in the thirteen-step scaffold at Clayton, New Mexico, that a few moments later would claim his head.

When the jury's verdict of death by hanging was announced, the judge is said to have asked Black Jack if he had any last wish. To which Black Jack is said to have responded: "I'd like to shave the District Attorney."

When in the prison at Santa Fe making ready to be taken to

Clayton for his execution, it is said that Black Jack purchased a snazzy striped bow tie, a jet black suit and a black derby "which he wore tilted in a sporting angle." It was said that Frank Harrington, the conductor who had shot Black Jack at his attempted solo train robbery, rode with Black Jack part of the way from Santa Fe to Clayton. Harrington was said to have reported that Black Jack seemed to be enjoying the ride and told him, "with your help I could have robbed the Treasury at Washington."

A window of Black Jack's jail cell at Clayton overlooked the enclosure in the adjoining courtyard in which he was to be hanged. Sitting at his window, watching the workers build the scaffold he is said to have remarked, "I wish they'd hurry up. I want to be in Hell in time for supper."

So the yarns went. It is probable that some of what was attributed to the man came from the fertile, imaginative and romantic minds of his chroniclers. Nevertheless, he achieved somehow, and doubtless will always be credited with, the reputation as one of the most devil-may-care bandits of all times.

When Black Jack's casket (a plain pine box) was lifted from its grave at 2:00 P.M. on Sunday, September 11, 1933, more than 2500 persons had gathered at the site. When the casket was opened, they trailed by for a look at Tom Ketchum's remains. Gerome W. Shields, ex-sheriff of Tom Green County, Texas, who had known Black Jack and his brother Sam in earlier days, was brought up from San Angelo, Texas, to identify the body. It was remarkably well preserved. This was apparently due to the fact that the grave penetrated — and the casket was surrounded by — a solid layer of caliche. This limestone deposit underlies all of the Texas High Plains area. Limestone's imperviousness to water is believed to alloy deterioration of bodies buried in it.

It was reported in the *Texan* that, "The black suit in which he was buried had turned a rusty brown, only the soles and heels and a little of the uppers remained of his shoes; his jet black hair and moustache were plainly visible but had also changed to a rusty brown. The right arm was missing."

Black Jack's body was then reinterred in the official Clayton Cemetery. In deference to the wishes of persons whose dead relatives also rested there, the gravesite assigned to Black Jack was completely separated from those of all others — and no headstone or other marker was ever placed there.

A Long Dead Outlaw Brings a Sense of Relief

So it remains today. Not surprisingly, however, it is one of the most easily recognizable gravesites in the cemetery and when I visited it in 1977, it appeared to be one of the best cared for. It was free of weeds and covered with relatively fresh looking flowers.

One man who objected to the whole disinterment and reburial procedure and the romanticism that surrounded it was John McCarty, editor of the *Texan* — who gave vent to his feelings in his column, "Cactus Sage and Loco:"

> I don't believe Black Jack should have been moved. I don't think the people who flocked out to see what a musty 32-year-old dead body looked like had anything like the right attitude or respect for the dead, even if in this case, he was a noted outlaw. I think further there is too much of a tendency to glorify such a character. What better and more fitting a permanent resting place could Black Jack have had than the knoll of that lonely cacti-covered hill, with rocks, badgers, prairie dogs, coyotes and owls all about?
>
> The state has exacted its toll of Black Jack and he has brought enough humiliation and disgrace upon a respectable family and a decent and useful father and mother without having the body dug up again and all the lurid details of a bloody criminal career flung in the face of a younger generation whose living bandit chiefs make the former tough men of the West look like innocent babes in the woods when it comes to slaying the populace. Why not let the dead rest?
>
> There is, however, one good point in reviving his history. It shows that Black Jack did his robbing in a more or less manly manner. He didn't mow down all the women and children in his path with machine guns and he didn't buy off the officers and politicians that sit in the seats of power and influence. He was a train robber and a six-gun killer and he made no bones about it. He wasn't a dirty, rotten, sniveling, stinking polecat of a gangster who couldn't use a six-gun well enough to hit anybody and was forced to use a machine gun where he couldn't miss. Black Jack had his good points when you compare him with the rats modern civilization is having to deal with, especially some of the wealthier and more powerful rats that influence your life and mine every day we live while we sometimes hail them as great high public officials or mighty kings of finance.
>
> There was no prayer said over Black Jack the first time he was buried, and no prayer the second time. If it is not too late, here is a prayer in all reverence and respect for the dead and for the Master:

Our Father in Heaven, we pray your blessings upon this departed man. We know he has left a crimson trail of sin and death as he traveled the rough and rock strewn road from the cradle to the grave. We realize, O Father, that he has misused the body and brain with which he was bestowed. We realize his career is such that all must look upon it with shame and humility but once he was a prattling babe whose tousled hair felt the sweet caress of a fond and loving mother. Once he was the chubby boy that gazed in fondness and admiration on a father whose record of service to Thee and to humanity was good.

We may never realize the weaknesses, the temptations or the little sin that may have turned his course like an arrow is deflected in its flight, but help us, O Lord, that we may profit from his horrible experience and teach us more forcefully than ever that the wages of sin are death. If the sacrifice of this one life can serve as a beacon of warning that may enable others to avoid the pitfalls on the way to Thee, then we thank Thee for his having lived. We plead in Thy Son's name, that Thou may have mercy on his soul and that Thy will be done in all things. Amen.

Thus this macabre episode, and the wild romantic yarns and sober reflections it stirred, made good, wholesome, entertaining reading, helping, for a fleeting moment, to divert the minds of the weary citizens far away from their otherwise humdrum, desolate, barren and almost hopeless existence.

Digging Out

Their farm homes were practically covered up with the sand that accumulated around the windows, and they actually had to shovel out the doors to get in and out. Not a green thing was growing. Not a chicken or a cow on the place. The children were ragged and the only food the family had was what they got through relief agencies. . . . I remember particularly one rather young mother with several children. I don't recall her name but she could not have been more than thirty-five years of age, and I remember her outcries when she was brought into the room. Not exactly what she said, but how she said — cried out — "Dust is killing me, it's killing my children, it's killing us all. *God help us.*"

— Wilson (Bill) Cowan
Former County Judge, later
Chief Judge of U.S. Court
of Claims in Washington

As this was written [1981–1983], about forty years had passed since the end of the Great Drouth of the 1930s which plagued the High Plains area of Texas, Oklahoma, New Mexico, Kansas, and Colorado — the area we came to call the Dust Bowl.

Many would prefer that it simply be forgotten. There is little left now on the surface of the earth to remind us how grazing lands were denuded of grass and farmlands were made useless by loss of topsoil or by drifting sand. It is difficult to describe adequately the hardships brought to the people of the area by that drouth.

When we are confronted with the near destruction of the land's usefulness which resulted, we must ask how could this have happened? How was the land made again to grow grasses on which livestock could live? How were the denuded fields restored to yield abundant crops? What is being done to prevent a recurrence?

From the mouths of old-timers who lived through it all, and from the pages of that courageous newspaper, *The Dalhart Texan*, we can gather some understanding as to how these questions may be answered.

We know that during the 1920s vast areas of the High Plains previously used only for pasturing cattle had been plowed up and converted into farmlands. This was mainly the result of availability of cheap land, better than average rainfall, and improved prices for farm products due to Europe's needs following World War I.

Also, there is evidence that cattle raisers, responding to the better prices for beef, had allowed cattle to eat up the stubble left in harvested fields or had increased their herds to a point where the grass on their pastures was weakened by over-grazing.

We know that the years of adequate rainfall came to an abrupt end late in 1931. In 1932, 1933, and 1934, rainfall was far below the normal. The average annual rainfall in the Dalhart area is about eighteen inches. West from Dalhart, toward the Rocky Mountains in Colorado and New Mexico, the average annual rainfall declines. The entire area is covered by a rich sandy loam topsoil deposited by millions of years of run-off from the Rocky Mountains. As long as it is not disturbed, the topsoil is held in place by thick grasses which nature adapted to it. When that sandy loam loses its grass cover because of plowing or other disturbance, it is prone to blow. And there is rarely a day in the area when the wind does not blow enough to move particles of sand in the topsoil where it is exposed. We know that the lands of the area, once put to plow, are likely to lose valuable topsoil in periods of dryness unless proper methods are taken to protect it from blowing. Also, we know that when the grass is weakened by overgrazing, it will cease to perform its function of holding the soil in place and the soil will become subject to blowing.

We know bumper crops of wheat, maize, corn and sorghum were grown in the area in 1931, but that these met a badly cratered economy in which the prices plummeted to a point where many farmers did not even recover the cost of harvesting. The rancher's cattle taken to market met a similar disastrous fall in prices.

As a result of the market disaster of 1931, the people in the High Plains who depended on farm and ranch produce for their livelihood were not in a strong financial condition to survive the impact

Digging Out

of weather conditions that would deny pasture grasses to the cattleman and deny harvestable crops to the farmer. Yet, just such weather conditions came in 1932, and continued unabated at least until in 1935. Gradually, commencing in 1935, weather conditions improved, but it was not until the great rains of 1942, that the dry cycle ended.

As noted, the crops harvested during 1931 met a disastrous market. The winter wheat planted in the fall of that year would normally have been ready to harvest in June of 1932. But early in 1932, most of it fell prey to hot winds and lack of moisture and that fall, the farmers' row crops (maize, sorghum, and corn planted in the spring) met a similar fate.

In the fall of 1932, the farmers again planted the winter wheat, hoping for a cash crop in the spring of 1933. By June of 1933, it was apparent that this crop was too sparse to justify harvesting, and the continued lack of rain cut down hope for a row crop harvest for that fall.

These conditions prevailed over much of the north Panhandle of Texas, most of the Oklahoma Panhandle, and over vast areas in northeast New Mexico, southeastern Colorado, and southwestern Kansas.

By June of 1933, it had become clear that the 1932–1933 winter wheat crop was a failure and the financial situation of the people of the area had become desperate. The farmers were particularly hard hit. Now two years of crop failure due to drouth had been added to the disastrous market conditions of 1931. The grasses of their pastures and the vegetables in their gardens had withered under the impact of drouth and hot winds, the milk production from their milk cows had been severely reduced and in many instances their stores of feed for all livestock had been used up. Many farmers were without the funds needed to buy feed for livestock, seed for planting, or even food for human consumption.

The town of Guymon, Oklahoma, lies in the approximate center of the Oklahoma Panhandle. It is also the approximate center of the High Plains area. On June 16, 1933, at the call of officials of Guymon's Red Cross and of its Chamber of Commerce, a giant meeting of concerned people from the High Plains area was held to develop the facts as to the distress caused by the drouth and depression and seek direct help from the federal government.

Businessmen, farmers, ranchers, newspaper reporters and editors, and others interested, attended, as did representatives of the governors of the four states, Texas, Kansas, Oklahoma, and New Mexico.

Albert H. Law, veteran reporter for *The Dalhart Texan*, attended the meeting. His report, carried in the June 17, 1933, issue of *The Dalhart Texan*, read in part as follows:

"The simple, honest sons of the soil told a story of disaster and desolation to the four-state relief meeting at Guymon Friday that beggars description and staggers the mind.

"Not a blade of wheat in Cimarron County, Oklahoma; cattle dying there on the ranch; a few bushels of wheat in the Perryton area against an average yield of four to six million bushels; with all stored surplus not more than fifty percent of the seeding needs will be met — ninety percent of the poultry dead in one Panhandle county because of sandstorms; sixty cattle dying Friday afternoon between Guymon and Liberal from some dust fever — milk cows going dry, turned into the highways to starve, hogs in such pitiable shape the buyers will not have them; cattle being moved from Dallam and other counties to grass; no wheat in Hartley County; row crops a remote possibility; cattle facing starvation . . ."

Those in charge of the Guymon meeting had reports prepared of the proceedings and copies of these were forwarded to the area's representatives in Congress with the urgent request that they be passed on to such of the agencies of Government as were thought to be in a position to render aid. The pleas were sort of blind groping with the general hope that somewhere among the maze of New Deal alphabetical agencies a responsive ear could be found.

Mrs. E. R. Stewart of Dalhart, the President of the Dallam County Red Cross, attended the Guymon meeting. Already the numbers of hungry and destitute persons calling for aid from the Red Cross had far exceeded the agency's ability to respond. Soon after the Guymon meeting, funds from a distress agency of the Reconstruction Finance Corporation enabled Mrs. Stewart to parcel out to a body of able-bodied men who had applied for relief the job of shoveling sand so as to reduce the size of some of the drifts in the edges of town. Each man was allowed to work not more than three days in any week and was paid one dollar per day.

Franklin Roosevelt had been inaugurated as President in March of 1933, and his New Deal administration had immediately begun its multifaceted drive to combat the depression. Of the programs initiated, many were aimed at restructuring the economy by forcing up prices for farm products while concurrently increasing employ-

Digging Out

ment and raising wages to enable the people to pay the increased cost of living thus created. Among other things, the RFC (Reconstruction Finance Corporation) was making loans to farmers on the security of produce kept off the market and stored on the farm; the Surplus Commodity Corporation was purchasing surplus farm products for redistribution to the needy, and the NRA (National Recovery Administration) was instituting codes within businesses and industry requiring reduced hours of labor with accompanying minimum wages.

Obviously, these programs were not well designed to help the farmers of the Dust Bowl region who had no produce either to store or to sell. Similarly, the programs were not well designed to help the businesses of the area, which could barely afford to meet their pared down payrolls.

True, the New Deal's Public Works Administration held out hope of providing jobs for many unemployed people and injecting Government funds into the economy through long range plans for public works. And its Agricultural Adjustment Administration was developing plans for paying farmers for taking lands out of production or reducing the numbers of pigs and other livestock. But, to the impoverished people of the Dust Bowl, even these programs seemed only remotely applicable to their needs.

Shortly after the Guymon meeting, another was held, this one in Amarillo. Here a suggested program was developed which seemed to promise a strong rejuvenation for the economy and provide constructive work for many farmers who were made idle by the drouth's forbidding them useful work in their fields.

Developed by W. H. Van London, the District Highway Engineer, the program envisioned was one of road construction, using the white, decomposed limestone (caliche) which abounded in the area and could be mined easily, and using the idle tractors, wagons, teams, and manpower from the farms. Van London proposed that the work be done under the Texas State Highway Commission and the men paid on a cost-plus basis.

The program was endorsed by the State Highway Commission and pressed on various government agencies by Congressman Marvin Jones, Senator Tom Connally, the area newspapers, Chambers of Commerce, and other agencies. The urgent and insistent plea was that the people did not want charity but useful constructive work.

Efforts to get some such work under way continued throughout the summer and into the fall without success. Finally, in November

1933, about five months after the Guymon meeting, a great sense of relief arose when the CWA (Civil Works Administration) under Harry L. Hopkins, Federal Relief Administrator, inaugurated highway work throughout the area.

Over 1,500 men in Dallam County had listed themselves as needing work and at first it seemed they were obtaining employment as fast as their applications could be processed. By the end of the first week, some 450 men were working, and the others were standing by with high expectations.

Then came the news that the program had been misunderstood. Its purpose was not to provide constructive work designed for wide application and a significant impact on restoring the economy; instead, it was designed to be a strictly work-relief program, on which only those otherwise living on relief handouts could qualify. Only one man per family would be permitted to work, and he would be limited to twenty-four hours of work per week at pay of thirty cents per hour.

The December 5, 1933, issue of *The Dalhart Texan* reported that men on the work rolls had taken up a collection to pay for a telegram to bring to the attention of Mr. Hopkins the true conditions of the County. The telegram was signed, "A. C. Johnson and 1500 others." The telegram read in part as follows:

> THE RECENT ANNOUNCEMENT OF C.W.A. WORK HERE DISPELLED GLOOM AND RAISED HOPES OF PEOPLE OF THIS DROUTH STRICKEN AREA THAT RELIEF WAS AT LAST IN SIGHT. DALLAM COUNTY HAS MORE THAN 1500 MEN NEEDING WORK. BUT NOW WE ARE TOLD THE C.W.A. ALLOTMENT IS FOR ONLY 285 MEN. NO AGRICULTURAL INCOME CAN ACCRUE UNTIL NEXT JULY FROM WHEAT AND NEXT NOVEMBER FROM OTHER CROPS. WE MUST HAVE WORK TO CARRY US THROUGH THE WINTER. WE ARE FIGHTING DESPERATELY TO MAINTAIN OUR HOMES, SCHOOLS, CHURCHES, AND VARIOUS ENTERPRISES TO MEET LOCAL NEEDS. WE DON'T WANT DOLE OR DIRECT RELIEF. WE WANT WORK.

Dallam County's quota of 285 men employable on the Civil Works Administration's program was based on comparative population rather than need. Responding somewhat to the cries of need, the C.W.A., late in December 1933, raised the quota to 400. These remained limited to men otherwise on relief. This left out some 1,100 to 1,400 additional men listed as unemployed and asking for work. So the C.W.A. program turned out to be only a relief program, not a constructive work program as many had hoped and expected.

The Civil Works Administration ceased to exist late in March 1934. Following a Panhandle-wide protest meeting in Amarillo, the C.W.A. employment program was replaced by one administered by the Texas Relief Commission. But, again, only one man per family could be employed and these must be persons on relief rolls who could prove they had no other means of support. Each man was allowed not over twenty-five hours of work per week, and the pay was thirty cents an hour.

By this time, disillusionment became widespread in Washington's ability or willingness to provide the area a meaningful work program, and at one point in May 1934, after the area farmers and ranchers had felt and smelled rain for the first time in months, an editorial in *The Dalhart Texan* suggested as follows:

> Farmers and ranchers of the North Panhandle, sick and disgusted with government bureaucracy, double-crossing and unfilled pledges on a promised work relief program, muttered to themselves that with another rain or so or a few more days of this one, and Mr. Harry Hopkins, Federal Relief Administrator, and all his drouth and relief cohorts could take a running start and go jump in the lake.

Gradually the residents began to turn away from the federal government as a source of their salvation and to look instead to themselves and the one resource upon which all else depended: the land!

Only the land could produce the grasses on which the farmer and rancher could raise his cattle, or produce the crops on which the farmer depended. The federal government could not make grass or crops grow on denuded land, nor could the federal government or any other restore the land so it could. Government could help — but the initiative for land restoration and protection must come from the people themselves.

For nearly three years now, the ranchers had watched the grasses on their pastures cut back by drouth and hot winds or covered by blowing sand. Many had moved their herds away to other areas where they could find grass. Even strongly established ranchers like Orville Finch and W. H. Lathem found it necessary to move their herds to Montana; Andy James moved his to California.*

By March 1934, the plight of the farmer became desperate. It was apparent that for the third straight year there would be no wheat harvest. Even the most solid, industrious, and frugal of the farmers were beginning to lose hope. Those who had been there long enough to understand the normal vicissitudes of farming on the plains had long since come to expect and to cope with years when the lack of rainfall or excessive heat and high winds would prevent or destroy crops. Heretofore, they had always been sustained in the belief that *next year* things would be better. They would simply tighten their belts and go back into their fields to prepare their lands for another planting. They had learned from experience that in drouth times they could lose precious topsoil to the winds, and so they kept themselves aware of the conditions of their land, and alert to the forces which could harm it.

The good, frugal, industrious farmers of the area had continuously struggled to save their farmland from severe erosion by repeated deep listing of their plowed fields and leaving stubble wherever a crop was permitted to grow and be harvested. Now after three years of preparing their land for "next year," but seeing the seeds fail to sprout due to lack of moisture or to sprout and be cut down by hot winds or blowing sand, many of the farmers — even the most settled and reliable — began to hold a deep fear that there might never be a "next year" when good times could return.

The good farmer's sense of discouragement and frustration was not due solely to the effect of lack of moisture and wind. For while he could protect his own land from blowing, he had no way to keep the soil from his neighbor's farm from blowing upon his. Perhaps a major cause of the destruction of farm and ranch lands in these bitter years was the blowing sand from land which had been plowed by speculative farmers and then abandoned when the speculation failed,

---

* The blowing sand, settling on the grass, then being picked up by the next high wind, cut down the grass on many pastures, even causing some pastureland to start blowing much the same as the plowed fields did.

There was one compensation from this destruction — the exposure of ancient Indian camping grounds where arrowheads could be found. Arrowhead hunting became a favorite diversion for many residents. On elevated spots chosen by Indians for campsites in order to see any approaching enemies, the soil, blackened by campfires, would become exposed to view when the grass was cut down. A search of these blackened areas was likely to yield many discarded arrowheads.

Digging Out

or sand from the land of farmers who, through lack of enterprise or lack of funds, failed to adequately work their fields to protect them from blowing.

By the spring of 1934, so much of the farmland in the area had been abandoned or neglected, and the problems for the remaining farmers and for the ranchers had become so acute that the Federal Land Bank, to which a great portion of the land was mortgaged to secure its loans, became alarmed. At its request a meeting was set up in March in the Dallam County Courthouse in Dalhart for the airing of the problem and discussion of ways and means of solving it. Over 150 farmers and landowners attended.

One of these was Andy James, one of the area's most prominent pioneer ranchers. His message to the group was about as follows:

> Folks, I am sure you all know that I have been around here about as long as anybody. In fact, I have been here ever since 1901 when my brother and I and our mother came here and went out to a spot about ten miles north of Dalhart where we bought four sections of land and started the James Ranch. The main reason we picked out that spot was because my dad, who had come here a couple of years before, had said that this was land that would never be plowed up. And the fact is there just weren't any farmers anywhere around here, and the whole area, as far as you could see, was covered with the prettiest waist-high bluestem grass that you ever saw, and beneath it was just a carpet of gramma and curly mesquite. It was the prettiest and best cow country a man can imagine. Since then, I have seen this country change from a ranching country to a farming country. I don't mind telling you that I hated to see the farmers come. There is no doubt about it; if they hadn't come, and torn up the grass the Old Man Up Yonder put here to hold this land in place, it wouldn't be blown away the way it is today. So, for a lot of years I literally hated farmers and I kept hoping that somehow they would all go away and this country could go back to being just cow country again. Finally though, I came to realize that the farmers were here to stay. As a matter of fact, I have been trying to do a little farming myself for the past few years but I would a damn sight rather be punching cows.
>
> Now, I guess you all know that our James Brothers Ranch that had its headquarters out there ten miles north of Dalhart went under after the big blizzard in 1919. And after that the Interstate Bank of Kansas City took over and lots and lots of our old ranchlands was sold to farmers. This included the old headquarters place, which my Dad had thought would never be plowed.

Well, I went out there to look at that headquarters place the other day and I can tell you that what I saw made me sick. There is not a blade of grass in miles of that place. The roads are all covered with sand. All the fences have sand held by tumbleweeds piled up on them to where you can walk over them. And right out in front of where the old ranch house used to stand, the tumbleweeds and sand had built a sand dune about as big as this Courthouse. In front of that, there used to be a pretty row of cottonwood trees that my mother planted. Now, they are all dead. In fact, there are only two of them that are still standing and all they have for branches are stubby, broken spikes. The only sign of life I saw out there was crow's nests. I ran off one old crow who was sitting in one of the trees and I looked at those nests. Those nests were made of bobwire and tumbleweed. I guess that is all the crows could find out there to build the nests with.

Now folks, this is a terrible way for us to treat our land. And, it didn't have to happen. There has got to be some way that we can do something about it.

I know it is true that our good farmers have always known how to take care of their land and keep it from blowing, but we have heard here today how even the best farmers are having their land ruined by the sand that is blowing from other people's farms that have been abandoned or just neglected.

I want us to find some way to get our grasslands back into grass and our farmlands made so they can be farmed again. That means we are going to have to get a big plan going, and we are all going to have to do what we can. We may have to get some help from the Government.

I have learned that there is such a thing as a Soil Conservation Service run by a Mr. H. H. Bennett of the U.S. Department of the Interior. It has been in operation since 1929, and they have been doing a lot of work up in Wisconsin, and down in Mississippi and Virginia, and so on, to stop water erosion, but evidently they have never thought about how the wind can erode land. I think we ought to form a committee to get together the facts about what the wind has done to erode this country and take it up to Mr. Bennett, and see if his Soil Conservation Service can't help us do something about our problem.

More than 150 farmers and landowners from Dallam, Hartley, Sherman, and Moore counties came to the meeting. After Andy James's speech, they adopted a resolution forming the North Plains Wind Erosion Control Association, the purpose of which was to search for a program to restore the denuded farmlands and pastures and hopefully find a way to control wind erosion in the future. Andy James was elected chairman and Malcolm Stewart, secretary. Under James's direction, questionnaires were developed and distributed. From the answers a report was prepared, designed to show the amount of land in the four counties damaged by wind erosion, the extent of the damage, and the location and ownership of such land.

James sent the report to the Department of Interior's Soil Conservation Service with the plea that it extend its work so as to include problems of wind erosion.

At that time, the Soil Conservation Service had twenty-five water erosion control projects throughout the nation but none directed toward wind erosion.

In July 1934, a few months after his receipt of James's Association report, H. H. Bennett, head of the Soil Conservation Service, announced that a wind erosion control demonstration project, the first for the nation, would be established near Dalhart.

H. H. Finnell of the A&M College at Goodwell, Oklahoma was enlisted as director of the Dalhart project.

The area initially chosen for the project was 16,000 acres about ten miles north and east of Dalhart, which included the site of the old James Brothers headquarters where, as James had described at the March meeting at the Dallam County Courthouse, there stood a great sand dune flanked by dead cottonwood trees holding crow's nests built of barbed wire and tumbleweeds.

In September, with the help of a committee of local farmers and ranchers, the owners of most of the land involved signed contracts agreeing to cooperate with the Soil Conservation Service for three years in such work as it should direct on their land for the purpose of restoring it to usefulness and preventing further erosion. Any improvements resulting on the land would belong to the landowners.

It was not the soil alone that had suffered serious erosion. The will of the people to hold on had also suffered serious erosion. All had read repeated magazine and newspaper articles suggesting that agricultural use of the lands in the whole area had proven a failure and that the Government should consider moving the farming people from the area to other climes and allowing the farmland to revert to pasture.

Consequently, it was heartening to hear from an authority such as Finnell that the conversion of the plains into farmlands had not been an unsound development and agitation for abandonment of the plains as submarginal was not founded on knowledge of their true potential. And most importantly, that these farmlands, now seemingly permanently damaged, could and should be restored to productivity.

Finnell brought his message to the Dalhart area people in a series of articles published in *The Dalhart Texan* in August and September, 1934. Here are some highlights:

> Putting the plains land under cultivation cannot be justly blamed for wind erosion. It *should* be in cultivation. The blame, if any, rests on the unwitting neglect of a certain factor necessary to the most profitable use of cultivated lands as such. The point that has generally been overlooked in High Plains farming is that the sky overhead belongs to the land, that is if we care to use it . . .
>
> We do not want a changed climate — all that is needed to reach a solution of many of the drouth problems is to make a better use of the rain that is received. Rainfall fluctuations from season to season and year to year are unavoidable and must be prepared for. Rainwater that falls on a man's land surely belongs to the man if he wants it. Good management dictates that none should go to waste. Here is where the moisture problem ties in with the wind erosion problem.
>
> It is through crop failure that the protective supply of stubble or stalks is lost and the soil exposed to the destructive drifting by wind. It may also be lost by over-pasturing or the ill-considered disposal of residues of the harvested crops, but the prevention of a widespread crisis such as that just witnessed on the plains can only be undertaken successfully by preparing in advance on a countrywide scale to reduce crop failure to a minimum during drouthy periods. Moisture conservation is the answer. Such methods of moisture conservation have been amply demonstrated. Control by cover crops and tillage methods must be used in an emergency, but the latter are but temporary in effect and very expensive.
>
> Protective crop planting and windbreaks have a function, but the maintenance of an adequate vegetative cover is the one important fundamental around which all other devices must be built. It is the only permanent solution compatible with economical production.

Finnell said measures to maintain a protective vegetative cover included terracing and contouring for moisture conservation, restricting grazing to conserve vegetation and leaving stubble on the ground after harvesting any crops.

On lands too badly blown out to permit the above procedures, he counseled deep plowing to raise heavier soil to the surface, then planting cover crops solely for erosion control, such as rye sown in the fall on sandy land or sorghum or millet sown in spring or summer on any land.

He promised that the 16,000-acre Dalhart Wind Erosion Demonstration Project "in which a community will band together with the Government" would work out a permanent system of wind erosion control. (In 1936, the Soil Conservation Service reported that the area being employed in this land-use demonstration project, through cooperation of the farmers, had grown to over 47,000 acres.)

The huge sand dune on the old James Brothers Ranch headquarters provided an ideal demonstration of how to restore badly hummocked farmlands to usefulness. Former County Judge Wilson (Bill) Cowan described the procedure as follows:

> I have spoken of the enormous sand dune that existed on the farm about ten miles directly north of Dalhart and the fact that the Soil Conservation Service made a special project of trying to restore this land. I've forgotten now just who the Conservationist was in charge but I remember he told me that the most effective way to deal with a problem of the kind was to use the wind itself as a factor in restoration. So he began by using a grader and moving some of the sand around the edges of the dune toward the direction from which the wind was blowing. And then he deeplisted adjoining areas, leaving the furrows into which the wind would blow the sand that was loosened from the edge of the large dune. This process was continued from day to day until all the dune was finally leveled or most all of it. And then as quickly as it was possible for him to do so with the available rainfall, he planted cane, a very fast growing and soil holding crop to prevent a recurrence of the dune building effect. And then later on he planted some more and better soil retaining crops like sudan grass and after a time — and I don't remember how long a period this was — this horrible example of wind erosion, perhaps the most horrible one that could be found in the Dust Bowl area was a farm that could produce again, or perhaps be seeded in grass and used as ranchland, but nevertheless it was a farm that could be put back in production by the methods used by the Soil Conservation Service.

An October 1934, editorial in the *Dallas Morning News* spoke of the wide interest in the Dalhart Wind Erosion Control Project and opined:

The new federal project in the Panhandle, which has for its purpose the stopping of erosion by wind, is not contemplated as a giant government enterprise involving large expenditures.

It will lead the way by experimentation and example and thus help the farmers help themselves.

There will be demonstration farming in the restoration of native grasses, strip planting, terracing and other means of combating erosion by wind, with the belief that farmers of that area will observe and follow the example. Some government assistance will be lent farmers in the form of technical advice and special equipment.

Some doubt the destructiveness of erosion by wind because they have not seen it. But out in the West, where a vast new farming industry has torn nature's covering from the soil, a new condition has been created. Nature has a way of balancing its own forces; it had done so on the great plains of North America by providing a covering to protect the soil from restless winds. The spread of farming removed the carpet of grass. For a number of years it has been apparent that damage was being done by wind erosion. The experience during the drouth of recent months has left no doubt.

The experiment to check destruction of soil, made possible by the new conditions, is simply man's defense of the breach that man made in nature's wall of defense of its own resources when man turned the grass lands into wheat and cotton fields. The experiment near Dalhart may mark the beginning of a new era in Panhandle farming.

The Dalhart Texan ran editorial and news story after editorial and news story urging the area farmers to heed the lessons being taught and demonstrated by Finnell's Dalhart Wind Erosion Control Project. Authorities such as W. C. Laudermilk and H. H. Bennett warned of the vast economic and social deterioration produced by wind and water erosion.

Laudermilk visited Dalhart and told his audience:

> There has always been erosion, but under nature's plan the rate of erosion was not greater than the rate of soil rebuilding, as a result of decaying vegetable matter and other methods. Now because of unprotected farmlands, over-grazing and the like, Americans are practicing suicidal production in which erosion is many times faster than replacement of the topsoil. As a result farm and sometimes pasturelands are being virtually if not entirely ruined, which condemns future generations to abject poverty and mere existence or perhaps to a complete starvation.

Thus Finnell and others lectured and demonstrated on the methods for restoration of the denuded lands and on means of protecting against further spread of the wind's erosion. *The Dalhart Texan* filled its columns with such information and with exhortations to the farmers to accept and follow Finnell's teachings. Many farmers and other landowners did so.

But the years of repeated crop failures had left many farmers too impoverished to afford the expense of tractor fuel for the required plowing and of seed required for erosion-resisting plants necessary for restoration of topsoil-stripped, and badly hummocked fields. In many cases those who properly handled their own lands, exactly as Finnell preached, found their efforts frustrated by the sand from the neighboring abandoned farmsteads which continued to blow. So the destructive effects of wind erosion continued to spread despite the efforts of the Soil Conservation Service, *The Dalhart Texan* and the concerned, intelligent and industrious farmers. By March 1935, the area badly affected by wind erosion had widened until it extended from the Canadian border to the Rio Grande. At that point, wind erosion became recognized by Congress as a national problem.

On April 11, 1935, a news release out of Washington declared:

> President Roosevelt today said all money needed will be allocated for emergency erosion control work in the dust ripped areas of Texas, Kansas, New Mexico, Oklahoma and Colorado.
>
> Meanwhile scores of families left the affected area, particularly northwestern Oklahoma. Even wagons were pressed into use as the coughing, choking humans fled before the fury of the stifling dust.
>
> More than a hundred families have been forced out of Cimarron and Texas Counties in Oklahoma, immediately north of Dallam County, Texas. Dust held the Scott City, Kansas, business district closed for the third consecutive day. Every school in De Baca County, Colorado, closed Wednesday. The dust held 180 school children and bus passengers in a school building and homes at Pritchett, Colorado. Even rail traffic has been stopped at points in the dust ridden area.
>
> Within the last 30 days 100 normally self-sustaining families have been driven out of Texas County, Oklahoma, according to Chester Lamar, FERA Administration. Floyd Hutchison of Cimarron County, Oklahoma, said all but three of the 40 families in

69 townships out of Boise City, Oklahoma, have been driven out. Mrs. Mabel Lather, relief worker at Guymon, says 4,000 of the 5,500 families in six northwestern Oklahoma counties are on relief.

At Buffalo, Oklahoma, the powerful wind hurled gravel, breaking windows. With the gravel was a silt so fine and black that it filtered into houses and offices, obscuring persons across the room from one another.

Dust has doomed wheat in Western Kansas, a major source of the nation's supply, says R. L. Throckmorton, head of the Kansas State College Agronomy Department. Not even rains will save it now, he stated.

President Roosevelt urged upon Congress the passage of a five billion dollar Work Relief Program to include wind erosion control work patterned on the lessons of the Dalhart Wind Erosion Control Project.

Local areas were urged to come up with their own suggested plans.

On March 18, 1935, at the request of the Dalhart Chamber of Commerce, a fifty-one counties meeting was held in the Dalhart Courthouse. The announced purpose: To secure immediate widespread and effective wind erosion control and soil conservation on the Southwestern High Plains.

Twenty-eight counties in Texas, twelve counties in Kansas, three in Colorado, three in Oklahoma and five in New Mexico were invited to send representatives.

A plan (which became known as the Dalhart Plan), was proposed:

1. Countour listing and wide-row planting of stooling sorghum on unprotected land, this to be achieved by the federal government furnishing seed and gasoline for tractors and the farmer paid forty cents per acre for tractor use or forty-five cents if horses were used.

2. Where wheat land has been abandoned, leaving no vegetative cover, seed and gasoline would be furnished but nothing paid for the labor of seeding.

3. Grazing of any crops resulting would be restricted through the spring and summer of 1935.

4. Any harvesting would have to leave a stubble satisfactory to the erosion specialists.

Proponents recognized the physical results might last only

through the windy season of 1935–1936. Even so, they argued that the educational value would be worth the cost.

Reporting on the result of the meeting, the March 19 *Dalhart Texan* said:

> More than 700 sturdy Panhandle Citizens, wind whipped and dust covered, Monday afternoon at a huge 51 county conference in Dalhart, voted to stand by their guns and once more make this country blossom as the rose.
>
> When it came time to vote on whether or not the farmers and their wives should continue the fight against erosion, every vote was aye.

By April 17, the great Work Relief Bill had become law and a Washington announcement had declared that, under it, $500,000 would be made available for erosion control work in forty-one Texas Panhandle Counties along the lines of the Dalhart Plan espoused at the March eighteenth meeting.

In preparation for this work, the County Agent for Dallam County made a survey of the cultivated land in the County and estimated that ninety percent of it needed the proposed wind erosion control work.

Meantime, a recruitment drive for the Civilian Conservation Corps had increased the number of young men and boys in that corps from about 300,000 to about 600,000. Of these, many were assigned to five newly organized camps in the forty-one wind-eroded Panhandle Counties earmarked for erosion control work under the President's Work Relief Bill. The CCC personnel, under direction of the Soil Conservation Service, surveyed and laid out contour lines on farms where asked to do so. And the farmers themselves, pursuant to the Dalhart Plan, proceeded with the work of terracing and contouring their fields and then strip planting of stooling sorghum.

Again in the spring of 1936, a similar terracing and contouring program was carried out in the drouth ravaged Dust Bowl area; this under direction of the Soil Conservation Service, acting in cooperation with state and local authorities.

Reporting on the results, the Soil Conservation Service said:

> During this emergency program nearly 2,500,000 acres were listed on the contour. From five to eight inches of rain fell late in May. The water caught and stored in the soil, as a result of the contour listing, meant the difference between a crop and a crop failure in nearly every instance. Measurements indicated that on

the average, one inch more of rainfall soaked into the contoured land than into similar land untreated or plowed in straight rows. This meant that the contoured soil was wet more than one foot deeper than the soil which was not contoured.

This amount of additional underground water storage increased the probability of crop production by seventy-five percent and meant additional protective residues for the prevention of wind erosion during the 1936-1937 winter-spring "blow season."

In 1929, fresh out of The University of Texas Law School, a young man named Wilson Cowan came to Dalhart. Five years later (July 30, 1934), he was elected County Judge of Dallam County.

Judge Cowan saw and dealt with the problems brought to the people by the continued drouth as perhaps no other person could.

The County Judge presides over the Commissioner's Court. That Court presides over and administers the business of the county. It is empowered to spend the County's tax revenues. In the 1930s the Court was constantly being reminded of the mounting tax delinquencies brought on by the drouth.

The County Judge is, by reason of his office, also the Superintendent of rural schools in the county, that is, all public schools not operated by Independent School Districts. Thus, Judge Cowan was Superintendent of the schools at Ware, Conlen, Perico and Kerrick. By the time Judge Cowan took office in 1934, many of the farm families served by these schools had given up and moved away, leaving their farmlands heavily burdened with delinquent county and state taxes and completely at the mercy of the winds. Soon the loss of patronage and delinquency in taxes forced most of these rural schools to close.

Farmers abandoning their farmsteads to begin their trek to other climes often came to Judge Cowan for help. Also, the Commissioner's Court heard lunacy trials. So Judge Cowan dealt with some for whom the privation had proven to be too much to withstand. In Judge Cowan's words:

"As I have earlier mentioned, many of the poor farmers of Dallam County who could no longer raise any crops simply gathered together what few possessions they had, loaded them in or on top of their old automobiles and sometimes a trailer as it had formerly been used to haul grain to market. Of course these people actually had nothing. They were able to get a little food from the local relief agency but they often called on me at the County Courthouse with a

Digging Out

request like this: Judge, we've had to pull out. We don't have anything but we are going to my wife's kinfolks in Eureka, Arkansas. Could you possibly buy an old secondhand tire? We've got a bad tire and would you buy us ten gallons of gasoline? This same plea was repeated to me many times and I got blanket authority from the Commissioners Court, the governing body of the County, to issue orders to a local filling station directing or authorizing them to furnish these poor people an old secondhand tire at a cost of about $3.50 and ten gallons of gasoline and it enabled them to get either to their destination or certainly a long ways.

"It was a pitiful sight. Often you'd see an old worn-out car full of a family with their children, a mattress, a sofa and two or three chairs tied on the top. And then sometimes an old grain trailer hooked on behind full of the pitiful odds and ends, the personal property that the family owned. Of course I have no recollection of how many cases there were of this kind. There were not hundreds of them, but they were in the scores.

"The County Court also had jurisdiction of lunacy trials. That is trials that are held upon complaint that a resident of the County has become insane and must be sent to an institution. A jury of six men is impaneled to hear the case and both expert and lay testimony is used. I think one of the most tragic portions of my experience as County Judge was the lunacy trials of two or three farm matrons, wives of farmers, who had simply gone stark raving mad because of the terrible conditions that were produced because of the wind erosion, the drouth, the lack of food, and the general discouragement and the frustration that followed. Their farm homes were practically covered up with the sand that accumulated around the windows and they actually had to shovel out the doors to get in and out. Not a green thing was growing. Not a chicken or a cow on the place. The children were ragged and the only food the family had was what they got through relief agencies.

"I remember particularly one rather young mother with several children. I don't recall her name but she could not have been more than thirty-five years of age and I remember her outcries when she was brought into the room. Not exactly what she said, but how she just said — *cried out* — 'Dust is killing me, it's killing my children, it's killing us all. *God help us.*' As I say, one of the saddest things I had to do was to sign a certificate committing this poor lady to the State Insane Institution at Wichita Falls, Texas, and there were at least two more of such cases, all caused by the extreme privation, hardship, worry and most of all — complete lack of hope which these poor women faced under those terrible conditions."

Of course, Judge Cowan and his Commissioner's Court were keenly interested in the progress of the land restoration and land saving programs demonstrated and spearheaded by Finnell's Soil Conservation Demonstration Project. And Cowan and Finnell conferred frequently about the progress and about the problems involved.

By mid-1935, the ranks of the established farmers of the area who had seen the benefits of the programs and gladly adapted them to their farms had increased dramatically. And gradually some harvestable crops began to result from moisture saving brought about by the terracing and contouring of the fields.

But a nagging and apparently insoluble problem was presented by the existence of the vast areas of farmland that had not received the terracing and contouring simply because it had been abandoned.

The constant intrusion of blowing sands from these abandoned farmlands often frustrated, or even destroyed the good terracing and contouring efforts of the prudent and industrious farmers who had stuck it out.

In his interview in his Washington office in 1973, Judge Cowan (then Chief Judge of the United States Court of Claims) explained how this problem was attacked:

> Because of the high rate of abandonment of farms by many of the farmers and their families who left the county, the already difficult problem of wind erosion was greatly accentuated because of the fact that there was no one left to deep list the farm in the spring of the year which was one of the simplest and best known ways to prevent the spread of wind erosion. All of the farmers who stayed there knew very well how to keep their land from blowing, at least to a very large extent, by this deep listing process and whenever there was any rainfall at all they added to that by what we call strip cropping. That is planting of such rapidly growing crops as sudan grass around the borders of the farm.
>
> However, it did very little good for an industrious farmer to take care of his land if there were two or three farms adjacent to him which nobody was taking care of. This became such an acute problem that early in 1935 County Judges of ten Panhandle counties, including Dallam, Hartley, Sherman, Deaf Smith, Randal, Odom, Ochiltree, Hansford and Lipscomb, formed an informal organization to see what could be done by enlisting the cooperation of both state and federal agencies to meet what was then the

most grievous and to us an almost insolvable problem. We formed an informal organization, as I have said, in which Judge Noel McDade of Dumas, Moore County, was the chairman. I was the secretary and Judge M. M. Stewart of Hereford, Deaf Smith County, was the vice-president. After we had several meetings and with the help of an interested attorney, Mr. J. O. Guleke, of Amarillo, we drafted a most unusual statute, the first of its kind in the history of the United States. And with the help of our Senator, Clint Small, we got it passed through the Texas Legislature very rapidly. In substance this new law provided that each of the ten counties was to be a Wind Erosion Conservation District — to be precise. And the Commissioner's Court, already the governing body of the County, was to be the governing body of the Wind Erosion Conservation District. The law went further to provide that in any case where the governing body determined that a landowner was neglecting his land and permitting extensive wind erosion to damage the land of adjacent and neighboring owners, the governing body could give him notice that unless he took measures to prevent this damage within thirty days, the governing body could itself enter upon the land, perform the work, and assess the cost against the landowner which would be entered upon the records as a lien in the same way as a lien for taxes. The State of Texas, as part of the law, also was to remit or give to the counties all state taxes that would be collected within a five year period to provide initial funds for these Wind Erosion Districts.

The Law provided that the acceptance by any county so as to make of it a Soil Erosion Conservation District and grant the Law's powers to the County Commissioner's Court was subject to the approval by a majority of the qualified voters of the county.

The Commissioner's Court of Dallam County set a date in August 1935, for the people to vote on acceptance or rejection of the proposal.

As a means of awakening the people to the seriousness of the problem and the need for approval, a group of leading citizens of the area were taken on a tour over the wind-eroded lands.

Albert Law, veteran reporter for *The Dalhart Texan*, went along and, in the June 28, 1935, issue of that paper, he reported:

Picture a man prone and naked. Tireless wolves tear at him. His armor has been carried away by well intentioned but ill advised friends who have meant no harm. Will he recover?

This is a picture personified of many Panhandle farms. They are not animate beings who can arise, seek shelter and defend themselves. They are naked because man, meaning well, but farming wrong, has allowed them to become denuded. There they lie under the teeth of every wind that tirelessly rips and tears at them.

Can nature intervene in time and adequately to save them from complete destruction? A group of more than 45 business and professional men of Dalhart, Amarillo, Channing, Texline and Clayton making a tour north and east of Dalhart Wednesday feels generally that human help must be had immediately.

There are occasional fields in good shape. They have been given protection by a vegetative cover, or their owners have spent hundreds of dollars in tillage to keep wind from ripping away the soil. But adjacent is a field with the soil blown out to a depth of two feet. The hard, unyielding subsoil, that does not even flinch from the lash of the wind, stares sullenly at the onlooker. Crops can be returned to it if it is plowed, catching fertile topsoil from other fields as the winds whip it about, and then anchoring that soil under proper farming methods.

On another field are frowning hummocks, mounds of dirt built up around tumbleweeds or other vegetation. They defy ordinary farming methods. They must be humbled first. As they stand one or several men could hide behind them. The fields in which they abound are ready-made for guerilla warfare.

On other fields small sand dunes are forming. The west portion of the fields are blown out to plow depth, perhaps lower. From 5 inches to a foot or more of soil has united in a big sand pile that grows larger with each wind. In increasing numbers these are developed into those vast, inexorable, mystic menaces; marching sand dunes. As the winds howl out of the southwest they move slowly northeastward. Nothing stops them. They have engulfed farm homes and improvements. They have laid waste hundreds of acres of farm and ranch lands in the past few years. They threaten hundreds of additional acres, and their hoard is steadily being recruited.

Just west of the E. Ross Smith farm about 8 miles North of Dalhart on the Dalhart-Boise City Highway, there are nearly a half section of giant dunes. Some of them must be 50 feet high. In addition to the actual dune acreage these moving monsters have laid waste at least to another half section. A mile or so south and west of this first devastated area is another section and a half tract, barren, shivering, quivering or stocially suffering under the same lash.

The area of these dunes was the first stop made on the tour. There on the rubbish-littered site of a once fine farm home, B. W. McGinnis, agronomist with the U.S. Soil Conservation Service in Dalhart, told how nature's sterile child, the Gobi Desert had been created through natural conditions, and how these dunes before their eyes would gradually spread waste and desolation.

The land on which the shifty, threatening, dunes stand was once a fertile farm. Some 20 years ago, the owner allowed cattle to pasture his stalk fields. They continued to lay out. Subtly but surely the wind whipped the loose soil, first into little piles, then into bigger ones and then before anyone realized the seriousness of the mobilization, into marching dunes.

One remedy is to drill sudan grass or cane on the back of the dune (the southwest side) when moisture permits such action. If the crop takes hold, the dune, when it starts its next march, will find a part of it is anchored. The next spring, sagebrush, wild plums, or tamarisk can be sewn along the stubble of the sudan grass and cane, which is not cut. The third spring native grass is introduced into the vegetative covering on the dune either by allowing nearby grass to go to seed by light grazing or by nature. Native grass seeds cannot be drilled.

This process is followed on that part of the dune marching on until eventually all of it is conquered.

The next stop, several miles to the northeast, was on a farm out of cultivation only 2 or 3 years. Corn stalks still lay about. But the wind had already whipped up massive sand piles only one stage removed from traveling sand dunes, said H. H. Finnell, Director of the Government's entire Panhandle Soil Conservation and Erosion Program, with offices in Dalhart.

You may think this an isolated example, he told his hearers "but it is not." There are thousands and thousands of acres headed for this condition. And unless something is done at once they will get into permanent blow-outs and traveling dunes.

Benefits of terracing and contour listing were viewed at the third stop on Hauhie Roberts's farm west of Chamberlain.

Recently a hard washing shower fell. Roberts's farm not only held, but equitably distributed, the water. No rubbage went dashing down the lister rows. But in adjacent fields they did, with the result that on the high points the crop was washed out. At low points it was covered up. Adjacent fields not only have to be replanted, but have lost much of the moisture from the rains, so when crops come on them again, they do not have the same good chances of maturing that the one on the Roberts's farm does.

Roberts saved the extra time and expense of replanting and regardless of whether more rain falls or not, he is assured of a vegetative cover for his soil.

"Dallam County's biggest challenge today," said Mr. Stubbs, "is to preserve its land. Moisture conservation is a basic step. Proper tillage cropping, prevention of over-grazing are other important parts."

The fourth stop was on a pasture where contouring was demonstrated as a means of increasing the grass. The pasture had been contoured to keep water that falls on it from running into a lake. The contouring was done with a two row lister, two rows plowed (on contour), two skipped. O. T. Williams, Extension Agent with the Soil Conservation Service, Dalhart, said contouring often doubles the grass capacity of the land; it makes the grass cover less likely to suffer in drouth because what water falls is conserved; the greater grass capacity provides a margin of safety against overgrazing which has been destructive to hundreds of acres of Panhandle ranges. In one to three years, the furrows are grassed over abundantly, depending on moisture conditions. Buffalo grass spreads by runners, other grasses by seeds. Gradually, the contours fill up; then the intervening spaces can be plowed so that finally the field becomes gently corrugated, able to handle the torrential rain.

At the Colony Schoolhouse, County Judge Wilson Cowan explained the new state law under which counties can form Soil Erosion Control Districts (with an affirmative vote of the citizens) boundaries are co-extensive with those of the county.

In a speech spiced with price tag statements and straight from shoulder logic, Lon C. McCrory, President of the Citizens State Bank of Dalhart, told the meeting in the schoolhouse that: 'My faith, for the first time, is being shaken in this country — just a few folks know that we have a serious erosion problem — we haven't become conscious of the seriousness of our own conditions — we need somebody to save us from ourselves. Now is the time for aggressive action.'

'People are actually hesitant about loaning $2.00 per acre on land now that formerly sold for $20.00 per acre; not because the land itself is damaged, but because adjacent soil is wind torn, dunes forming and the ugly leer of desolation spreading on the horizon,' he declared. 'Approval of the Soil Conservation District, is our only hope.'

At the August 1935 election, the Dallam County voters over-

Digging Out

whelmingly approved making that county a Wind Erosion Control District as provided for in the pioneer law designed by Judge Cowan and the other County Judges.

The voters of the other counties did likewise. Judge Cowan told of problems met in carrying the law into effect:

> We sent notices out to many of these landowners who had neglected their property and we got a good response. Most of them were nonresident owners or mortgagees who had taken back title to the land after purchasers had defaulted and left the area. But there was lots of abandoned land we couldn't reach this way, and the taxes remitted to us by the State (only about $20,000 the two years 1935–1936) was a pitifully inadequate amount to do all we needed to do. We decided to try to get help from the federal government. And so it was that in the latter part of May, 1936, Judges McDade, Stewart and I, after correspondence with our Congressman, Judge Marvin Jones, went to Washington. We had conferences with M. L. Wilson, then the Assistant Secretary of Agriculture, Dr. Rexford Guy Tugwell, one of Roosevelt's original brain trusters and then head of the Resettlement Administration, Dr. H. H. Bennett, who was Chief of the Soil Conservation Service and several others. We outlined our needs to these people in rather concrete form. We told them that we needed some technical assistance from soil conservationists trained in wind erosion but more than that what we needed was a great deal of heavy equipment to work on this badly hummocked land and to level it out. This equipment consisted of bulldozers and road graders plus plows for deep listing. At the time we got a lot of sympathetic expressions but actually we got nothing more than an agreement to study the matter carefully and to see what could be done. And then on August 18, 1936, the President's Great Plains Committee visited Dalhart to look at the situation. It consisted of Dr. H. H. Bennett, the Chief of the Soil Conservation Service, Dr. Rexford Guy Tugwell, head of the Rural Resettlement Administration, John Page, Chief of the Bureau of Reclamation, Colonel C. E. Howton, one of the Chief Engineers of the Work Progress Administration, Colonel Richard Moore of the Corps of Engineers, Louis C. Gray, head of the Land Utilization Division of the Resettlement Administration, Dr. H. H. Finnell, then the Regional Conservator of the Soil Conservation Service at Amarillo and a number of others.
>
> I remember that the morning after the group arrived I had breakfast with Dr. Tugwell and renewed the acquaintance I'd made with him in Washington and told him again that we urgently

needed this help from the federal government. And he said he thought so but wasn't sure just how it could be done. One of the ideas he advanced to me was that perhaps the best thing to do would be for the government to buy up a lot of this abandoned land and move any farmers left on or near it to more humid areas of the country where there was at least enough rainfall for them to raise subsistence crops. I disagreed with Dr. Tugwell. I told him that the people who were left were a very hardy strain and all of the weak ones, all of those who couldn't stand the terrible conditions, had already left and I thought those that were still here with a little help (far less than it would cost to buy up the land) would survive — would stay until we started having rainfall again. I said to him that they'd learned a great deal themselves about controlling wind erosion and that they were taking active steps.

Well, finally after the committee had visited Dalhart, some months later we did get help of two kinds. First, the Soil Conservation Service provided each of the counties with a trained Soil Conservation Agent to work directly on this bad land. Second, they also provided us with a quantity of equipment, not a great deal, possibly about four units in Dallam County, that would be four tractors and bulldozers, four road graders and perhaps four big plows. What we got was a great help to us because we also used all the equipment which the county had. And we did a great deal of good in working on some of the worst lands in the county and removing the hummocks.

Historians affirm that the drouth on the High Plains in the 1930s was not the first nor even the most severe drouth to hit the area. But it was easily the most destructive. And the reason was that so much of nature's cover of the soil had been stripped away by the plow and the naked land left unprotected.

Perhaps the blinding, choking sand and dust storms, and the physical losses to the people which resulted, was Mother Nature's way of teaching man's dependence on his environment and his duty to protect it.

Certainly it is true that the courage and resourcefulness; in short, the character, of the people of the area were given the supreme test. John McCarty, in his February 26, 1935, editorial in *The Dalhart Texan* likened those who had stuck it out to the Spartans of old:

> Spartans (no other word can better describe most of the citizens of the North Plains Country and of Dalhart.) Spartan in training, Spartan in living and Spartan in their thinking, these people com-

bine courage with vision, dreaming with toil, and persistent effort with optimism, to the admiration and wonder of all who know them.

Gathering strength from the sheer impossibility of the task of carrying on and reconstruction that confronts them, the farmers and ranchers, our first citizens, are staying with the soil and wagering heavy odds they will win. Their faces are open books wherein may be read sincerity of purpose, dogged determination, and the love for the elemental forces of nature they are fighting.

Perhaps, as Judge Cowan suggested, all of man's efforts in leveling the sand hummocks, following Finnell's advice by terracing, contouring, saving crop residues, etc. could only operate to enable the people to hold on until the rains came.

And, in the long run, of course, it was the rains provided by a forgiving Mother Nature that restored productivity to the land and a returning prosperity to its people.

The experience of the 1930s brought to the area new tools by means of which man may be able to prevent future drouths from doing the damage the drouth of the 1930s did. For now, in addition to the vastly improved plows and tractors and other equipment, the people have a permanent federal Soil Conservation Service to advise them, and locally manned and locally oriented Soil Conservation Districts available to keep a watchful eye on man's treatment of his land. The 1930s taught men the land's entitlement to the sky overhead and how to maintain vegetative cover by better use of the water that came from that source.

But in 1937, man, in his restless quest for ever more bounty from nature, found the semiarid High Plains could be irrigated by deep wells, tapping what is known as the Ogallala Aquifer. A new era of High Plains agriculture resulted.

Knowledgeable persons in the Dalhart area estimate that at least sixty percent of the cultivated land in Dallam County, dependent on rainfall prior to the advent of irrigation, now uses water pumped from the Ogallala. Since such irrigation began, at least 60,000 acres, up to then in virgin grass, have been put in cultivation and are drawing water from the Ogallala.

On the resultant increase in production of grains and roughage, feedlots in Dallam County now fatten over a hundred thousand cattle. Feedmills, fertilizer outlets and other related businesses are directly the result of availability and use of the water from the Ogallala.

So that source has obviously contributed greatly to the current prosperity of the Dalhart area. The same condition exists to a large extent throughout all the High Plains, for most if not all of that area is served by the Ogallala.

Where water from this source is available, the farmers do not have the Dust Bowl farmers' concern with the problems of retaining moisture and soil cover. After all, the soil of a field, while soaking wet, does not blow and crops will survive and mature on water pumped from below with little need for water from above.

But all know the underground water is being used up many times faster than nature can replace it. Some predict the Ogallala Aquifer, at the present rate of use, will cease to provide High Plains irrigation within the normal lifetimes of all but the most aged residents. Many stockmen say the irrigation movement is drying up the shallow wells upon which they must depend for survival of their herds.

When the Ogallala Aquifer is used up, the agriculture and stock raising and the related businesses of the area will again be dependent on such moisture as falls from the skies. Will the people then occupying the High Plains be able to cope with drouthy conditions which history tells us will surely return?

If they have the courage, the inventiveness and the love of the land which their predecessors of the 1930s had, they will.

About the Author

John C. Dawson was born in Stanley, Kentucky, April 2, 1903. He was the youngest of three sons born to Dr. George Waller Dawson, a pioneer Dalhart Doctor, and wife Willie Catherine. Dr. Dawson moved with his family from Kentucky to Channing in 1907 and then to Dalhart in 1912, where he became the doctor of the High Plains and established the Trans-Canadian Sanitarium. The Sanitarium became one of the largest rural medical centers in North Texas.

John grew up in Dalhart and attended Dalhart schools. He went on to Northwestern Military Academy in Lake Geneva, Wisconsin; University of Wisconsin (where he became president of the student body); and law school at Northwestern University and the University of Texas. He then entered law practice in Houston with the firm of Liddell, Dawson, Sapp, and Zively, where he practiced for forty years. John was married to Lucylle Rowan, and they had two sons, John Jr. and Robbin. John Jr. lives in Houston, is married to Neva Chambers of Wichita Falls, and is a partner in the law firm of Vinson & Elkins, L.L.P. Robbin, formerly managing partner of the Houston law firm of Sheinfeld, Maley, and Kay, now lives in Panhandle, Texas, where he is engaged in the title company business and ranching, and is married to Alice Surratt of Panhandle.

Following his retirement from law practice, John C. Dawson became one of the founders of the Retina Research Foundation of Houston. He was actively engaged in support of basic research in the quest to learn the causes and cures of retinal blindness.

John's long-held ambition to write a book about his boyhood hometown, Dalhart, and the people who endured the hardships of the early days in the High Plains, was fulfilled in 1985 when his book, *High Plains Yesterdays*, was published. The XIT Museum held an open house for an autograph party during the XIT Reunion 1985, when John led the XIT Rodeo Parade as its honorary Grand Marshal.

John's interest in people continued until his death January, 8, 1988. He died unexpectedly while dictating passages for a book he was writing about his neighborhood in Houston, Texas.

John has been very generous to Dalhart, as the royalties from the sale of his book are donated in equal shares to the XIT Museum Trust Fund and Dalhart's Memorial Park Cemetery Perpetual Care Trust Fund.

John had a passion for life, both its ups and its downs. His outlook is summed up in the epitaph on his gravestone, which he wrote several years before his death, "...while I was looking at the beautiful world about me while high up on the Matterhorn."

> I want no grieving here.
> I want remembrance of
> the zest and joy of life.
> Life was fun. It should
> be remembered so.
> I am not at all sure
> about the future, but
> if there is a hereafter,
> I hope it will be
> more of what was here.

Index

A

Adair, John, 184
Adams, Pete, 66, 67
Adobe Walls, 3, 21
Adrian, 153
Agua Fria, 24, 25
Alamocitos Pasture, 153
Alamosa, Colorado, 182
Alexander, Sheriff George W., 143, 144, 145
Allen, Frank, 113
Allender, Dan, 97, 103, 105
Allender, Joe, 99
Alma, New Mexico, 231, 232
Altus, Oklahoma, 44, 45, 50, 51
Amarillo, 76, 97, 123, 124, 160, 224, 225, 226, 241, 257, 258
Amarillo Globe News, 215, 217, 218, 227
An Eleventh Commandment, 206
Arkansas River, 182
Art Schlofman's Boot and Saddlery, 37
Arterbury, Fatty, 18
Atkinson, D. C., 126

B

Baca Company, 96, 183, 188, 189, 209, 210
Bailey County, 10
Barbed Wire Crow's Nests, 214
Barkley and Meadows, 128, 129, 130
Bass, Joe, 35, 36, 63, 173
Batis, Slim, 15, 16, 36
Beall, Mr., 54
Beals, David T., 48
Beaver River, 52
Bennett, Bill, 77, 112–117, 175
   H. H., 246, 247, 250, 261
   Mr., 94
Betsy, 79, 83, 84, 175
Beverly, Bob, 173
Billy the Kid, 34, 229
Bishop, 2
Black dust black storms, 180
Black Dusters, 180, 181, 184, 186, 188, 216, 217
Black Jack Ketchum [See Ketchum]
Black Sunday, 183

Blair, Mr., 19
Blair's Dam, 19, 22
Blocker, Ab, 11
Boise City, 75, 80, 160, 182, 183, 192, 200, 202, 203, 252
Boise City Funeral Home, 203, 204
Boise City High School, 198
Boggy Creek, 38
Bonner, Smokey, 55, 173
Boot Hill Cemetery, 35
Bowman's Livery Stable, 18
Boyce, Anna Lou, 16
   Colonel, 10
   Henry, 173
Brashears, R. S., 227
Brazos River, 38
Brown, Eck, 172
Brown's Hole, 231
Buffalo, Oklahoma, 252
Buffalo Springs, 11, 12, 22, 25
Bull, Cave, 114
   Cave Jr., 114
   Daddy, 46
Burkburnett, 125
Burke, Joe (Shorty No Legs), 35

C

Cactus Plant, 156, 160, 161
California, 244
California Gold Rush, 4
Campbell, B. H. (Barbecue), 11
Canadian River, 1, 42, 44, 50, 51, 75, 79, 167
Carawaka Cattle Company, 46
Carnegie Hero Fund Commission, 158, 161
Carnes, Agnes, 16
Carol, 204
Carr, Gene, 164
Carrizo Creek, 220
Carson County, 4, 152
Carter, Shine, 140, 173
Cassidy, Butch, 229, 231
Castro County, 10
Cecil, Bertie Whaley, 148–151
Chamberlain, 224, 259
Channing, Texas, 7, 8, 9, 10, 12, 17, 25, 74, 75, 128, 150, 169,

267

219, 258
Charles Summers and Sons Clothing Store, 118, 172
Charlie Hill's Barber Shop, 34
Cherokee Strip, 193
Cheyenne Wells, Colorado, 183
Chicago Rock Island and Pacific, 4
Chickasaw Indian Nation, 44
Chief, 113
Childers, Sally (Aunt Sally), 163, 174
Childress, 227
Childress Index, 227
Chisholm Trail, 38
Ciboleros, 24, 25, 26
Cimarron County, 45, 46, 191, 192, 201, 207, 240, 251
Cimarron, New Mexico, 230
Cimarron, River, 10, 148, 150
Citizens State Bank, 150, 171, 172, 260
Clarendon, Texas, 184
Clayton Cemetery, 234
Clayton, New Mexico, 67, 69, 154, 228, 229, 230, 231, 234, 258
Clovis, New Mexico, 213
Cochran County, 10
Coldwater, 55, 205, 208
Cole, Newt, 120
Coleman's Jewelry Store, 94
Collier, Tom, 39, 41
Colorado, 3, 76, 182, 237, 238, 239, 251, 252
Comancheros, 3, 24, 25, 26
Comanches, 2, 24
Combs, Tennessee, 67
Commercial Hotel, 57, 58, 67
Conlen, 84, 113, 224, 254
Connally, Senator Tom, 241
Cook, R. M., 47, 48, 49
Coon, H., 142
    W. H. (Uncle Dick), 16, 120, 172, 173, 174
Corona, New Mexico, 172
Coronado, 24
Cowan, Judge Wilson (Bill), 237, 249, 254, 256, 260, 261, 263
Crabtree, 47, 53
Cross-eyed Mac, 140
Crouch, Cary J., 39, 40
Culbertson, Bill, 172, 173
Curry, 231

D

Dalhart Courthouse, 252
Dalhart Fire Department, 148, 221
Dalhart Haven, 83, 120
Dalhart Plan, 252, 253
Dalhart Quartet, 217
Dalhart Texan, 41, 59, 62, 83, 105, 106, 119, 125, 141, 142, 152, 153, 154, 168, 169, 173, 180, 182, 183, 191, 215, 223, 230, 238, 240, 242, 243, 248, 250, 251, 257, 262
Dalhart, Texas, 4, 7, 9, 10, 11, 12, 15, 17, 42, 45, 54, 97, 223, 229
Dalhart Wind Erosion Control Project, 249, 250, 252
Dallam County, 4, 10, 11, 37, 45, 120, 152, 169, 171, 211, 240, 242, 246, 253, 256, 257, 260
Dallam County Courthouse, 245, 247
Dallam County Red Cross, 119, 121, 240
Dallas Morning News, 249
Dalton, Al, 36, 112–117, 167, 173
Damron, Earl, 145, 146
Dawson, Artis, 8, 9, 19, 22, 23, 26, 27, 28, 29, 30, 42, 55, 78, 95, 99, 135–138, 146, 166, 180, 184, 186, 187, 190
    Berkley, 173
    Dr. G. W., 10, 53, 55, 68, 69, 72–87, 99, 105, 106, 113, 127, 136, 141, 146, 169, 174, 187
    G. W., 8, 9, 19, 22, 27, 29, 30, 55, 84, 85, 135–138
    Harriett, 95, 186, 187
    John Jr., 86, 187
    Robbin, 86, 187
    Willie (see Mitchell, Willie), 10, 55, 57, 76, 77, 88–102, 105, 127, 128, 141, 167, 174, 175, 186, 187, 215
Deaf-Smith, County, 10, 256, 257
Deere, John, 110
Dellinger, Bert, 144, 145
    Chock, 19, 27, 29, 30, 36
    Lon, 143, 144, 145
    Mrs. Lon, 145, 146
    Ode, 143, 144
    Oral (Spud), 144, 145, 146
Delp, C. W., 126, 128, 129
Denson Farm, 39, 40
Denton, Pem, 126

Index

Denver, 55, 226, 230, 231
Desdemona, 125
De Soto Hotel, 17, 35, 37, 58, 61, 62, 63, 64, 65, 66, 116, 120, 167, 172, 174
De Soto Hotel Barbershop, 173
Diamond Brand, 45
Diamond Ranch, 52
Dinwiddie, Charlie, 140, 173
Dinwiddie's Pool Hall and Domino Parlor, 34, 35, 37, 68, 112, 115, 116, 140, 173
Doan's Crossing, 38, 44
Dodge City, Kansas, 38, 44, 182, 183
Duke, Bob, 173
Dumas, 80, 150, 178, 219, 257
Dunlap Ranch, 188
Dust Bowl, 178, 179, 180, 215, 237, 241, 249
Dust Devils, 181
Dyche, Bobby, 172

E

Eastin, Stephen, 183
Eckley, Colorado, 183
Eklund, Carl, 231
Eklund Hotel Bar, 230
Eldridge, Tom, 224, 226
Elkhart, Kansas, 200
El Llano Estacado, 25
Ely, George, 126
Ely-Hesse Produce Store, 174
Ely-Hesse Wholesale Grocery, 37
Engels, Laura, 182
Enid, 202
Enlow, Zumie, [see Lucas], 192
Esquibel, Jesus, 143, 144
Everitt, H. H., 230
Exum, Hugh, 173

F

Farwell, Charles B., 11
  Frank, 173
  John V., 11
Felton Opera House, 17, 37, 58, 59, 119, 124, 165
Ferris, Bob, 160, 161
  Mrs., 161
Fezjlo, [Dawson horse], 9, 74, 77
Finch, Orville, 16, 42, 172, 173, 244
Finnell, H. H., 218, 247, 248, 256, 259, 261, 263
First National Bank, 185
Folson, New Mexico, 232

Forbes, Weldon, 121, 146
Ford, Doris, 16
Fort Bascom, 9
Fort Worth and Denver Railroad, 4, 10, 34, 37, 58, 63, 65, 66, 128, 132, 150, 160, 167
Fountain, Lydia, 174
Four Ways, 219
Foust, Harvey, 139, 145, 146, 147
Fowler, S. L., 125
Fox Hardware, 219
Fruth, Dr., 67

G

Gable Well, 53
Garcia, Salomi, 231
  Sheriff, 229
  Vincent, 231
Gibbons, Blondie, 116, 117
Gibbs, Billy, 55
Gibney, Marie, 83
Giles, 2
Golden Cycle Oil Company, 124–133
Goodnight, Charles, 3, 24, 184
Graham, Texas, 39, 40
grasshoppers, 87, 97
Gray, Elmer, 113, 114
  Justice, 40
  Louis C., 261
  Tom, 231
Great Plains, 178
Greenough, H. P., 122
  Mrs., 95, 174
  W. H., 174
  Lee, 126
  Willa, 16
Groom, 226
Guleke, Mr. J. O., 257
Gunnels Farm, 145, 146, 147
Gunnels, John, 145
Gushwa, I. J., 16, 35, 57–64
  Phoebe Anna, 61, 62, 63, 174
Guy McGee's Drugstore, 37, 166
Guymon, Oklahoma, 182, 217, 226, 239, 240, 241, 252
Guymon Quartet, 217

H

Hamilton, W. L., 126
Hanks, Camilla, 231
  Deaf Charley, 232
Hansford County, 256
Harrington, Frank, 233, 234

Hartley County, 10, 145, 169, 171, 212, 240, 246, 256
Haverstick, 54
Hawk, Wilbur C., 215, 217
Hedrick, Dr., 75
Hereford, 257
Herzstein, Levi, 231
  Morris, 231
Hill County, 38
Hockley County, 10
Hogtown, 34
Hollis, 41
Hopkins, Harry L., 242, 243
Horan, James D., 231
Houghton, Ted, 142, 148, 173
  Mrs. Ted, 148
Houston, 7, 11, 178
Houston, Temple, 35
Howe, Gene, 215, 227
Howton, C. E., 261
Hutchison, Floyd, 251

I

Influenza epidemic, 118
Interstate Bank, 54
Isaacs, R. W., 231

J

J A Ranch, 8, 184
Jack Jesse's Saloon, 18, 34, 66, 67
Jacques, Gus, 218
  T. L., 173, 218
James, Andy, 43-56, 113, 129, 169, 170, 171, 172, 173, 214, 244, 245, 246, 247
  Captain Andy, 16, 44, 45
James Brothers Ranch, 43-56, 170, 172, 194, 214, 245, 247
James, Jesse, 45, 49, 50, 113, 154, 229
  Sue Cole, 44, 51, 52
  Walter, 44, 45, 46, 47, 49, 169, 170, 171, 173
  Walter Jr., 51
Jarrett, Billy, 173, 224
Jenkins, Jess, 16, 34, 35, 36, 129, 154, 172, 173
Jesse, Jack, 19, 77
Jim Pigmaw's Abstract Company, 37
Joe Langhorne's Barbershop, 35, 36, 66
Joe Scott's Ford Dealership, 37, 92
John Adair-Charles Goodnight Ranch, 184
Johnson, A. C., 242
  Charles E., 227
  Ed, 39
  Rube, 52, 55, 113, 114
  Sid, 66, 140
  U.S. Deputy, 40, 41
Jones, Congressman Marvin, 241, 261
Jesse, 120
Justice, A. A., 183

K

Kansas, 4, 5, 74, 150, 219, 220, 237, 239, 240, 251, 252
Kansas City, 54
Kendrick, C. R., 18, 19
Kentucky, 8, 69, 72, 74
Kerrick, 254
Ketchum, Sam, 231, 232, 234
  Tom (Black Jack), 69, 228, 230, 231, 232, 234
Killen, Mr., 95, 174
  Mrs., 95, 174, 175
  Araminta, 167
  Blondie, 16
  Sam E., 126
Kilpatrick, Ben, 231
Kiowa Indians, 2, 24
Kovarik, Martin, 69, 70

L

Lamar, Chester, 251
Lamar, Colorado, 182, 183
Lamb County, 10
Lane, Mr. and Mrs., 95
Langhorne, Bob, 154, 185
  Joe, 16, 31, 34, 35, 36, 63, 154, 173
Las Casas Amarillas, 26
Las Ruedas Canyon, 8, 9, 24, 25
Las Vegas, New Mexico, 144
Lathem, Glen, 18
  W. H., 35, 124-133, 172, 173, 244
Lather, Mrs. Mabel, 252
Laudermilk, W. C., 250
Law, Mr., 154
  Albert, 10, 154, 191, 215-227, 230, 232, 240, 257
Lawson, 121, 122
Lay, Elza, 231, 232
Lazy J Ranch, 148
Lemman, O. R., 126
Letts, Miss, 55
Lewis Company, 96
Liberal, Kansas, 183, 240
Liberty, New Mexico, 231

Index

Lipscomb County, 256
Llano Estacado, 1, 2
Locked J Brand, 45
Lofgren, Geneva, 78
Logan, 226
    Eugene (Cyclone), 36, 37-42, 173
    Harvey, 231, 232
    Kate, 40
Long, Stephen Harriman, 1
Longbaugh, Harry, 231
Loretto Hospital, 76, 121, 146
Lovell, Dr., 78
Lowe, M. D., 126
Lubbock, 10, 25, 168
Lucas, C. C., 191-214
    Carlie, 193, 195
    Dee, 193
Lucas Family, 191-214
Lucas, Grandmother, 205
    Hazel (see Shaw, Hazel), 193, 198
    John J., 192
    Loumiza, 202
    Virginia, 191, 192, 193, 194, 195, 197, 198, 199, 202, 205, 206
    Zumie, 192, 193, 194, 195, 197, 198, 199, 201
Lucase, 47, 53

M

Machokta, Frank, 226
Magenta Station, 167
Major, 9, 74
Mann, J. T., 16, 142
Marcy, Randolph B., 1
Marlow Brothers, 39, 40, 41
Martin, P. A., 40
Matador Ranch, 8, 54, 153
Mayo, Dr. Charles, 80, 128
Mayo Clinic, 80, 128
McCandless, John (Scandalous), 16, 18, 114, 135, 136, 173
McCarty, John, 62, 142, 180, 189, 215-227, 235, 262
McCrory, Lon C., 16, 172, 260
McDade, Judge Noel, 257, 261
McGee, Guy, 35
McGinnis, B. W., 259
McKinney, 168
Meadows, Mr., 129, 131, 132
Midway Bank, 43, 128, 130, 172
Mission Theater, 37
Mitchell, Willie Catherine (see Dawson, Willie), 74
Mitchell's Saloon, 67

Montana, 149, 244
Montgomery, Porter, 186
Moore boys, 55
Moore, Colonel Richard, 261
Moore County, 4, 152, 169, 246, 257
Moore, Ealy, 173
    Henry, 18
    Weaver, 19
Moreman's Slaughterhouse, 19
Morris, Al, 63
    Jess, 140
Mount Dora, New Mexico, 167

N

Nall, Garry L., 1, 2
Nara Visa, New Mexico, 25, 68, 75, 226
Nettie's Place, 140
New Mexico, 5, 9, 25, 41, 44, 74, 76, 182, 219, 231, 237, 238, 239, 240, 251, 252
Night Flyer, 232, 233
North Plains Wind Erosion Control Association, 246
North Ranch, 46, 47, 51, 52, 53, 54, 113
Number 126, 139-147, 173

O

Ochiltree County, 256
Odessa, Texas, 180
Odom County, 256
Ogallala Aquifer, 263, 264
Oklahoma, 2, 5, 44, 74, 76, 182, 237, 240, 251, 252
Oklahoma Indian Territory, 39
Oklahoma Land Rush, 193
Oklahoma Red Lands, 182
Oklahoma Strip, 112, 168, 173
Oklahoma Territory, 191
Oldham County, 10
Old Kid, 18
Old Loco Column, 218
Old Loco's Last Man Club, 216
Old Man Scrooge, 163, 164, 165, 166
Old Mobeetie, 34, 35
Old Tascosa, 34
Old Walt, 108, 109, 110, 111
101 Ranch, 34, 154
Opera House Hospital, 120
Owensboro, Kentucky, 93

P

Page, John, 261
Palo Duro Canyon, 3, 44, 184, 185
Palousers, 180
Panhandle, [North], 168, 173, 178, 243
Panhandle, Oklahoma, 10, 41, 171, 191, 192, 193, 219, 220, 222, 223, 225, 227, 239, 250, 253
Panhandle, Texas, 44, 74, 171, 182, 191, 219, 220, 221, 222, 223, 225, 227, 239, 250, 253
Parmer County, 10
Pate, Ben, 85
Peeples Funeral Home, 66, 70
Peeples, W. L., 66
Pendleton, Fay, 78
Penney, J.C., 227
Perico, 55, 254
Perkle, 121, 122
Pieratt, Dr. Carl, 78, 95, 146
 Mrs., 95
Pinard, Sheriff Saturnino, 233
Pinkerton Files, 231
Pitts, Tobe, 173
Potter, Jack, 230
Powder Springs, 231
Powell, J. V., 126
 Val, 31, 32, 33, 174, 175
Priestly, Mrs., 47
Prince, 83, 84, 175
Pronger, Mr., 156
Pronger's Ranch, 156
Pueblo, 85, 226
Punta de Agua, 24, 25, 148, 220

Q

Queen, Mr., 10
 Beale, 7-12, 15, 25, 153, 154, 184, 188, 210
 Ralph, 8, 9, 25
 Thelma, 9
Quigley, George, 141

R

Randal County, 256
Ranger, 125
Ranger Ledger, 183
Rathjen, Frederick, 2
Red River, 1, 38
Reese, Judge, 135, 136
Reynolds, Bob, 156, 157, 158, 161
 [children], 156, 159, 161
 DeWitt, 56

 Kenneth H., 162
 Joe, 173
Rita Blanca Canyon, 19, 21, 22, 23, 90, 154, 164
Rita Blanca Lake, 55, 220
Rittenhouse, Nettie, 140
Robbins, [Mr.], 160, 161
Roberts, Hauhie, 259, 260
 Oran M., 11
Robinson, Dr., 52
 L. O., 126
 W. R., 126
Rochester, Minnesota, 80
Rock Island Depot, 167
Rock Island Railroad, 19, 37, 42, 57, 63, 66, 90, 219, 226
Rock Island's *Golden State Limited*, 174
Rocky Mountains, 182, 238
Romero, 148
Roosevelt, President Franklin, 240, 251, 252
Ross, Earl, 67, 68

S

San Angelo, Texas, 234
Sand Augers, 181
San Jon, 226
Santa Fe, 233
Sayre, Oklahoma, 226
Schroeder's Well, 22, 26, 27, 30
Schuhart, A. J., 126
 E. G., 126
Schuhart Feed Store, 37
Schuhart Grain Company, 165
Scott, Dr. and Mrs., 95
Scott City, Kansas, 251
Scott, Joe, 16, 38, 71, 82, 117, 140, 148
Selby, Grace, 78, 95
Seyller, Mr., 153
 Mrs., 153
Shaw, Mr., 204, 205
 Hazel (see Lucas, Hazel), 176, 198, 204, 205
 Ruth Nell, 202, 203, 204, 205
Shawnee, 193
Shelton, Malcolm, 173
Sherman County, 4, 152, 169, 246, 256
Shields, Gerome W., 234
Shorty, 92
Shorty No Legs (see Burke, Joe), 16, 36, 63, 65-71, 173
Simooms, 180

Index

Small, Senator Clint, 257
Smith, E. Ross, 258
    Flossie, 18
    Rats, 19, 27, 29, 30
    S. T., 126
Sneed, Arch, 173
South Plains, 97
South Ranch, 47, 51, 52, 53, 54
Southern Pacific, 232
Spearman, 75
Spencer, Dan, 87
Springfield, Colorado, 182
Stanley, Kentucky, 7, 85
Steel, Charles, 150, 172
    Charles Jr., 150
    Lawrence, 16
    W. W., 149, 150, 178, 191
Steinle, Charlotte, 78
Stewart, E. R., 35, 84
    Mrs. E. R., 80, 118–123, 124, 174, 240
    Judge, M. M., 257, 261
    Malcolm, 53, 56, 173, 247
    Vic, 173
    Walter, 53
Stone, Joe Billy, 19, 27
    W. N., 126, 128
Stout, Mrs. Roy, 40
Stratford, Texas, 80, 84, 87, 150, 154, 155, 158, 182
Stubbs, Mr., 260
Summers, [Charles Summers and Sons Clothing Store], 35, 118
Sundance Kid, 231
Swearingen, Mrs., 174
    Ada Mae, 16, 35
    Eula, 16, 35
    T. L., 35

T

Tandy, Henry, 126, 173
Taos, New Mexico, 167
Tascosa, 35, 50, 75, 219
Tatum, Frank, 35, 36, 69
    Judge Reese, 65, 67
    Regina, 16
Taylor, Uncle Joe, 52
Texan, 234
Texas, 240, 251
Texas Caprock Escarpment, 2
Texas Cattlemen's Association, 38
Texas County, Oklahoma, 251
Texas High Plains, 234
Texas Pacific Coal Company, 125

Texhoma, 71, 193, 203, 204, 205
Texline, Texas, 45, 55, 80, 226, 258
Thomas, Charles C., 230
Thompson, A. W., 230
    Roy W., 126
Thornton, Tex, 223, 224, 225, 226
Throckmorton, R. L., 252
Tom Green County, 234
Trans-Canadian Sanitarium, 37, 75, 76, 78, 79, 89, 115, 119, 174, 175
Trinidad, 233
Tucumcari, 41, 42, 45, 226
Tugwell, Dr. Rexford Guy, 261, 262
Turkey Canyon, 231
Turner, T. W., 126
Twin Mountains, 233

U

Uncle Bob, 50
Union Chapel Community, 192

V

Val Powell's Blacksmith Shop, 31
Van London, W. H., 241
Vaughn, New Mexico, 226
Vega, 226
Vernon, Texas, 38, 112
Vici, Oklahoma, 182, 203, 205
Vineyard, Toots, 19, 27
Vitamin K. Relief, 224, 227

W

Wade, J. M., 126
Waggoner, Sam D., 40
Walker, Herbert, 215
    Lillian, 140, 141, 142
    Marcella, 16
    W. H., 35
Wallace, Deputy, 40
    Marion A., 39
    Marion D., 39
Wanser, Bill, 173
Ware, 254
Webb, Jim, 134–138
    Walter Prescott, 2, 4, 5
Wellington, 50
West Texas Utilities Company, 219, 221, 222
Whaley, George Thomas, 150, 151
    Mrs., 150
Whaley Ranch, 150, 191
Wharton, Minnie, 71
    Sheriff Rube, 68
    Rue, 149
    Webb, 70, 71, 173

White Deer, 50
W. H. Lathem's Land Office, 37
Wichita Falls, 125, 128, 132
Wilbanks, Mr. [children], 86
Wild Bunch, 229, 231
Wilderado, 226
Williams, O. T., 260
Wilson, Mr., 157, 158, 159, 161
  Mrs., 157
  M. L., 261
Wohlford, Mrs., 157
  Sam, 152–162, 191
Wolf, Shorty, 35, 36, 70, 173
  W. A., 126
Wood, Clint, 130, 131
Woods, C. R., 60, 61

  Charlie, 172
  John (Polecat), 53, 55
Woodward, 182
Wyatt Cattle Company, 55
Wynn, Fred, 171
Wyoming, 226

X

XIT Museum, 72, 75
XIT Ranch, 9, 10, 12, 22, 54, 57, 74, 75, 77, 149, 171, 172

Y

Young County, 38, 39
Young County Massacre, 39
Y T Ranch, 55
Yuma County, 183

Editor: Shirley Denise Ratisseau

www.ingramcontent.com/pod-product-compliance
Lightning Source LLC
Chambersburg PA
CBHW051117160426
43195CB00014B/2245